Snip, Burn, Solder, Shred

SNIP, BURN, SOLDER, SHRED

SERIOUSLY GEEKY STUFF TO MAKE WITH YOUR KIDS

by David Erik Nelson

no starch press

San Francisco

14 13 12 11 10   1 2 3 4 5 6 7 8 9

ISBN-10: 1-59327-259-6
ISBN-13: 978-1-59327-259-3

Publisher: William Pollock
Production Editor: Serena Yang
Cover and Interior Design: Octopod Studios
Developmental Editor: Tyler Ortman
Technical Reviewers: Sara Swanson, Vince Russo, Tom Clark, and J.P. Sweeney
Copyeditors: Rachel Kai and Lisa Theobald
Compositor: Riley Hoffman
Proofreader: Linda Seifert

For information on book distributors or translations, please contact No Starch Press, Inc. directly:

No Starch Press, Inc.
38 Ringold Street, San Francisco, CA 94103
phone: 415.863.9900; fax: 415.863.9950; info@nostarch.com; http://www.nostarch.com/

Library of Congress Cataloging-in-Publication Data

Nelson, David Erik.
 Snip, burn, solder, shred : seriously geeky stuff to make with your kids / by David Erik Nelson.
    p. cm.
 ISBN-13: 978-1-59327-259-3
 ISBN-10: 1-59327-259-6
 1. Handicraft. I. Title.
 TT145.N45 2009
 745.5--dc22
                        2010032248

DEDICATION

To my wife, Cara Jeanne, and our son, Otto Sam, without whom this all would not only be impossible but also kinda pointless.

ACKNOWLEDGMENTS

This book would never have come to exist without the enduring patience, kindness, charity, and friendship of hundreds of folks, from loving kin to affable store clerks to the many industrious makers who've tinkered in solitude and shared their findings online. Two standouts in this latter group are Steven L. Sachs (who, unbeknownst to him, taught me most of what I know about didgeridoos) and Tim Escobedo (much-loved throughout the Internet for his simple and fun sound circuits).

More immediately, I'd like to thank everyone at No Starch Press for both their patience with my innumerable revisions and faith in this project—thanks that should be especially amplified for Bill Pollock (No Starch's publisher), Tyler Ortman (my editor), and Riley Hoffman (both a dear friend and a fantastic compositor and graphic designer). I similarly would like to thank my technical readers: Sara Swanson (along with her son, Oscar, and father, Doug Schneider, who tested most of the toys; her brother, Matt Schneider, who crafted the first PVC teepees I ever saw; and her husband Fritz, for pizza boxes, diddley bow feedback, and sharing his boyhood experience with NASA's Finest Paper Airplane), Vince Russo, Tom Clark, and J.P. Sweeney (especially for his help with the Marshmallow Muzzleloader firing circuit and the Ticklebox schematic). More casual toy testing—as well as vital enthusiasm—was provided by my own son, Otto, and my nephews Jake and Griff.

Lots of folks provided little notes that had a big impact on specific projects: My brother-in-law Paul Spindler schooled me on the limitations of step-up transformers; David Helder provided input on the Spring Reverb and the $10 Electric Guitar; and my own father, David Robert Nelson, had surprisingly helpful suggestions on business in general and the specific design of the $10 Electric Guitar's tuning machine. The $10 Electric Guitar likewise benefited from the luthiery opinions and anecdotes of Adam Stein (*http://www.steininstruments.com/*). The flying toys in this book owe their existence to Ted Bailey and Hamil Ma. In the summer of 1996, Jason Michael drunkenly demonstrated his potato canon to me, doing fatal damage to a sober pumpkin. I was impressed. There's no way of getting around the fact that I basically stole and miniaturized that design thirteen years later. Thank you, Jason. I also stole a propane torch from Dean Melmoth and deeply appreciate the fact that he has never pursued me on this matter. Finally, I'd like to thank Dale Dougherty of *MAKE* magazine, whose enthusiasm for this book—and for making in Detroit—gave me a needed boost as I rounded the final bend.

BRIEF CONTENTS

CONTENTS IN DETAIL

In my old life, before my son was born, I taught at a small, innovative private school where students were asked to take control of their educations, make their own choices, and then reap the rewards or endure the consequences. Staff and students were required to treat each other as equals. Because of the realities of private education in America, such a school had to be run on a shoestring budget and largely served "troubled" kids.

The big-hearted, late-1960s ethos of the place was unspeakably foreign to me: I had myself attended an elite prep school and Big Ten university and had no training in education; fortunately, at that time, Michigan's stringent requirements for a private school teacher was that he or she be hired by a private school to teach something. I passed the background check. I was not given a drug test.

The environment was stressful for everyone, but it was good for the students: Many came in with drug problems, having just left psychiatric institutions, or having spent months or years out of conventional school because of anxiety or abject misery. They left our school feeling better about themselves and their futures; went on to attend colleges, universities, or vocational programs or enter the work force; and now are musicians, sound engineers, academics, artists, carpenters, or deep in the mire of grad school.

What's between these covers represents the best of what I learned as a teacher at this radically egalitarian school with a good heart and no budget. Many of these are the same projects I built with those kids. Every single project in this book has three key qualities:

▶   You will make a wicked awesome Thing.

▶   You will do it for cheap (or free!).

▶   In making this Thing you will pick up a transferable skill or fundamental understanding of the Thing and thus be able to modify or make new Wicked Awesome Things.

What's in This Book?

The 24 projects in this book are grouped into three parts. Within each section, the projects are organized roughly by how challenging they are to build, with easier projects coming first—that said, you should build whichever project strikes your fancy right now.

"Part I: Kid Stuff" showcases projects suitable for a range of ages (both in their construction and the final product). The skills taught include basic sewing, carpentry, and electronics. The toys and games go from toddler-friendly (the Lock-n-Latch Treasure Chest and the PVC Teepee) to more suitable for middle school–aged and older kids. Heck, most adult men will get a kick out of the Tickle-box, and the whole family can make a game night out of Go, Tafl, or Shut-the-Box.

"Part II: The Electro-Skiffle Band" is all music projects and calls for slightly more advanced carpentry and soldering skills—several of these (including the Dirt-Cheap Amp and the core of the Cigar Box Synthesizer) were projects I used to teach soldering to young high schoolers. The resulting instruments are safe for all ages (my four-year-old and his friends love the drums, Electro-Didgeridoo, and $10 Electric Guitar) and can make real music.

The final section, "Part III: The Locomotivated," is dedicated to flying and projectile toys. Some—like the Cardboard Boomerangs and FedEx Kites—are safe and easy even for elementary schoolers, although they captivated even the most jaded teenage smokers back when I was teaching. Others—like the Marshmallow Muzzleloader and Putt-Putt Boat—are going to require a little more technical acumen and manual dexterity.

Every project is written with the absolute beginner in mind—this can be the first time you've ever threaded a needle or warmed up a soldering iron, and you can expect to get a decent result. And these projects run the gamut: If you're a sewer who's never touched a saw, I've got projects for you. If you're a musician who's never soldered, flip to Part II and start building your electro-skiffle band *today*. But before you jump in, I want to impress a few safety tips that I picked up while teaching at the Hippie School for Troubled Youths:

▶ In order to learn about the real world, you need to use real tools; nothing in this book is dumbed down or babyfied. Show caution, heed the warnings, and wear goggles, masks, and work gloves when advised to do so: Sawdust and PVC chips can wreck up your eyes; soldering irons, torches, and fire can burn you; saws and knives can cut you; pins and needles can poke you; electricity can zap you.

▶ Work outside when advised to do so; I mention phosgene gas (released when PVC is heated) several times—*please take this seriously!* The same goes for spray-paint or anything else fumey.

▶ Just like working out of Betty Crocker, make a point of reading *every step* of a project before doing *anything*; you want to have a full understanding of what's going to be asked of you and what you'll need at hand before launching into making.

▶ And lastly, don't let these warnings dissuade you from making these projects! Drug-addled teens were able to complete them without injury or mishap.

Further Reading

About half the projects in this book are devoted to musical instruments and electronics—areas of homebrew tinkering that seem to invariably capture the adolescent imagination. If any of these projects end up tickling your fancy, then go out and get a hold of these books:

Handmade Electronic Music: The Art of Hardware Hacking by Nicolas Collins. This is a great book on building experimental electronic instruments (even simple, high-quality microphones), modifying noisy toys into instruments, and creating sound-art installations. You'll clearly see its influence on projects like the Spring Reverb (Project 14) and the Blinkie Tremolo (Project 15).

Electronic Projects for Musicians and its companion, *Do-It-Yourself Projects for Guitarists*, both by Craig Anderton. Some of Anderton's pro-grade designs are a little out-of-date, but you can buy complete kits for them online (mostly through PAiA, *http://www.paia.com/*). Both books offer plenty of great design ideas and improvements you can add to electric guitars yourself (and adapt to other electrified instruments).

Guerrilla Home Recording: How to Get Great Sound from Any Studio by Karl Coryat. This is a hardware/software agnostic primer on audio engineering and will help you squeeze great recordings out of any old setup you can hack together.

If robots are more your speed, then get copies of *JunkBots, Bugbots, and Bots on Wheels: Building Simple Robots with BEAM Technology* by David Hrynkiw and Mark Tilden and *Robot Builder's Bonanza* by Gordon McComb and Myke Predko.

Electronic tinkerers and makers of all levels will benefit from a handful of books by Forrest M. Mims III. A great place to start is *Getting Started in Electronics*, which offers a solid foundation in basic electronic theory and skills, as well as scads of great, simple circuits. His books are often sold in RadioShack stores; they are sparse (mostly schematics with little further explanation), but the designs are robust, with lots of opportunities to adapt them to new and novel projects. Circuit benders (folks that make a hobby of torturing new, noise-musical sounds from old electronic toys) *love* Mims's designs and frequently hack them into their creations.

Support and Contact

The *Snip, Burn, Solder* Blog lives at *http://www.davideriknelson.com/sbsb/* and features videos, tutorials, Q&As, templates, and archived webpages of some resources that have recently become scarce online (such as Steven L. Sachs's didgeridoo pages and circuit designs by T. Escobedo). The best way to contact me is through my website. If you drop me links to pictures and videos of what you make, I'll add them to the online gallery.

PART I

Kid Stuff

Generally speaking, we are born with all of the gear we're ever going to have: Heart and lungs are fully formed; the maximum number of fingers and toes are in place; infant ovaries contain the total number of eggs that the female human will ever release, regardless of how many hundreds of years she might live. The brain, on the other hand, is a little trickier. Although we are born with the total number of neurons we'll ever have (more or less), these are largely unwired at birth. It is the connections between neurons (called *synapses*) that are the gross physiological feature responsible for juggling, remembering phone numbers, and signing a bill into law. During the first three years of life, the brain is furiously wiring up these neurons; a toddler's brain is roughly twice as active as an adult's and twice as dense with synapses—toddlers have about one trillion. The brain vastly overwires in the first three years and then spends childhood and early adolescence thinning out the unneeded connections on a use-it-or-lose-it basis (a process that developmental researchers call *pruning*). From toddlerhood forward, a child is performing relentless, round-the-clock experiments to figure out which synaptic connections are important in her environment (*What language is spoken here? How important is foraging? Are stairs an issue?*), reinforce those connections, and lose the ones that aren't applicable. (This is why Hispanic toddlers can effortlessly trill their *rr*s and Anglo-Midwestern college students can't.) More than genetics, our environments form our brains, and they do it years before we ever pick an extracurricular activity or say "I wanna learn to play piano."

In a strict evolutionary biology sense, the job of any toy is to exercise as many of these synapses as possible, so they don't get lost. The following toys and projects are fun and encourage open-ended creative play, exploration, creative expression, curiosity, strategic planning, and impishness.

More so than any other project in this book, the following list of supplies is a suggestion; you can probably hack this together with whatever boards, hinges, and latches you have kicking around your garage or basement. If you are bereft of these supplies, be sure to hit your local resale shops, garage sales, and hardware store Dumpsters before shelling out for new supplies. This particular design has a double-door lid, a barn-door front, and a mouse door in the back, each with individual latches.

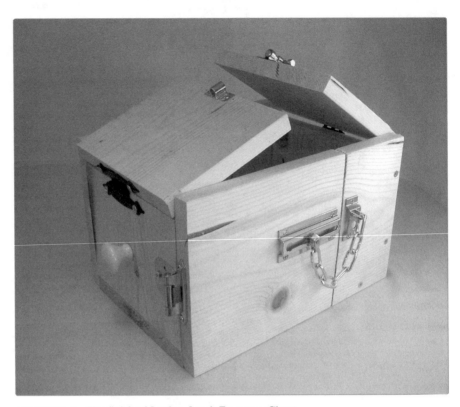

FIGURE 1-1: *The finished Lock-n-Latch Treasure Chest*

Tools

▶ a wood saw (Your plain old crosscut saw will work, but a Japanese pull saw will leave a smoother edge.)

▶ a keyhole saw

▶ an electric drill with bits

▶ sandpaper (Any fine-grit paper will work; 150-grit paper—which has 150 abrasive grains of aluminum oxide per inch—is good to keep on hand.)

Supplies

▶ a 1"×8" board at least 5' long.

✴ **HINT:** *Pine is cheaper and easier to work than a hardwood like oak (for some important notes on wood sizing and selection, flip to "About Board Sizes" on page 10).*

- a dozen 1 1/2" wood screws (for building the box)
- about three dozen 3/4" wood screws (for mounting hardware to the box)
- a variety of locks and latches (I've used a barrel bolt, a chain lock, and a window latch. These are easy to scrounge at resale shops or garage sales; if all else fails, a barrel bolt or window latch is only a couple bucks new at the hardware store, but a new chain lock tends to run at least $10 or $12.)
- hinges (You'll want to keep an eye out for a pair of narrow cabinet hinges that can close flat in order to make the double door–style lid. Since the hinges are largely exposed, it pays to choose something a little more snazzy; brass screams class.)
- a few knobs (You can use these to fancy up the doors, but you're well advised to put one on each end; a toddler is going to want to haul this around, and you might as well make it easier to carry, rather than making it easier to crush a toe.)
- (optional) about a dozen orange juice can lids (These make great "coins" for toddlers—they are free, made of safe, inert stainless steel, make a great sound, have a pleasing weight and texture, and offer no sharp edges or choking hazards.)

FIGURE 1-2: *Tools and supplies*

Building It

Step 1   Measure and mark four 12" lengths and two 5 3/4" lengths on your board. These will be the four sides and two ends of your box, respectively. Cut the board, then sand the raw edges. Use a pencil to mark the four long pieces "bottom," "top," "front," and "back."

Step 2   Quickly mock up the box as in Figure 1-3, just to be sure you have a sense of how this is all going to come together. Note that the end pieces are oriented so that their cut edges are at the top and bottom, not left and right.

FIGURE 1-3: *The mocked-up box*

Step 3   Take apart your mock-up. Measure 6" along the edge of the "top" board. Use this as a guide to draw a line across the middle of the board, then saw it in half. These are your double doors.

Step 4   On your "front" board, measure 4" from one end, mark it, and saw it; this is the barn door.

Step 5   Now for the mouse door (shown on the far right of Figure 1-4). Take the "back" board and measure 3 1/2" in from each end and 4" up from the bottom. Use these as guides to draw your back door, and then cut it out using either a manual keyhole saw or an electric jigsaw. If you're using a keyhole saw, you will probably have to drill a hole in one of the upper corners of your door in order to make the last cut across the top. Sand down the rough edges.

FIGURE 1-4: *From left to right: the top, front, and back, sawed and ready to go*

Step 6   If you're going to stain or paint your box, do so now.

Step 7   Now it's time to start building the box. Stand the two end pieces up on your work-table, about a foot apart, with a cut edge down. Place the bottom (the piece that has no extra cuts) on top of the two ends, as shown in Figure 1-5 (you can also place the front and back in place, in order to help you center the end pieces). Pre-drilling guide holes, rather than driving the screw directly into the wood, will help prevent cracking. Guide holes should be a tad smaller than the actual screws: Find the bit that's the same thickness as your 1 1/2" screws, and then use the next smaller bit. Drill a set of guide holes through the bottom of the box and into one end, and then drive 1 1/2" wood screws through the bottom and into the end piece. Repeat with the other end piece.

Step 8   Install the back board and the anchored side of the front board (see Figure 1-6 for the final result). For the back, drill two guide holes along each side edge and two along the bottom edge, then drive in the screws. For the anchored side of the front, screw the shorter length of the board to either the left or right end piece. Don't forget to drill those guide holes first!

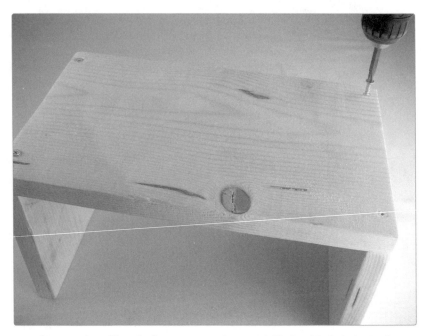

FIGURE 1-5: *Installing the bottom; note the pre-drilled guide hole in the front right corner*

FIGURE 1-6: *The back installed (the anchored side of the barn door, attached to the left end piece, is also visible)*

Step 9 Now for the hinges and doors. The lid hinges are attached to the exposed outer edge of each of the double doors, then anchored to the face of each end piece; note that the pins of the lid hinges are on the outside of the box. The hinge for the front barn door is mounted on the door's edge, then anchored to the outer face of the box's end piece (this sounds confusing, but looks simple; let Figure 1-7 guide you). The mouse door hinge is mounted on the outside face of the box. (You may need to sand down or trim the mouse door a bit so it can swing freely.)

FIGURE 1-7: *Hinge orientation for lid (top) and barn door (right)*

Step 10 Install your locks, latches, and knobs. Use the 3/4" wood screws to secure your latches; the knobs should come with whatever mounting hardware they need.

Step 11 (optional) Fill the Lock-n-Latch Treasure Chest with some toddler treasures, like orange juice can lids.

About Board Sizes

Be aware that a board isn't necessarily flat or straight; crooked boards are fine for many construction jobs, and there are many opportunities for a board to warp between the lumber mill and the checkout line. Before buying a board, look down its length, and be sure that the board runs straight without bowing (curving up from end to end, like an archery bow), cupping (curving along its length, so that it forms a gutter instead of a flat board), twisting, or warping. Also look out for cracks or loose knots; knots smaller than a quarter are usually *tight*, which means they are well-integrated with the surrounding wood and will stay put. Larger knots, especially those surrounded by a dark ring, often fall out as the wood ages—hence the term *loose knot*.

Savvy readers are probably wondering why the Lock-n-Latch Treasure Chest's end pieces are cut to 5 3/4", instead of 6". After all, the height of the box is the same as the width of the board (nominally 8"). Subtract 1" of thickness for each of the top and bottom boards (since they are cut from a 1"×8" board), and it should call for a 6" tall end piece. But as it turns out, a 1"×8" board is actually more like a 3/4" by 7 1/4" board. There's a variety of reasons for this: When the boards are initially milled, some of the lumber is eaten up by the thickness of the blade (called the *kerf*), so both the width and height of the boards end up about 1/16" to 1/8" smaller than expected. Then the boards are smoothed with a plane and kiln dried, processes that further reduce the finished dimensions. Since lumber dimensions were much more variable in the past, building techniques and codes tolerate wild variation. As mills became more precise, it became possible to deliver sturdy, high-quality lumber with less waste. Lumbermen realized that they could actually make each board a little smaller from the start with no ill effects; saving 1/8" per board doesn't amount to much more than a fraction of a cent, but over the course of a few million board feet of lumber the interest compounds. In the end, it's all about the Benjamins, baby.

Crosscut Saw vs. Pull Saw

Any old wood saw you have lying around is almost certainly a *crosscut saw*. These are designed to cut across the grain of a piece of wood, slicing on the forward stroke, when you are pushing. Since they need to stay rigid under pressure, crosscut saws must have fairly thick blades (i.e., a wider kerf). This often also means having larger teeth, which tend to tear up the wood, resulting in ragged edges and lots of splinters. Since a *Japanese pull saw* cuts on the back stroke, it's under tension rather than compression. Thus, the blade can be significantly thinner (i.e., it has a narrower kerf) and the teeth finer, resulting in a very neat cut. As an added benefit, that flexible blade can cut very close to walls and floors when installing wood trim. While Japanese pull saws come in lots of styles and sizes, the one you're most likely to find in the States is a *ryoba* (shown at the top of Figure 1-8), which has a double-sided blade. One edge has fine, alternating teeth and is used for cutting across the grain, while the other has large, jagged teeth and is used for *ripping* (cutting with the grain of the wood).

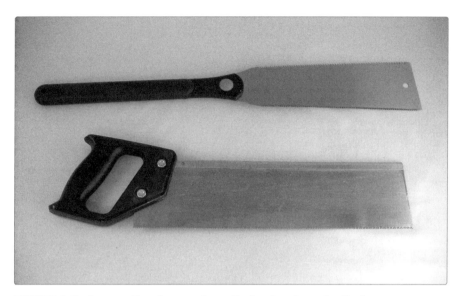

FIGURE 1-8: *A conventional crosscut saw (bottom) and a ryoba (top)*

FYI, the thin blade of the pull saw can be tapped and waggled to make a neat wacky-musical-saw warble—keep this in mind when you start building your electro-skiffle band in Part II.

2   SWITCHBOX: A SOLDERING PROJECT FOR GREENHORNS

As a first-timer electronics project, this junior steampunk curio offers plenty of practice soldering with relatively difficult-to-damage components and will run you through the basics of reading circuit diagrams, wiring switches, and so on. (Soldering technique and electronic fundamentals are fully discussed in the appendix.)

The Switchbox is a cigar box kitted out with three toggle switches, a push-button switch, a buzzer, nine LEDs, batteries, and a few yards of wire arranged in five interdependent circuits. The Switchbox buzzes, clacks, and glows; for a child, it's part puzzle (*What do these switches do? How do I get all the lights on?*) and part prop: It's a ghost trap, a warp-drive control unit, or the SCRAM panel for Chernobyl Reactor Room #4 playtime fun.

Most tobacconists have piles of cigar boxes on hand. Sometimes they'll give them away; usually they'll sell them for a buck or two. The boxes for upscale brands are quite sturdy but can still be worked with common hand tools and little expertise. At this price, they are the perfect project enclosure (and will pop up throughout this book). As a bonus, they smell wonderful and look really cool with a few brass knobs and batwing switches installed.

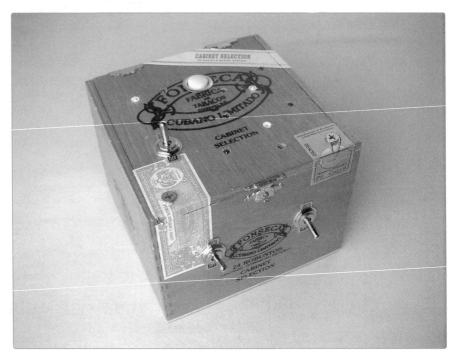

FIGURE 2-1: *The finished Switchbox*

Tools

▶   an electric drill with 1/8", 3/16", and 1/2" bits

▶   a soldering iron, solder, wire strippers, and diagonal snippers (i.e., the standard soldering kit; see the appendix)

▶   cyanoacrylate adhesive (often abbreviated as CA and casually referred to as "superglue"), such as Krazy Glue

▶   wood glue (or better yet, Gorilla Glue)

▶   (optional) a jigsaw or keyhole saw

Supplies

- a wooden cigar box
- some scrap wood (enough to supply two 3/4" blocks)
- two 1" brass wood screws
- a pair of AA batteries and a battery holder
- several toggle switches (This design uses the toggle switch three-pack sold by RadioShack as part #275-322.)
- a "normally off" momentary push-button switch (e.g., a doorbell switch)
- nine LEDs (Stick to red and yellow, unless you plan on using a 9-volt battery and doing some math.)
- three 47 ohm resistors (These have yellow-violet-black stripes; resistor codes are discussed fully in the appendix.)
- a piezo buzzer (RadioShack part #273-059 is readily available, but any piezo buzzer you come across will work, provided it can be driven by 3 volts DC.)
- 22- or 24-gauge insulated wire (Either stranded or solid-core is fine; using two colors—red and black are traditional—will make it easier to keep your connections straight later on.)
- (optional) Velcro strips with self-adhesive backing

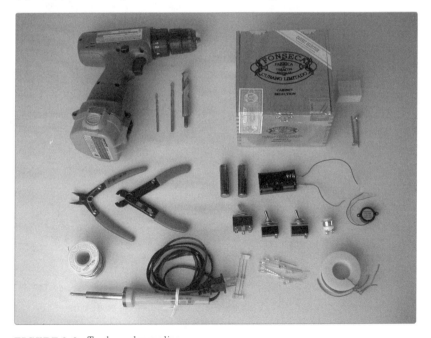

FIGURE 2-2: *Tools and supplies*

Building It

Step 1   Consider the cigar box and decide how to best orient your switches. Although you could use plain old light switches for this project—they're cheap, and very easy to scrounge—it is much easier to drill a hole than to cut a slot. The switches listed in the supplies are reasonably priced—around $5.50 for all three—include nifty metal ON/OFF labels, make a satisfying clack, and have easy-to-install 1/2" round shafts. If you decide to go with wall switches, you can use the inner rectangle of an old switch cover plate as a stencil, then cut your slots using a keyhole saw or jigsaw.

Step 2   Drill holes for the switches; you'll want to leave a little space around each switch (so you have room to run the wires later) and be sure that the box will still close nicely once your switch is installed. Cigar boxes are made of thin, cheap, fine-grained wood and shouldn't splinter too badly if you run the drill fast and put a little weight behind it.

Step 3   Temporarily mount the switches and use them as a reference as you choose positions for the LEDs. A 3/16" hole, which is what you see perforating the box's lid in Figure 2-3, will hold a standard LED quite snugly. Drill one extra hole so that the buzzer won't be terribly muffled.

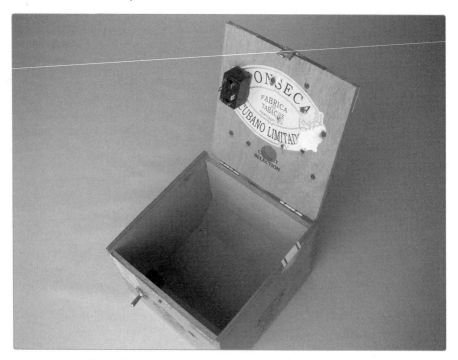

FIGURE 2-3: *The drilled box with two switches in place*

Step 4   You'll ultimately want to prevent unauthorized toddler access to the interior; the pair of brass screws will accomplish this. Cut two 3/4" blocks and glue them to the inside front corners of the box (see Figure 2-4 for orientation). Let the glue fully set (usually overnight), then close the box and drill guide holes a touch slimmer than the body of your screws (you'll probably end up using a 7/64" or 1/8" bit).

FIGURE 2-4: *The blocks installed, with guide holes drilled*

Step 5   While you're waiting for the glue to dry, solder together the LED arrays illustrated in Figure 2-5. The triangle with two arrows shooting out of it represents a light-emitting diode (LED), and the jagged line a resistor (there's a component symbol cheat sheet in the appendix). LEDs have two characteristics, apart from emitting light: They only allow current to pass through them in one direction (i.e., they have *polarity*), and they only do so if the current exceeds some minimum voltage, called the *forward voltage*. For most orange or red LEDs, the forward voltage is around 2 volts, hence the two AA batteries (totaling around 3 volts) powering this project.

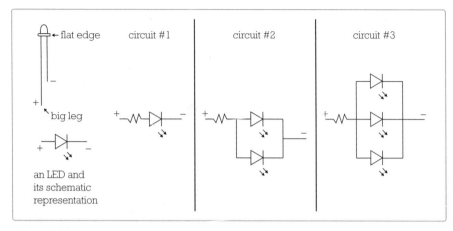

FIGURE 2-5: *Circuit diagrams of the LED arrays*

As a rule, never attach a battery directly to an LED. The LED will quickly become overwhelmed, often getting hot enough to burn you before snuffing out with an audible pop. In this design, a 47 ohm resistor limits the current going into the LED. (There's some nifty math behind this; see "Voltage, Current, and Resistance" on page 22 if you want to try using different colored LEDs or a different battery.) Figure 2-6 is a photo of the three light circuits. To make the first circuit, just solder a 47 ohm resistor to the positive leg of one of the LEDs (the positive leg is usually longer; the negative leg is always marked by a flattened or notched edge on the LED's lens). On schematics, the negative leg of the LED always coincides with the black line on the LED symbol.

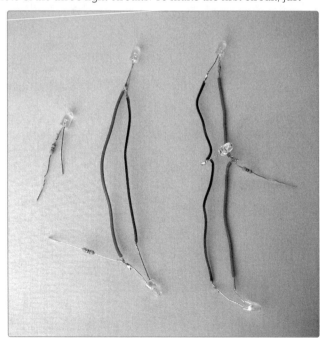

FIGURE 2-6: *The LED arrays*

The second circuit adds a second LED connected in *parallel* with the first (by contrast, the resistor in the first schematic is in *series* with its LED). Construct the second circuit, using black wire to connect the negative legs and red for the positive (color-coding is optional but makes it easier to keep your wires uncrossed later).

The third circuit adds one more LED in parallel. Make two of these arrays.

If the LEDs were connected in series, then the forward voltage would add up and be around 4 volts after just two LEDs, exceeding the power our little pair of AAs could furnish. By wiring them in parallel, you can keep the voltage lower and buffer each array with a single resistor.

Step 6   Wire up the switches. The schematic in Figure 2-7 shows how the switches are inserted into the circuits and the arrays wired together. You'll want to run relatively long wires—probably 5" or 6", depending on the dimensions of your cigar box—to and from the switches and battery pack to give you plenty of room to work when you install the wiring in the box in Step 7.

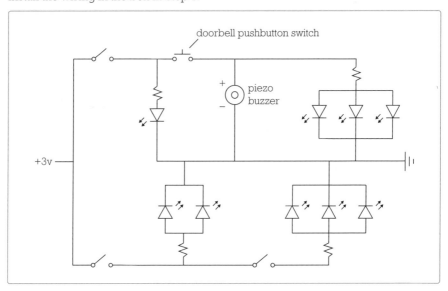

FIGURE 2-7: *The full circuit diagram for the Switchbox*

Your switches may have screw terminals, like the middle two switches in Figure 2-8, or may have solder lugs (flat tabs that you solder the wires to, like the other two switches); all work fine for the Switchbox. The three-switch pack from RadioShack comes with two SPST switches and one DPDT switch; just wire the DPDT up as though it were SPST, using one central and one end terminal along the same edge.

Types of Switches

This design calls for *single pole single throw (SPST)* toggle switches, which are the kind you are most familiar with: A single circuit is completed by a single throw of the switch (a standard bedroom light switch is an SPST switch). Other common toggle-switch configurations are:

1. *single pole dual throw (SPDT)*—flick the switch one way to complete, or *close*, one circuit, and the other way to turn off, or *open*, the first circuit and complete a different circuit
2. *dual pole single throw (DPST)*—throw the switch to close two separate circuits simultaneously
3. *dual pole dual throw (DPDT)*—throw it one way to turn on two circuits and the other way to turn off the first two and turn on two more circuits

Figure 2-8 shows all four common varieties of toggle switch.

FIGURE 2-8: *From left to right, an SPST, SPDT, DPST, and DPDT switch; on the second and fourth switches the* common terminals—*those shared by the circuits hooked to each pole—are in the middle*

A few notes: The switches always break the positive lead, which means that they should have red wires connected to both terminals; one terminal is connected to the red lead from an LED array, and the other terminal connected to the red lead from the battery pack. All of the black wires get connected and go to the negative terminal of the battery pack, which is represented on the schematic by the triangle composed of three parallel lines (on the far right of the circuit diagram). This symbol technically means *ground;* for all of the projects in this book, that's synonymous with the negative terminal on the power pack. The piezo buzzer, much like an LED, is polarized; its black (i.e., negative) lead connects to the black wire on the battery pack, and its positive lead (the red one) goes to one of the doorbell switch's two terminals. The other doorbell switch terminal is connected to the red wire from the battery pack. (Despite what's implied by Figure 2-9, you'll probably have to mount the doorbell switch in the top of the box before hooking it up.)

The schematic (Figure 2-7) is orderly and clear; contrast that to the tangle of wires and switches pictured in Figure 2-9. This is why the good Lord saw fit to create the circuit diagram (on the fifth day, after marine mammals but before birds). God bless the circuit diagram.

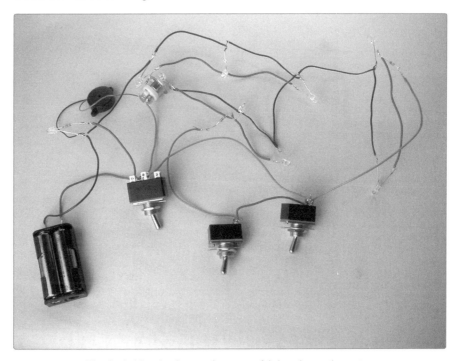

FIGURE 2-9: *The Switchbox's electronic guts; a frightening rat's nest*

Step 7 Mount everything in the box as in Figure 2-10. The LEDs will probably be held snugly enough by the holes, but you can always smear their edges with a little CA (cyanoacrylate adhesive) before inserting them. Since you don't want clever little hands uninstalling the switches (and possibly eating a nut in the process), smear a little CA on the threads of each switch's collar, then tighten the nut down firmly. Clean your hands and tools, and let the glue set overnight; no one will be removing these nuts without tools and good manual dexterity. Glue the buzzer to the inside of the box. Securing the battery pack using Velcro, rather than glue, will make it considerably easier to change the batteries in the future.

Step 8 Tuck in the wires, close up the box, and drive the brass screws home, sealing the Switchbox shut.

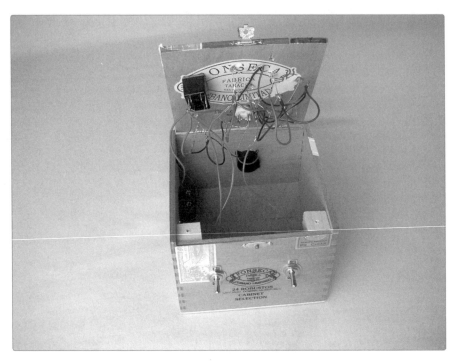

FIGURE 2-10: *Interior of the finished Switchbox*

Voltage, Current, and Resistance

Back in 1827, Georg Ohm described the relationship between voltage, current, and resistance in an electrical circuit—demonstrating that voltage and current varied in direct proportion to each other. This was codified in *Ohm's Law*:

V / I = R

In the equation *R* stands for resistance (measured, predictably, in *ohms*), *V* for voltage (measured in *volts*, which take their name from the foppish inventor of the electric cell—early forerunner of those AA batteries—Count Alessandro Volta) and *I* for current (measured in *amperes*). Since an amp is a very large amount of current—most houses run on 10 amp supplies, and less than an amp can stop the heart—you'll usually see current measured in *milliamperes (mA)*, which are 1/1000 of an amp.

Electricity is almost invariably described with water analogies, so: Imagine a building whose water is supplied by a water tower. The supply of water in that tower is the voltage, the water flow is the current, and the diameter of the pipes determines the resistance. Since the pipes aren't going to change, then it stands to reason that, as the water drains out of the tower, the water pressure will go down. Make up some arbitrary numbers, and you'll see that holds in the formula: If R is fixed, then as V decreases, so does I. Similarly, if you replace all the plumbing with narrower pipes, you'll have less water flowing to the taps, lower pressure, and will drain the tank more slowly.

To model the LED circuits in the Switchbox, you need to rearrange Ohm's Law, breaking the voltage into two components:

$$(V_S - V_L) / I = R$$

V_S is the voltage of the power supply (the batteries), and V_L is the forward voltage the LEDs require. You can usually assume that an LED draws around 20 mA (0.02 amps)—but check the package or data sheet for your LEDs to be sure. Plug in the numbers for the circuit you built in Step 5, and you'll find:

(3 volts – 2 volts) / 0.02 A = 50 ohms

Ideally, you'd want to buffer the LED with a 50 ohm resistor or larger. 50 ohm resistors are rare, but 47 ohm resistors are ultra-common; the difference between the two is basically within the margin of error for the components. As you add each additional LED wired in parallel, you load another 0.02 amps of current draw to the circuit; hypothetically, you could make the second circuit in Figure 2-5 with a 25 ohm resistor.

If you'd rather use blue or white LEDs, which usually have a forward voltage near 4 volts, then you'd need to use a bigger power supply, such as a 9-volt battery. To make the first circuit in Figure 2-5 with a blue LED and 9 volts:

(9 volts – 4 volts) / 0.02 A = 250 ohms

250 ohm resistors aren't commonly manufactured, but 240 and 270 are. Although the 240 is within the tolerance and probably fine, be safe and go with the 270 (marked with red-violet-brown stripes), since a 9-volt battery can make a pretty impressive burn and blue LEDs can be pricey.

For a more complete discussion of electrical components, thumb to the appendix.

3 THE SOCK SQUID

Mysterious, charming, and delicious, squid have fascinated and terrified humanity ever since Pliny the Elder reported a giant squid attack on seaside Spanish fish-brining tanks, with several dogs and fisherman bludgeoned in the melee (recounted in his *Naturalis Historia*, circa 77 CE). Hence, the squid is a natural subject for adorable handicrafts.

The noble squid is distinguished from the lowly octopus by having an elongated *mantle* (or *headsac*) with two stabilizing fins, eight to ten *arms* with suckers all down their length along their inside surface, and two significantly longer hunting *tentacles* that only have suckers on their club-shaped tips.

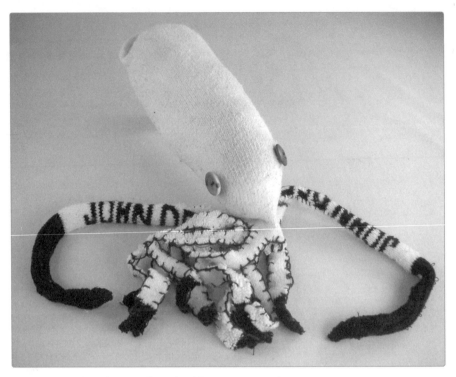

FIGURE 3-1: *The finished Sock Squid*

Tools

▶   a sewing needle

▶   a tapestry needle (A standard embroidery needle will do in a pinch.)

▶   a ruler

▶   scissors

▶   (optional) needle-nose pliers

Supplies

▶   a calf-length or knee-length sock (A tall, relatively heavy athletic sock will work; you can always use the red-heeled wool socks of sock-monkey fame.)

▶   sewing thread that matches your sock

▶   embroidery floss that contrasts with your sock

▶   a few fistfuls of stuffing (called fiberfill and generally made from spun polyester fibers)

▶   (optional) a pair of buttons

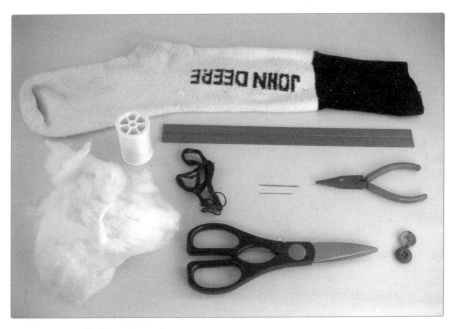

FIGURE 3-2: *Tools and supplies*

Building It

Step 1   Lay your sock out flat and measure the width of the top (the sock's opening). You are going to snip all of the sock above the ankle into strips, which will ultimately become our squid's arms and tentacles. As Figure 3-3 illustrates, you'll want each of

the arms to be roughly half the width of the two big tentacles. If your sock is around 3 1/2" wide (which isn't unusual), you'll want each arm to be about 1/2" wide and the tentacles a bit over 1" wide (wider tentacles will be easier to work with). To generalize this: In terms of squid appendages, the top of your sock is $6x$ inches across, where each arm is x inches wide, and the tentacles are $2x$ inches wide. If you do the math for this hypothetical sock, you'll find that the arms should be 0.58" wide each. This is a terrible number; round the arms down and the tentacles up, and be happier for it.

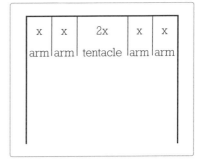

x	x	2x	x	x
arm	arm	tentacle	arm	arm

FIGURE 3-3: *Your sock's top divvied up into squid's arms and tentacles; the sock is doubled, so this gives eight arms and two tentacles.*

Step 2   Picture an imaginary line across the ankle of the sock, and snip each squid append-
age up to that point. Cut through both sides of the sock simultaneously (thus saving
time and keeping the squid symmetrical), then cut up the folded sides (the arms at
either edge in Figure 3-3), freeing the squid's end arms, as illustrated in Figure 3-4.

FIGURE 3-4: *A sock with appendages separated*

Step 3   Fold one tentacle (one of the two double-wide appendages) in half, with the
inside out, and trim the tip to a point (hacking off the corner at 45 degrees is good
enough). Starting about 1" from the tentacle's base (i.e., the point where it joins the
sock), use matching thread to sew the tentacle edges together using a whipstitch
(shown in Figure 3-5, this is a looping overhand stitch that passes over the edge of
the seam, so that each stitch enters the same side of the cloth; the path of the thread
describes a helix). Repeat on the other tentacle.

Step 4   Carefully turn your tentacles right side out. This is much easier if you use a pair of
needle-nose pliers. Starting where the tentacle meets the body, slide the tip of the
pliers into the inside-out tentacle, open them gently to stretch out the tentacle, clamp
a little bit of fabric about 1" down, and slowly pull it through. Repeat until the whole
tentacle is right side out. Then give the tentacle a few stretches and sew up the
inch of seam you left open at the base of the tentacle. Repeat on the other hunting
tentacle.

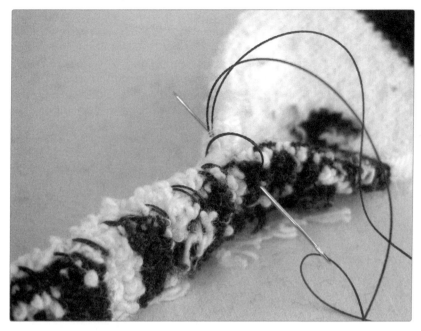

FIGURE 3-5: *The whipstitched tentacle, still wrong side out (sewn with contrasting thread, for clarity)*

Step 5   To give each tentacle its characteristic broad, spade-shaped tip, hold the tip of the tentacle with its seam toward you and running down the center (like the main vein on a leaf). Flatten the tip with your fingers, and then whipstitch around the edge using matching thread. To finish the tip, pinch the whipstitched edges together about 1" below the tip, and use a few stitches to dart the sides together, forming a skinny "wrist" (as in Figure 3-6).

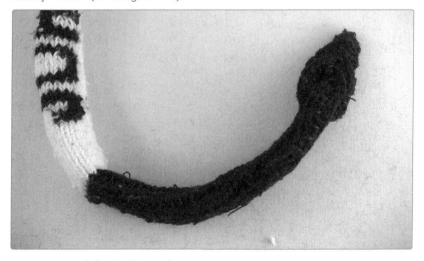

FIGURE 3-6: *A finished tentacle*

Step 6 Now for the eight arms. Trim 3" or 4" from each arm, rounding the tips. We're going to use the tapestry needle to finish the edges of the arms with the contrasting embroidery floss. Embroidery floss is colorful, shiny yarn composed of six cotton threads. For most embroidery projects you only use a few strands of floss at a time. Since we want a thick line to both decorate and reinforce the arms, we'll use all six strands together. This will be easier if you use a tapestry needle instead of an embroidery needle, as the former is fatter, blunter, and has a nice big eye.

Step 7 Finish the rough edges of the squid's arms with a *blanket stitch*.[1] Pick up your sock and hold it so the appendages dangle down. Start at the base of one arm, with the inside (the ugly side) of the sock facing away from you. Thread your tapestry needle (as shown in Figure 3-7), tie a big knot in your embroidery floss, and then bring the needle up through the fabric, setting the knot on the inside of the sock. To execute your first blanket stitch, bring your threaded tapestry needle up through the fabric from the ugly side again and pull all of the slack through. Then thread your needle back under the stitch you just made, looping in from behind as shown in Figure 3-8. Take out all of the slack, and bring your next stitch up from the ugly side. Repeat, sewing

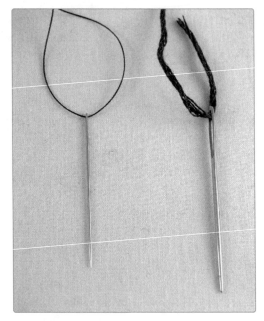

FIGURE 3-7: *A threaded sewing needle (left) and tapestry needle (right); note that you do not double up the embroidery floss the way you do sewing thread.*

down the arm, then flip the squid over when you get to the tip and continue down toward the arm's base. Keep going onto the next arm until you are out of floss. As you get the hang of it, you'll find that you can work quickly by starting the next stitch in the same motion that finishes the previous. (If the blanket stitch is stressing you out, you can always just whipstitch the edges; it will hold up but will tend to curl the arms along their length and won't look as tidy.)

Step 8 Add fins to the mantle (see Figure 3-9 for a close-up). Lay your sock down right side out, with the toe flattened, and imagine two lines giving the toe a triangular tip. Use your sewing needle and matching thread to sew a running stitch along these

---

1. A *blanket stitch* is a fancified version of a whipstitch, usually used to finish the edge of a woven blanket so that it doesn't unravel.

FIGURE 3-8: *A close-up of the blanket-stitched arm*

FIGURE 3-9: *The mantle with fins, sewn with contrasting thread for clarity*

imaginary lines (the running stitch is a classic, simple stitch; see Figure 4-9 on page 43 for an example).

Step 9   Stuff the squid's mantle. You can buy brand-new fiberfill for this at any fabric store (it's pretty cheap; three dollars' worth will fill dozens of sock animals), pull a little out of a throw pillow, use some rags, or use the other sock of the pair, which you won't be needing for anything else (unless you plan on making a Sock Cthulhu; see "Sock Cthulhu" on the next page). Once your squid is appropriately plump, press the mantle flat at the base of the appendages, so that the hunting tentacles are on the left and right. Pinch the fabric at the sock's heel, and fold it so that the two tentacles come together behind the mantle. Now use your matching thread to sew a running stitch through all four layers of sock along the base of the tentacles as shown in Figure 3-10.

FIGURE 3-10: *Closing up the mantle (again, contrasting thread used for clarity); arms are to the front, tentacles to the back*

Step 10   Add eyes. You can either sew on a pair of buttons or use more embroidery floss to craft whatever eyes you deem fit. Slightly mismatched eyes are slightly creepier.

Sock Cthulhu

If you are the kind of person who wants to sew a Sock Squid, you are almost certainly the kind of person who'd want a Sock Cthulhu. To make a Sock Cthulhu, start by making a Sock Squid (which only calls for one sock), but cut the arms significantly shorter (trim at least 5" or 6" off of each, instead of 3"), and stop before sewing up the mantle. Set this aside—it will be the Sleepless Dreamer's head. For the body, sew a classic sock monkey body (Figure 3-11) from the other sock in the pair: Turn the sock inside out, flatten it on the table with the heel up, and make a cut going down the ankle to within roughly 2" of the heel. These are the Sock Cthulhu's legs. (You may also want to round off the ends of the legs, as I have done in Figure 3-11, but this is far from mandatory.)

FIGURE 3-11: *The body, with right leg stitched and left leg ready to be sewn*

Starting about 2" from the crotch, whipstitch down each leg, closing it off. Turn the body right side out, stuff it, and sew up the crotch. Sew the head to the body, tack down the tentacles to make arms, add eyes, and then a pair of felt wings (you can stiffen these with bits of coat hanger along the top, although the perky wings of the Sock Cthulhu shown in Figure 3-12 needed no such extra support). *Ph'nglui mglw'nafh C'thulhu R'lyeh wgah'nagl fhtagn!*

FIGURE 3-12: *A finished Sock Cthulhu*

Resources

For almost a decade, Poor Mojo's Giant Squid has penned a weekly advice column: *http://www.squid.poormojo.org/*.

To learn more about the Elder Gods, check your local library or visit these websites:

- *http://www.mythostomes.com/*
- *http://www.cthulhulives.org/*
- *http://www.hplovecraft.com/*

4 THE PVC TEEPEE

A good indoor/outdoor play tent can easily keep toddlers and early elementary-age kids busy for hours. While store-bought tents are usually made of flimsy nylon, which will eventually disintegrate after hours of exposure to the sun, this teepee is made from durable, easy-to-clean cotton canvas, has enough heft that a stiff breeze can't send it into the hedge, and is supported by a cheap and easy-to-replace frame; there is nothing sadder than a broken-backed pop-up playhouse slumped forlornly in the back yard.

There are two secrets to fast-and-dirty sewing: folding and pressing. Properly folded material can be cut quickly, without measuring and re-measuring in a fruitless attempt to keep pieces matching and symmetrical. Pressing each piece with a clothes iron prior to sewing will make the stitching go much faster and save you a lot of time (and pain) pinning, since most neatly ironed pieces can be easily held together by hand while you stitch.

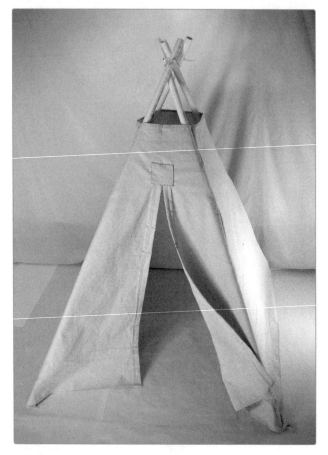

FIGURE 4-1: *The finished PVC Teepee*

Tools

▶ sharp, hearty scissors (Paper scissors from your desk drawer probably won't do it; go with a decent pair of fabric scissors or, ideally, the heavy-duty *trauma shears* carried by paramedics and EMTs.)

▶ a sewing machine or needle and thread

- a clothes iron (If your iron doesn't have steam, then you will also need a small spray bottle of water.)
- an electric drill with a 1/4" bit
- straight pins
- (optional) a saw[1] (Most hardware stores will cut your PVC to the lengths you need.)

Supplies

- a 4'×15' 8-ounce canvas drop cloth
- four 5' lengths of 3/4" PVC
- two magnets less than 3/4" in diameter
- two longish bolts or other pieces of magnetic metal
- 1' or so of cord less than 1/4" in diameter

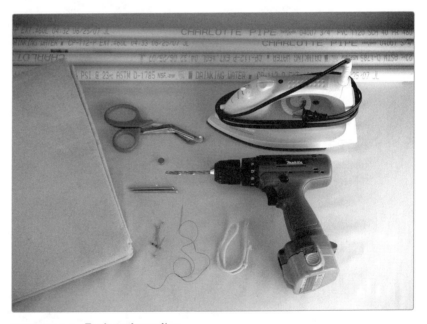

FIGURE 4-2: *Tools and supplies*

---

1. If you cut the PVC yourself, *always wear goggles* and be aware that the friction from a saw can heat PVC sufficiently to cause it to release phosgene, a chemical cousin of chlorine gas, best known as a WWI-era chemical weapon. Go slow and work in a well-ventilated space. For more on PVC safety, flip to Project 11, the Electro-Didgeridoo.

Building It

Step 1   Lay out the long, rectangular canvas tarp on the floor horizontally, fold it in half once crosswise, and then again (also crosswise), so that it is a rough square with four layers of fabric. Your 4' by 15' tarp is actually a bit smaller than that (the finished size—the actual size of the tarp once it's been hemmed at the factory—is usually closer to 3 3/4' by 14 3/4'), so this square is roughly 44" tall by 47" wide. Now fold it once lengthwise, along the vertical axis, resulting in a packet of cloth that has eight layers and is 44" tall by 23 1/2" wide).

Step 2   Starting at the folded edge, measure 5" along the top of your folded canvas and mark this point. Draw a line from your mark to the opposite lower corner (the longest possible line that can be drawn from this point—see Figure 4-3).

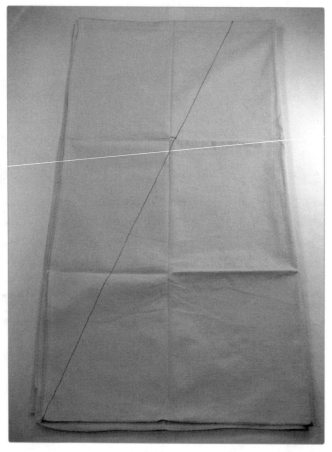

FIGURE 4-3: *The folded canvas, marked and ready to cut; the folded edge is to the right*

Step 3   Set the clothes iron to its "cotton" setting (usually the highest temperature). While the iron is warming up, find the mightiest scissors you can muster, and cut along the line from Step 2. This will probably be a royal pain in the ass; work slowly, and give your thumb a periodic break.

Step 4   If you were to completely unfold the tarp right now, you'd have a set of simplistic canvas paper dolls. Do not do this! Unfold the final lengthwise fold of the tarp so that you have a trapezoid, slip the scissors into the creases at the top and bottom of your trapezoid, and trim the connecting edges. The result will be four identical trapezoids and a whole lotta scrap, as in Figure 4-4; save the scrap.

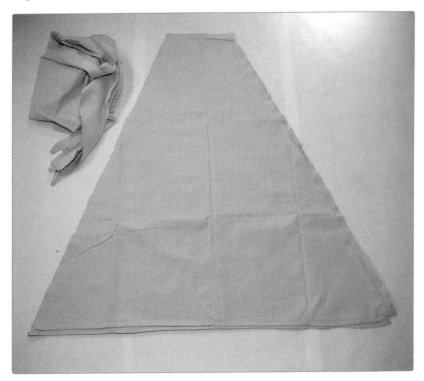

FIGURE 4-4: *Your scraps and trapezoids; the scraps are to the left*

Step 5   Prepare each trapezoid to be hemmed. Assign an outside (front) and inside (back) to each trapezoidal wall. Lay out one wall, front down, fold in roughly 1/2" along the top edge of the trapezoid, and press it with the hot iron, making a nice sharp crease (see Figure 4-5; if your iron doesn't have steam, then spritz the cloth with water before ironing). Repeat this on the bottom and then along each angled side (which will be a little trickier). Do this for each trapezoid. Leave the iron on the same setting, since you'll be ironing again in a few minutes.

FIGURE 4-5: *Pressing a hem*

Step 6   Pick one trapezoid to be the door wall (Figure 4-6). Find the center of the top edge of the trapezoid, measure roughly 9" down, make a mark for your endpoint, and then cut up from the bottom of this piece (the crease from Step 1 makes a handy guide).

Step 7   Time to return to the scrap pile. You are going to need the following pieces: two long rectangles that are 36" by 4" (you can probably find a 4" strip that's 72" long; use it, as it will save you some time in Step 8), four rectangles that are 4" by 8", and one rectangle that's 4" by 4" (this piece will reinforce the top of the door flap cut and can be replaced with a cool patch or other decorative flourish).

Step 8   Start with your long strip, which will be the edging for the door flaps. If you found a 72" long piece, then fold it in half so you have a 36" long piece that's double thick, and press the crease. Fold this long strip once along its length (i.e., make it into a 36" long, 2" wide strip that has a central crease and four layers) and press it again. Unfold it, bring both edges in to the center line as shown in Figure 4-7, press the long edge creases, then fold it closed again and freshen up the edge and central creases.

Step 9   Unfold, slide your scissors into the short crosswise crease, and free the two 36" strips from each other. Refold each and give them one more press for good measure. Set them aside carefully to preserve the creases and avoid crumpling.

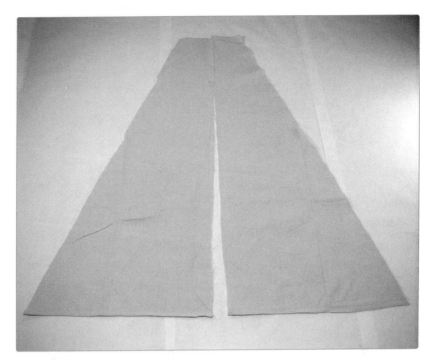

FIGURE 4-6: *The door wall*

FIGURE 4-7: *The door edging, just prior to its final pressing*

Step 10   The four 4" by 8" rectangles will be the pockets that hold the feet of your four teepee poles. For each of your 4" by 8" rectangles: Fold in 1/2" on each side, press, then fold it in half (so that you have a roughly 4" by 4" square with two layers) and press the crease (the result is shown unfolded on the left side of Figure 4-8). If you're going to use a plain piece of 4" by 4" canvas to reinforce the top of the door flap, then fold in 1/2" along each of its edges and press them now. Set these all aside.

FIGURE 4-8: *A finished, unfolded pole pocket (left) and the back of the door flap reinforcer (right)*

Step 11   Time to sew! Start by sewing the top and bottom hems for each trapezoid. You can do this by hand using a running stitch (see Figure 4-9; the running stitch is the most basic stitch, the one a classic TV bachelor thinks of when you say "sewing") or save time by running them through a sewing machine.

Step 12   Add the edging to the door flaps: Lay the door wall out flat, and slip the long edging strip over the edge, pinning it down in several places along its length. Sew the edging in place, leaving roughly 3/4" between your stitch line and the opening edge of the flap. As you sew, slip the magnets in against the crease of the edging (see Figure 4-10; you want one magnet near the middle of the door and one at the bottom)—you'll do likewise with your magnetic bolts on the other flap. You can secure them for the time being with a little tape or fabric adhesive.

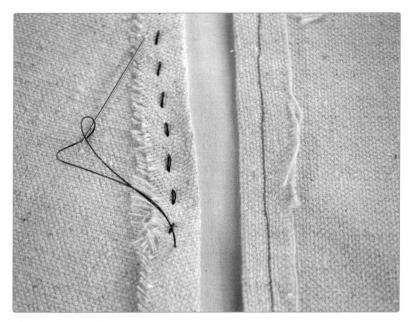

FIGURE 4-9: *On the left is a hand-sewn hem using a running stitch; on the right is a hem that's been sewn using a sewing machine.*

Step 13   The edging will be 1" or so longer than the door opening. Fold the excess up under the door, and stitch it to the inside of the flap. Some sewing machines can power through this many layers of canvas, but it might be easier to hand stitch. Finally, go back and add a line of stitching above and below each magnet or bolt, thus trapping it in a little pocket.

Step 14   To finish the door, sew the 4" by 4" door flap reinforcement square (or awesome and culturally appropriate patch) over the top of the door flap cut, as in Figure 4-11; this covers the messy ends of the edging and keeps the cut from running.

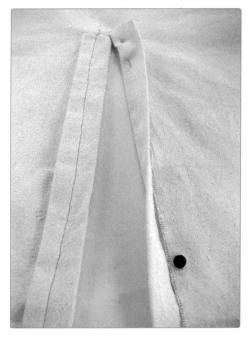

FIGURE 4-10: *A partially pinned door flap edge with magnet*

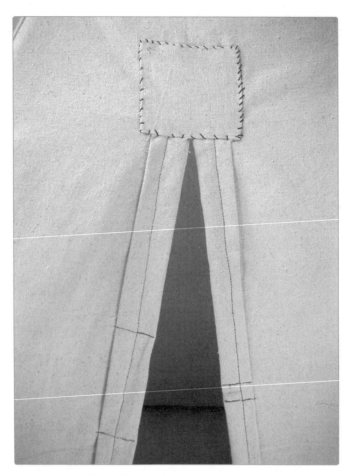

FIGURE 4-11: *Door flap reinforcement square and magnets, installed*

Step 15   Now you're ready to construct the teepee body. Take two of the walls, lay them flat, place them front to front, and run a line of stitches down the left angled edge. Now take the other two walls and do likewise, this time running stitches down the right angled edge (resulting in the two sets of canvas batwings shown in Figure 4-12). Make sure that you are sewing them with the insides facing out!

Step 16   Take your two halves, open them up, place the pretty front of one half to the pretty front of the other, and stitch up your last two sides. You now have an inside-out teepee. Leave it that way for the final bit of sewing.

Step 17   Install the pole pockets. Center a folded pocket over the foot of one long seam, as close to the bottom as possible with its bottom toward the corner. Sew it down, leaving the top of the pocket open as shown in Figure 4-13. Repeat on the other three corners, then turn the teepee's canvas body right side out, and set it aside.

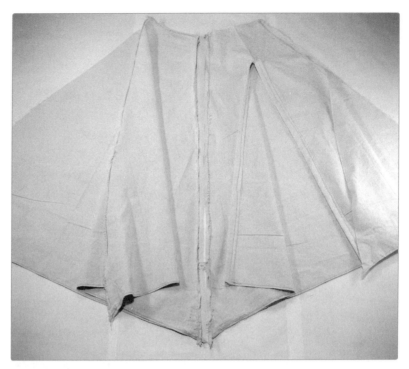

FIGURE 4-12: *The state of your teepee just prior to Step 16: two halves, with ugly sides facing out*

FIGURE 4-13: *A pole pocket, in situ*

Step 18   Take each length of PVC, measure 3" from one end, and drill a 1/4" hole all the way through. Knot the end of your cord, and string the four poles on it loosely, like femurs on Kali's necklace. Leave some slack (as shown in Figure 4-14), and knot the other end.

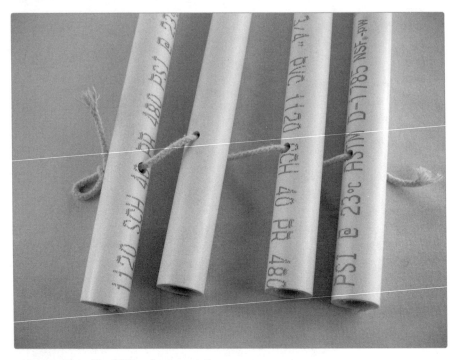

FIGURE 4-14: *The PVC poles on a string*

Step 19   To pitch the teepee, slide the poles in through the "smoke hole" at the top of the canvas body, lining it up so that the pole cord follows an invisible line connecting the middle of the door wall and the middle of the back wall. Divide them into a pair of front poles and a pair of back poles. Flip the tent, then slip the front two poles into the front two pole pockets and the rear two into the rear two pockets. The teepee will now look a bit like a closed umbrella. Flip it back, set the feet of the poles against the ground, and slide them apart, so that each pair of poles makes an inverted V. Interlock the vertices of the two inverted Vs, as shown in Figure 4-15. Adjust as needed (you may want to add or take up slack in the cord). Now is a good time to snip any unsightly stray threads, before the local band of Lunar Lakota take possession of their new home.

FIGURE 4-15: *Detail of the tops of the poles once the teepee is pitched; notice that the cord joining the poles allows for a good deal of play*

Building Tip

The tarp used in this project is a touch pricey (around $15); if that's a problem, feel free to replace it with several cotton sheets (which you can usually get at the Salvation Army for a buck or two per). The sheets will be easier to cut and sew but won't hold up to the weather or block out light as well as the canvas; 3/8 of the coolness factor of any play tent is the degree to which it is dark and cozy, like a little animal's den.

5 CHEAP MESH SCREEN PRINTING

Invented in China roughly 2,000 years ago, silk screen printing is the cheapest, most pleasing way to directly reproduce images and designs. A screen (once silk, now usually polyester, but in all cases permeable to ink) is stretched over a wooden frame, and *screen filler* is applied to all portions of the screen that *are not* part of the intended design, forming a stencil. (The Chinese used to do this by weaving human hairs into the screen in order to make portions impermeable.) Once the filler has dried, you apply ink to the screen and pull the ink across the open design with a *squeegee*, flooding the mesh and pressing through onto your *substrate* (usually paper or cloth). You then repeat this process, adding more ink as necessary. Using this technique, hundreds of copies of a single design can be more or less perfectly reproduced in about an hour.

Beginner screen printing kits are a little pricey and are not necessary to get a feel for the method. There's nothing magical about the "silk" mesh used on commercial screens, apart from being very fine and sturdy. Any mesh will do. Nylon tulle (used to make veils, wedding centerpieces, etc.) is cheap (a few bucks a yard), sold at any craft or fabric store, and works fine. Your prints will end up a little lo-fi (sort of blocky, à la Super Mario), so you might prefer a finer mesh; fabric stores have bolts of mesh backing materials used in dressmaking, such as organdy or organza. Avoid anything with much stretch to it, like old nylon stockings, as these will distort easily as you work the screen. I made my first screens from fabric scrounged from grimy old negligees a friend found while cleaning out her dearly departed granny's house. Worked like a charm.

The screen frame is, likewise, nothing special. We'll use an embroidery hoop in this project, since they are essentially free at many garage sales and cost less than $1.50 brand new. Old picture frames or the frames from recessed metal light fixtures also work well, or you can build frames from scrap wood.

Most commercial screen fillers can be washed out with solvent, and the screens reused with new designs. Our screen filler can't be washed out—meaning that you can only use each screen for a single design—but it should weather repeated gentle washes, making limited mass production possible; it's perfect for adding a repeating motif to your PVC Teepee (see Project 4).

FIGURE 5-1: *A finished printing screen with ink and an ID-card squeegee*

Tools

▸ scissors

▸ a small paintbrush, size #3, #4, or #5

▸ wide tape, such as packing or duct tape

▸ a water-resistant glue like Elmer's or Mod Podge

▸ a Sharpie fine point marker

Supplies

▸ an embroidery hoop

▸ a few feet of relatively fine mesh material

▸ an old credit card, library card, ID card, etc.

▸ screen printing ink (Specific inks are sold for printing to fabric and paper; although they are kinda-sorta interchangeable, it's worthwhile to get the right kind for the job you're doing, especially if you're printing to fabric and intend your design to withstand washings.)

▸ (optional) acrylic extender base (You can mix this with ink in order to increase transparency; it also makes the ink flow a little easier.)

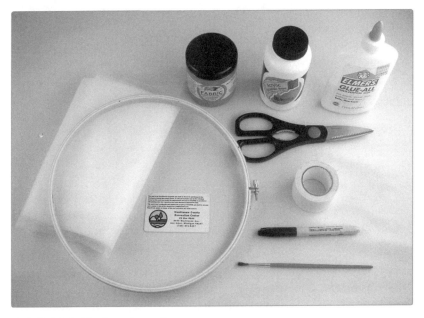

FIGURE 5-2: *Tools and supplies*

Building It

Step 1   Lay out a single layer of mesh and, using your frame as a guide, cut out a square piece, allowing roughly 2" of extra material on each side.

Step 2   Mount the fabric in the hoop, as in Figure 5-3. Try to get it as taut as possible, and tighten the hoop as much as you can. Henceforward, the *face* of the screen is the surface that is flush with the hoop's edge (and thus later, when you are ready to print, can be placed directly in contact with a T-shirt or piece of paper).

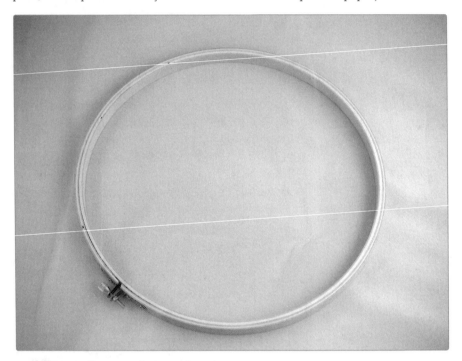

FIGURE 5-3: *Frame and trimmed mesh*

Step 3   Prepare the image you are going to use for your prints; the Internet is replete with black-and-white clip art just waiting for you to resize and print it. Lay your screen face down over the image, so that the mesh is in direct contact with the picture. Use your Sharpie to trace the image to the screen.

Step 4   Flip your screen over, face up, and place it on some scrap paper. Squirt a little puddle of glue onto an old dish (or another piece of scrap paper), and use your small paintbrush to dab glue onto the non-image portion of your screen, filling the areas where you do not want ink to be able to pass through. Working over a piece of white paper will make it easier to see your tracing and ultimately reduce insanity. Work slowly; you are basically stretching a thin glue membrane—your screen filler—across each square of the mesh. Use glue sparingly to minimize sagging and drips. Periodically re-tighten the screen as you work around the image; this will probably open tiny single holes in your filler. Holes will also naturally form as the glue dries and contracts. Check your work often and patch these holes as they crop up. Once you've filled in the finer details around the edge of the design (as in Figure 5-4), you can mask off large portions of the screen using tape applied to the face of the screen.

FIGURE 5-4: *A screen with some fill applied; note the stenciled image*

Step 5   Tighten the screen once more, touch up any holes, and leave it to dry overnight, face up. When the screen is dry, use tape to seal the edges where the screen meets the wood frame (this prevents leaks).

Step 6   Now you can pull a test print (the process is illustrated in Figure 5-5). Place the screen facedown on a clean sheet of paper. Spoon a little dab of ink onto one of the glue-filled portions of the screen, and then use your old ID card as a squeegee to drag the ink across the open portion of the screen in a single smooth stroke. Feel free to make several passes at varied angles in order to flood the image with ink. When you're done, carefully lift the screen away, and set your print aside to dry.

Step 7   When you are through printing, carefully clean your screen in tepid water. With a relatively large-gauge mesh (like tulle), some ink will stick in the image; a wipe down with a damp paper towel will probably clean it up. Otherwise, a quick rinse should do it. Hang the screen up to dry, since some fillers (like Elmer's) will get a little tacky during the rinsing and might want to stick to the table.

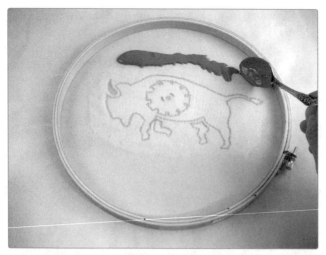

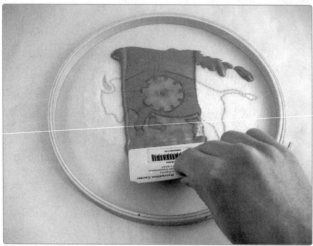

FIGURE 5-5: *Three steps: Ink the screen, pull the print, then lift the screen.*

Printing Tips

▶ Any medium that will dry to a water-resistant film can be used as screen filler, including *acrylic medium* (used by painters to extend paint and alter its luster and dried surface), *gesso* (used by painters to prepare canvasses and other surfaces), many different types of household paint, and even screen-printing ink. Although Mod Podge and gesso are more tolerant to repeated washings than Elmer's Glue (which will soften up under warm water), a carefully handled Elmer's-filled screen will last well enough, and it's hard to beat the price.

▶ For simpler images or text, you might consider tracing your design onto the paper backing of self-adhesive contact paper, cutting it out (keeping in mind that you are going to use the *negative* of your design and discard the piece that matches the design itself), peeling off the backing, and sticking that stencil directly to the *face* of your screen—an example of this is shown in Figure 5-6.

FIGURE 5-6: *A screen made with a contact-paper stencil*

▶ If you have trouble with the screen sticking to the substrate, try taping short stacks of pennies to the edges of the frame, so that the screen pops back up after you flood the design.

- If you decide you like screen printing, you can get supplies online at a good price. *Monofilament polyester screen fabric* is about $13 per square yard and can hold very high-resolution images. Making your own frames requires minimal woodworking skills; staple the polyester screen to the frame using a staple gun, first tacking the middle of each edge and then working out to the corners one at a time, tightening as you go.

- What draws most folks to screen printing is the prospect of using photo emulsion to transfer complicated designs to the screen. The chemicals for doing this (e.g., Speedball Diazo Photo Screen Printing Emulsions) are around $20 and very easy to work with; the process is much more tolerant of mistakes and stray light than developing photos in a darkroom. If you have a reasonably dim closet, access to a bright lamp, and some way to make transparencies (most copy shops will duplicate onto transparency paper for under a buck), then this is within your grasp.

Resources

For screen printing supplies, check Dick Blick's website, *http://www.dickblick.com/*.

6   SHUT-THE-BOX: A PIRATE DICING GAME

Shut-the-Box is a dice-based strategic game of chance for one or more players. The game's components include a counting box with nine numbered tiles and a pair of standard six-sided dice. Players take turns rolling dice, flipping down numbered tiles, and accruing penalty points until they are knocked out of the game; the last player left is the winner. Also called Tric-Trac, Canoga, or Batten Down the Hatches, Shut-the-Box is a game with an enduring, if foggy, history. It seems to have first gained notice as a game played by Hudson Bay Company sailors. Descriptions of the game go as far back as the 12th century, when it was popular with sailors on the English Channel. Although it is now often associated with pirates, no accounts of pirates playing Shut-the-Box are known to exist. But since all pirates began their lives as commercial or naval sailors, it isn't much of a stretch to imagine Edward Teach (the notorious marketing genius Blackbeard) hoisting a flagon and playing a few rounds between sewing silk pants and bouts of high-seas mayhem.

FIGURE 6-1: *The finished Shut-the-Box set*

Tools

- a wood saw (Since the cutting is minimal, any old saw will work.)
- an electric drill with small bits (You'll probably want the 3/32" or 7/64" bit, although you could get by with one as big as 1/8".)
- wood glue (or of course, Gorilla Glue)
- clamps (A couple of fat binder clips will work.)
- a marker, paints, woodburner, or soldering iron (to number the scoring tiles)
- sandpaper
- (optional) small bolt cutters, tin snips, or pliers with wire cutters

Supplies

- a cigar box
- an 18" length of 1/2"×1" wood (A trim molding scrap will work and is fine-grained and attractive; many lumberyards have scrap bins you can pick through for free.)
- 10 pennies
- a wire coat hanger
- a pair of dice
- (optional) a piece of felt or velvet
- (optional) spray adhesive, white glue, or fabric adhesive

FIGURE 6-2: *Tools and supplies*

Building It

Step 1 Cut eleven 1 1/2" lengths from your piece of wood; 9 of these will be the scoring tiles, and the other 2 are end pieces.

Step 2 Using a drill bit just a shade thicker than your coat hanger wire, drill a centered hole through each of your 9 tiles, 1/2" from the bottom, as shown in Figure 6-3.

FIGURE 6-3: *A drilled scoring tile*

Step 3   Use this same bit to drill a centered hole halfway through each end piece, 3/4"
from the bottom (Figure 6-4).

FIGURE 6-4: *A drilled end piece; note that this hole does not pass all the way
through the block*

Step 4   Measure the width of your cigar box, subtract 1/2", and cut that length of wire from your coat hanger. Small-gauge bolt cutters will slice right through a hanger, as will most tin snips. Wire cutters probably won't, but you can use them to score the hanger, and then bend the wire back and forth until it snaps. If the ends of the wire have been mangled in the process, straighten them with pliers.

Step 5   We're going to use the pennies as spacers, so that the scoring tiles can be easily flipped independently of each other. (There are no washers that cost one cent each.) Although you could use a hammer and awl to pound holes through the pennies, after a dozen or so this will dull your awl enough that it will want to split the pennies rather than pierce them. Also, you'll probably wreck your table doing this. Instead, working on top of a piece of scrap wood, drill a hole through the center of each penny. Drill with the tails side up; the bit will more easily bite into the bas-relief columns of the Lincoln Memorial than Abe's neck. Hold the penny down with pliers or a clamp, since the high-speed bit will just as happily chew into your fingertip as legal tender. Run the drill at full speed and put your weight behind it; the bit should pop right through.

Step 6   Sand down any rough edges, then number your scoring tiles one through nine. Although you can do this numbering with a Sharpie or poster paint, most will prefer the pirate-y wood-burned look shown in Figure 6-5. This uses tally marks to show the numbers and is accomplished with the clean chisel tip of a normal soldering iron. (For more detail on using a soldering iron for wood burning, check out Project 8, Small-Board Go/Tafl.)

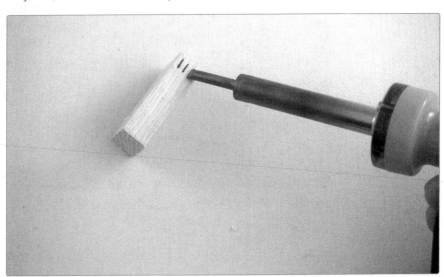

FIGURE 6-5: *Numbering a scoring tile with a soldering iron*

Step 7   Although optional, lining the bottom of the box will both add class and drastically cut down on annoying dice clatter. Craft stores sell 8 1/2"×11" sheets of self-adhesive felt that can be cut to size. An even cheaper option is to head to the fabric store. You'll need a piece of fabric no bigger than about 7" square, so ask about the remnant bin and scraps. The fabric will likely be less than a dollar (or even free). If you go the fabric-store route, glue the fabric into the box with either spray adhesive or a thin schmeer of a white glue (e.g., Elmer's Glue). Don't use Gorilla Glue (it foams as it cures) or a CA like Krazy Glue (which has an exothermic reaction with cotton and wool fibers! Fire!).

Step 8   Assemble the scoring tiles. First, line up all of the numbers in order (you'll kick yourself if you get them all strung on the wire and then realize you've swapped 3 and 8). Starting with tile 1, slide each scoring tile onto the wire, then a penny, then the next scoring tile, and so on, as shown in Figure 6-6. Finally, place a penny on each end, and add the end pieces.

FIGURE 6-6: *A half-assembled set of scoring tiles*

Step 9   The scoring tile assembly needs about a 1/2" of clearance from the back of the box. Measure and mark 1/2" from the back of the box on each side. The back edge of each end pieces will line up with these marks, as shown in Figure 6-7.

Step 10   Carefully slide the scoring tile assembly into the box, checking to confirm that everything fits nicely. You may need to drill the holes into the end pieces a touch deeper, but be careful not to go through, as that will make final assembly a more challenging juggling act.

FIGURE 6-7: *Measuring the clearance for the scoring tiles*

Step 11 Slide your scoring tile assembly forward and smear a little Gorilla Glue where the end pieces will anchor to the right and left sides. The best way to control the glue is to squirt a dollop onto a piece of scrap cardboard and use a toothpick to apply it to the surfaces. Be careful with Gorilla Glue! It's bad for your skin and ruins clothes. Consider wearing rubber gloves. Once you've applied the glue, slide the end pieces back into position, wipe up any excess glue (as the Gorilla Glue cures, it expands by about 300 percent; a hard-to-spot stray gob will blossom into an ugly mess), and then clamp the end pieces in place using big binder clips or clamps. Let the glue cure for 24 hours.

Game Play

There are many variations of Shut-the-Box, both in terms of equipment and rules. Boxes can have any configuration, and sets with up to a dozen tiles are not unusual. You could also quickly gin up a set from some playing cards and dice, if you had a hankering to play but no box. Play begins with all the numbers visible, and the goal is to be the last player to accrue 45 penalty points.

Standard Play

In each turn:

Step 1   Roll the dice, and add them together.

Step 2   Flip down any combination of tiles with the same sum as the dice.

Step 3   Repeat until you either (a) have flipped down all of the tiles ("shut the box") or (b) can no longer find a combination of tiles that matches the sum of the dice. Then count up your penalty points (explained below), reset the box, and pass the dice to the next player.

If your turn ends

► with the box still "open," then add up the exposed numbers on the tiles and jot them down; these are your *penalty points*. Each round's penalty points are added to the previous total.

► when you shut the box, then your entire penalty score drops to zero.

The last player to accrue 45 penalty points is The Winner.

Play Example

On your turn you roll a 6 and a 2, for a sum of 8. You may flip down any of the following combinations of tiles:

► the 1 and the 7

► the 2 and 6

► the 3 and 5

► the 1, 2, and 5

► the 1, 3, and 4

► the 8

If, at the end of your turn, the 8, 9, and 1 tiles are still open, then you have 18 penalty points. If you manage to shut the box on your next turn, then all of your penalty points disappear. But if that next turn ends with the 1 and 2 tiles still up, then you'll have a total of 21 penalty points (almost halfway to losing!).

Play Variations

► **Solitaire**   Favored by marooned pirates. Play like the standard game, with the goal of shutting the box before accruing 45 penalty points. Weep into your beer at your lonely plight.

► **Gambling**   The game begins with each player staking a wager. Play continues as normal, with each player having an opportunity to raise the pot, see raises, or fold at the end of each round. Any player who hits 45 penalty points is out, and the first player to shut the box wins the pot. Drink to excess. Call other players "scalawags."

7

TICKLEBOX: JOLT YOUR FRIENDS

Long before police were tasering belligerent drunks, prepubescent Midwestern boys were tearing apart broken camera flash units and making simple cattle prods to surprise and delight their friends: the Ticklebox—a sinister name for a sinister toy. This particular design, and its packaging, was the brainchild of a boyhood friend's teenaged cousin. Jiggle the foil-covered box and enjoy a brisk, but safe, 100-volt jolt. You could make up a game using the box (LARP *Operation*™? *Hungry-Hungry Don't Tase Me Bro!*?) but what's the point? High-voltage, low-current self-administered electrocution is its own joy.

The heart of the Ticklebox is a *step-up transformer*, a device that cunningly uses electromagnetism to *step up* a low voltage to a higher voltage. In this case we'll be slightly abusing a RadioShack audio output transformer, which is actually a *step-down transformer*, wiring it backward so it works as a step-up transformer.

The rule to remember is this: Whenever you have an electrical current flowing through a wire, it creates a magnetic field, and whenever you have a magnetic field moving past a wire, it will induce an electrical current to flow through that wire.

A transformer is composed of a square iron donut with two opposing sides wrapped in coils of thin enameled wire (thus, each side can function as an electromagnet). Our step-up transformer has a few wraps of wire on its primary side (the side we're applying current to), and many more windings on its secondary side (the side that we're using to shock folks). When a current pulses through the primary coil, it creates a magnetic field in the iron donut, which in turn induces a current in the secondary coil. Since the secondary coil has more loops (and is thus a longer wire), a larger voltage is induced on the secondary side. Handily, the ratio of wrappings between the secondary and primary coils determines the factor by which that voltage is multiplied. Since our RadioShack transformer has 11 times as many coils on the secondary side (when we wire it our way, which is backward to what it was designed for), the voltage on the secondary side is 11 times higher. So, when we pulse 9 volts through the primary coil, the secondary will produce a brisk 99 volts, give or take. (Compare this to the static shock you get while pulling off a sweater, which can be several thousand volts.) But you can't get something for nothing: When a transformer steps up voltage, it steps down current by the same factor. So, in this case, the final shock is 100 volts but a very safe handful of milliAmps. Contrast this to a fat wintertime doorknob static spark, which might be 7,000 volts, but just a few microAmps. On the other end of the spectrum, a paramedic's defibrillator paddles can zap you with a few hundred volts at several dozen amps—which is several thousand times the current delivered by the Ticklebox. (For a more complete discussion of voltage, current, and personal safety, flip ahead to the appendix or back to "Voltage, Current, and Resistance" on page 22.)

FIGURE 7-1: *The finished Ticklebox*

Tools

▶ a standard soldering kit (See the appendix.)

▶ a thumbtack or thin nail

Supplies

▶ a 100 μF electrolytic capacitor

▶ an audio output transformer, such as RadioShack part #273-1380

▶ an SPDT relay, such as RadioShack part #275-0248

▶ a *tilt switch* (I've used a mercury bubble switch—it looks like a fat Christmas tree light bulb in the picture—but these are pretty rare nowadays. Any tilt switch, such as Mouser part #107-2008, will do.)

▶ 22- or 24-gauge insulated wire, either stranded or solid-core

▶ a 9-volt battery and a battery clip

▶ aluminum foil

▶ a small box (A jewelry gift box is ideal.)

▶ electrical tape

▶ (optional) glue or double-sided tape

FIGURE 7-2: *Tools and supplies*

Building It

Start by examining the schematic in Figure 7-3. If the heart of the Ticklebox is the step-up transformer, then the brain is the *relay*, represented by the dashed box containing squares and little pennants. This is an electromagnetically controlled switch: When you power up the coil, it creates an electromagnetic field that pulls the switch closed, thus completing a circuit and turning your gadget on. When the coil loses power, the magnetic field dissipates, the switch opens, and the gadget turns off. Like other switches, relays come in SPST, DPDT, and other varieties (for a full discussion of different kinds of switches, see "Types of Switches" on page 20).

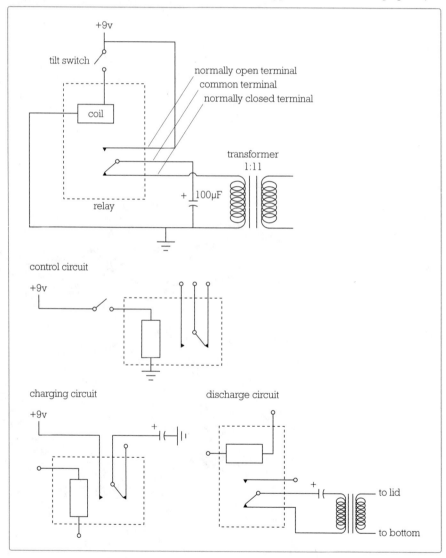

FIGURE 7-3: *The Ticklebox's full circuit diagram at the top (it is a very simple Taser), and the same circuit broken into its three component circuits*

Demystifying the Ticklebox

This design calls for a SPDT relay, which has five terminals. Two go to the coil: passing current through them activates the switch. One of the remaining legs is the *common terminal*, and the other two are the *normally open* and *normally closed* terminals. When current is sent through the coil, the switch is activated and the normally open terminal is connected to the common terminal, completing that circuit. When current is removed from the coil, the relay clicks back to its default state, which is to have the normally closed terminal completing a circuit with the common terminal.

Look at the schematic again and you'll see that the Ticklebox comprises three circuits. One loops from the battery's positive terminal to the tilt switch, connects to the relay's coil, and returns to the battery's ground (negative) terminal. Think of this as the *control loop*. The second circuit connects the normally open terminal of the relay switch to the battery's positive terminal, thus making it possible to connect the battery to the capacitor wired to the common terminal. This is the *charging circuit*. The third circuit connects the normal closed terminal of the relay's switch to the backward audio output transformer, then to a capacitor wired to the common terminal of the relay's switch. This is the *discharge loop* (although it might be more honest to call it the *shocker loop*).

The tilt switch contains a little conductive ball (these used to be made with a drop of mercury, but now are usually a tiny ball bearing). When someone picks up the Ticklebox, that ball slides to one end, connects two leads, and completes the circuit for the coil. This generates an electromagnetic field, which closes the switch, connecting the common terminal to the normally open terminal, which connects the battery to the capacitor, charging the capacitor in a matter of milliseconds. When the tilt switch is tilted the other way, the coil loses its power, and the relay clicks back to its normal mode, disconnecting the charging loop and completing the discharge loop. Now the capacitor is connected to the transformer and dumps its stored charge. The transformer steps up the voltage (by around a factor of 11 in this case), and whoever jiggled the box gets a shock.

Even though it will lead to a little re-soldering, we're going to build the three circuits one at a time, for clarity's sake. If the diagram is suitably clear to you, feel free to just put the circuit together as you see fit. Otherwise, use the following steps.

Step 1 Before you start soldering, you'll need to determine which terminals are which on your relay. Often they are labeled, either on the relay itself or its packaging (*nc* stands for normally closed, and *no* for normally open). If not, snap the 9-volt battery into its clip, and briefly connect the red and black wires to sets of terminals on the relay. When you find a pair that produce a snappy clack when the voltage is applied, those are the coil terminals—label them. You can then rig up a little circuit with an LED, a resistor, and a battery (such as the one from the Switchbox shown in Figure 2-5 on page 18), or use a multimeter (as discussed in the appendix), and poke around among the remaining three terminals to determine which are the normally closed, normally open, and common terminals of the relay's SPDT switch. Once you've identified all of the relay terminals, move on to Step 2.

Step 2   Solder together the control loop. The red wire of your battery clip is the positive lead, so the tilt switch should come between it and the coil. Solder the black battery lead (the ground) to the other side of the coil (the resulting circuit is shown in Figure 7-4).

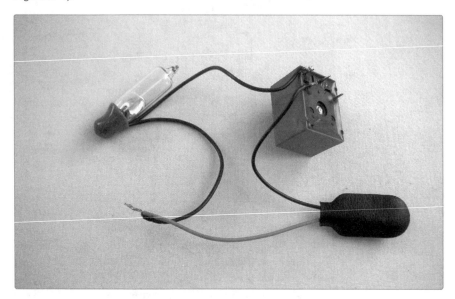

FIGURE 7-4: *The relay with the control loop installed*

Step 3   Build the charging loop. Since the capacitor is polarized, be sure to connect its negative leg (the one that lines up with the stripe on the capacitor) to the black lead on the battery clip (the ground). The other leg connects to the common terminal on the relay, and then the normally open terminal connects to the positive lead on the battery clip.

Step 4   Finally, build the discharge loop. Your audio output transformer should have two wires on one side and three on the other. (If you're using the RadioShack model, one side will be red and white; the other will be green, black, and blue—if you have a multimeter, the resistance across the red and white wires should be around 8 ohms, and roughly 1000 ohms for the green and blue.) You can clip off the middle wire on the three-wire side (the black wire on the RadioShack transformer), and strip the remaining four. Solder the normally closed terminal to either the red or white wire and then the remaining wire from that side back to the ground (the black battery lead), as shown in Figure 7-5. The green and blue wires will be your contacts. You might want to solder little extensions to them, depending on how long they are, in order to make it easier to install the circuit into the box.

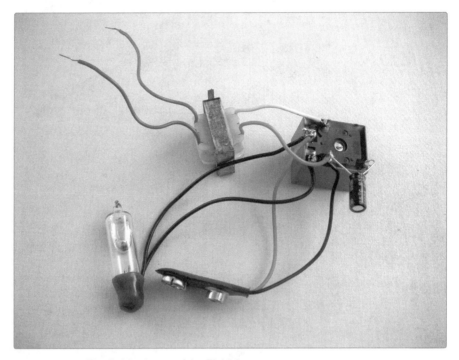

FIGURE 7-5: *The finished guts of the Ticklebox*

Step 5   Hook up the battery, jiggle the tilt switch, and shock yourself a few times. If it doesn't work, double check to be sure you have the relay wired properly.

Step 6   Experiment with putting the contacts different distances apart. Yelp occasionally. Reveal military secrets.

Step 7   Finish the enclosure you see in Figure 7-6. Use a thumbtack or thin nail to pop a small hole in the bottom of the box and thread one of the two contacts (the green and blue wires on the transformer) out. Use electrical tape to secure this flat against the outside of the box, being sure to leave as much of the copper core of the wire exposed as possible. Secure the other parts to the inside of the box; you can glue the relay and tilt switch down, but probably want to tape the battery in place. Cut out a square of aluminum foil a few inches larger than the box. Smooth the foil along the outside of the box bottom, making sure there is solid contact between the tip of the wire and the foil (with many boxes, it's easiest to get good contact along the edge). Trim off the excess foil, and use strips of electrical tape to secure the foil and insulate it from the top of the box.

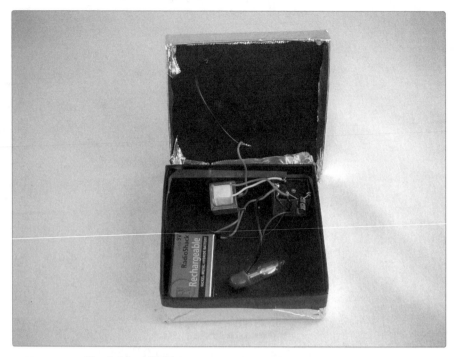

FIGURE 7-6: *The finished Ticklebox, opened to reveal the guts*

Step 8   Pop a hole in the top of the box, thread the wire through, and tape the wire down. Cover the top of the box with foil (no need to use electrical tape to secure it; the added foil and tape on the bottom half of the box will make for a snug fit as is). It is virtually impossible to avoid shocking yourself throughout this operation. If you haven't been getting shocked, then probably something got broken. Open the box, be sure that the foil on the box's top and bottom don't touch, then check all the connections to make sure none of the wires are creating a short circuit.

Step 9   Close up the box and give it a jiggle. Zzzap!

Scrounging Tips

When tilt switches were cheaply made using mercury, they were ubiquitous. Today they are much less common, although non-mercury tilt switches are easy to get by mail order. If you are having trouble finding a tilt switch, you have two options: (1) Old thermostats (the round kind with a dial in the middle) used a SPDT mercury bubble switch. Since these now have to be disposed of as hazardous waste, which is inconvenient in most cities, such thermostats can often be found kicking around the junk boxes in landlords' offices or among the hardware clutter at resale shops and garage sales. (2) Make your own tilt switch from a small ball bearing, two wires, and a section of drinking straw or the barrel of a disposable pen.

The relay used here (RadioShack part #275-0248) is nice but a little pricey (around $5). You might pay just a buck or two for a relay at a surplus retailer (like the inimitable American Science and Surplus, *http://www.sciplus.com/*). Be sure to get one with a full enclosure, since exposed switches are likely to get fouled with the other wires in Step 7, necessitating a lot of annoying troubleshooting, and their switch contacts get gunked up with dirt and grit, making for a much weaker zap. Alternatively, you can scrounge a fully enclosed DPDT relay out of a VCR or off an old internal modem card. Resale shops, like Goodwill and Salvation Army, frequently have boxes of old computer gear, including outmoded modems, for a buck apiece (or even free).

The Mean-Ass Jingle Bear

If you have a slightly crueler streak, or just hate Christmas, you might consider an alternate package for the Ticklebox: Get a small Christmas-themed teddy bear from the Salvation Army (like the one in Figure 7-7) and a pair of largish (roughly 1" in diameter) metal jingle bells from a fabric store. Cut open the bear's back, and install the Ticklebox guts, running the two contacts down through his arms and out of his palms. Solder these to your bells, then feed the slack wire back into the arms and sew the bells to the bear's palms. Display him prominently in your cubicle after Thanksgiving. Invite office workers to "Hold his hands and give him a jingle; it's really cute!"

Do not give the Jingle Bear to a child. That's just too much. Honest.

FIGURE 7-7: *The Mean-Ass Jingle Bear*

Unlike Shut-the-Box (Project 6), which *might* have a romantic historical pedigree, the Tafl family of board games have bona fide Viking credentials. Go, similarly, has an established place in the strategic and tactical thinking of Japan's shoguns, samurai, ninjas, and robot geishas.

Both Go and Tafl rely on the tension between *strategy*, which is the players' over-arching goal, and *tactics*, the immediate actions that need to be taken to achieve that goal. Go is a symmetrical game, in which both players have the same goal, pieces, and repertoire of tactics, while Tafl-type games are asymmetrical, fought out between unequal forces with differing capabilities and intentions. It is left as an exercise for the reader to determine how these differences have played out in terms of Western and Eastern approaches to foreign policy and international finance.

Go is usually played on a 19-line board; such games can be very long (several hours) and dauntingly intellectually exhausting, especially for beginners. A nine-line board is a great place to start and is also favored by seasoned players looking for a quick game. (Both board sizes are shown in Figure 8-1.) Although not all of the tactics and nuances of the small board translate to the full-size field, the fast pace of the smaller games facilitates a quick understanding of the game's core principles.

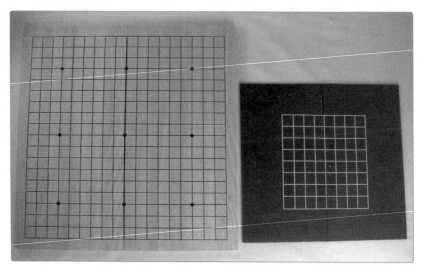

FIGURE 8-1: *A full-size Go board (left) and a nine-line Go board (right); the dots on the board are called stars.*

There are many variants of Tafl, but the best understood is Tablut (Figure 8-2): dark *raiders* (who start in the T-shaped *bases*) try to capture a light *king* (guarded by eight *king's men*) before he travels from his starting point at the board's center (his *throne*) to any corner.

This *pyrography* (woodburning) project combines simplified variants of these two games onto a single board (shown in Figure 8-3). On our combined board, the Go board's stars are rendered as boxes, and the Tablut board's bases are Xs.

FIGURE 8-2: *A conventional Tablut board layout*

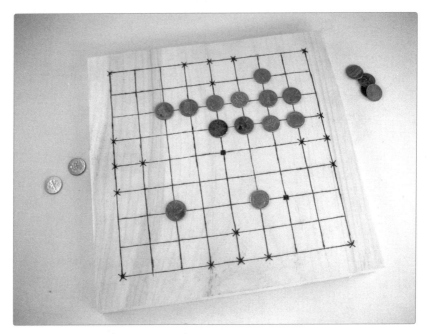

FIGURE 8-3: *The finished Small-Board Go/Tafl set*

Woodburners look and function very similarly to soldering irons. They have roughly the same form factor, and a beginner's woodburner generally heats to 600 to 900 degrees Fahrenheit. A 25-watt soldering iron (the kind normally used for soldering small projects, like those in this book) heats to about 750 degrees. The major difference is the tip: A woodburner has a brass tip shaped a bit like a very thick hobby knife, whereas a soldering iron tip is made of chromed or nickel-plated copper and usually shaped like a either a chisel or the point of a pencil. To use a soldering iron for pyrography, get a new, clean chisel-point tip (keep separate tips for soldering and woodburning). Since carbon build-up on the tip can be a problem while woodburning, you'll want to keep a piece of fine-grit sandpaper on your workbench; occasionally dragging the tip down the sandpaper will clean it off and hone its edge.

Pine, which is both cheap and pale, is a good wood to use in a beginner's pyrography project. You'll want a board that is as free as possible from surface defects. Boards of this quality are often called *B select and better* and are used for finish carpentry, furniture making, and so on. Avoid knots, as they are full of sap and burn very slowly. This project calls for a roughly 10" by 10" chunk of pine. If you buy your wood at a large chain hardware emporium, you'll likely have to get an entire 1"×10" board (the shortest length is usually 6') in order to get your 10" by 10" piece. Lumber yards, which are accustomed to working with carpenters who might just need a small piece to finish a project or make a repair, are sometimes willing to make deals and often have scraps or smaller pieces they'll give you for free. Any lumber purveyor should be more than happy to cut the piece to size for you.

Tools

- a metal straight edge ruler
- sandpaper (including a *medium grit*, like 80–120, and a *fine grit*, e.g., 150)
- a soldering iron with a chisel tip
- (optional) an electric sander

Supplies

- a 10" by 10" board
- 50 pennies, 50 dimes, and a nickel for playing pieces
- (optional) spar varnish

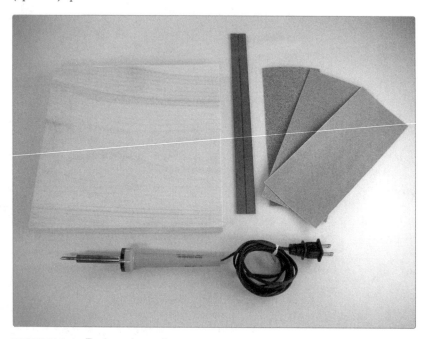

FIGURE 8-4: *Tools and supplies*

Building It

Step 1   Prepare the surface of the board. First use the medium-grit sandpaper to take the splinters off of the sawed edges and remove any gouges from the surface you are going to burn. Take the time to get your burning surface as smooth as possible, as this will vastly reduce your frustration in Steps 3 and 4. Once the surface is free of ridges, divots, and bumps, use the fine paper to buff out the signs of the heavier sanding.

Step 2   Use your straightedge to lightly pencil in an eight-by-eight grid of 1" squares, as illustrated in Figure 8-5. After you've drawn the grid, add the Go board's stars (the 5 small, dark boxes) and the Tafl bases (the 20 Xs). Double-check your work against Figure 8-6, since it's easy to erase pencil and hard to erase charred pine.

FIGURE 8-5: *Penciling in the design*

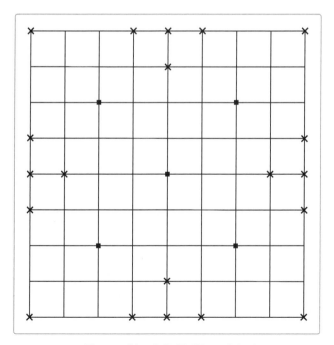

FIGURE 8-6: *The combined Go/Tafl board design*

Step 3   Burn in the lines. The trick to wood burning is that darkness is determined by time, not pressure. Always rest the iron lightly on the wood (it's very easy to accidentally gouge the soft pine), and slowly work down your line 1" at a time. It's often easier for beginners to get a straight line by pulling the iron toward themselves. Although it's tempting to use the straightedge as a guide, you'll quickly discover that it's more of a hindrance than a help. Use the flat tip of the chisel, as shown in Figure 8-7, and feel free to go over the lines several times. Burn the outermost perimeter first, then work through all of the vertical lines, then all of the horizontal lines (or vice versa; if you find it easier to work in one direction, then rotate the board as you work). Take your time; slow and easy wins the race in woodburning.

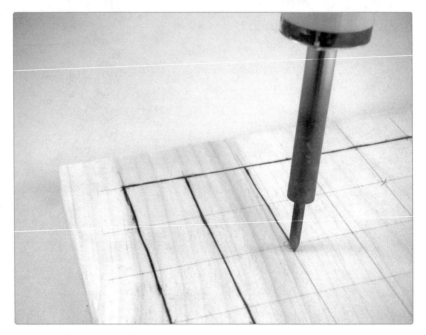

FIGURE 8-7: *Beginning to burn a line; note how the tip is flat against the board, and the iron vertical*

Step 4   When the grid is done, burn in the stars and bases. The stars are dark boxes, each one chisel width per side (as in Figure 8-8). To darken the center of the box, take advantage of the chisel tip by laying the iron over 45 degrees and dragging the broad, hot face across the box. Each base is an X made by pressing the chisel tip to the board.

Cunning crafters have already noticed that a nine-line Go board has the same dimensions as a standard chess or checker board. If you want to add checkerboard functionality, you can use the face of the chisel to lightly toast alternating squares, or you can give these a wash with watercolor paints.

FIGURE 8-8: *A half-burned star on the right, two completed bases on the left*

Step 5   (optional) To preserve the surface of the board, consider giving it several coats of spar varnish. Also called marine varnish, this finish is thick, glossy, and waterproof, and it will put up with a lot of abuse.

Game Play

This board is set up to play two very different strategy games, Japanese Go and Norse Tafl.

Playing Go

In Go, players alternate placing light and dark *stones* (here pennies and dimes) at intersections on the board (as in Figure 8-9) in an attempt to control territory and capture enemy stones.

Liberties and Capturing Stones

When a stone is placed on the board, every intersection directly connected to it is a *liberty*. If you occupy all of the liberties of an opponent's stone or group of stones, then those pieces are *captured*; they are immediately removed from the board by the capturer, never to return.

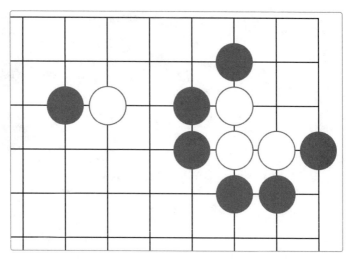

FIGURE 8-9: *The dark stone on the left has three liberties; the light chain on the right has only one and is about to be captured.*

When a set of stones of the same color are connected by lines, they are called a *chain*; they share their liberties, are harder to capture then scattered stones, and are better able to control territory.

In order to capture the chain in Figure 8-10 (the dark stones on the left), you need to take all eight of its liberties; you can't just pick off one stone. On the other hand, you can capture any of the stones in the *group* in Figure 8-10 (the light stones on the right) by occupying that stone's four liberties. With beginners, it is customary to say *atari* when you are one move from capturing a stone (a bit like saying *check* in chess); with more experienced players, it's often considered rude to say atari, as it implies that your opponent could be surprised by a capture.

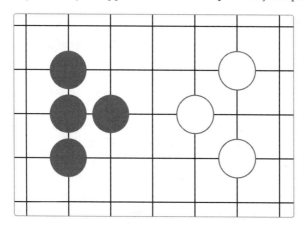

FIGURE 8-10: *On the left there is a chain of four dark stones; on the right a group of three light stones.*

The Ko Rule

The only complication to the capturing rule is *ko* (which means eternity). Look at the groups in Figure 8-11.

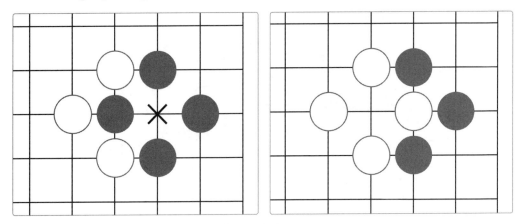

FIGURE 8-11: *The classic ko problem, before and after*

When the light player drops a stone at the point marked with an X, he will (1) capture a dark stone and (2) make a formation that is the mirror of the original (as you can see on the right). If the dark player were to then drop a piece back where her captured stone had been, she'd take the light stone that had just been placed by her opponent, and the board would look exactly as it had two moves prior. Stubborn players could carry on this pointless tit for tat until the heat death of the universe. In order to avoid such a state of affairs, the *ko rule* is: When a stone is captured in a *ko* formation, then the responding player must let at least one turn elapse before he can reply in that formation.

Live and Dead

The vital fundamental concept in Go is the notion of a *live* or *dead* group. The dark chain on the left of Figure 8-12 has two *eyes* (that is, two internal liberties) and thus cannot ever be captured by the light stones: If the light player tosses a stone into either eye, it is immediately surrounded and thus captured. This dark chain is live, since it cannot be killed.

Conversely, the chain of light stones on the right has only one eye and is therefore dead (watch it get captured in Figure 8-13). It might last for a while, but sooner or later the dark stones will surround it. When the final dark stone is dropped into the eye, it immediately kills the entire chain.

The point of the game, then, is to construct live chains such that you control the most territory.

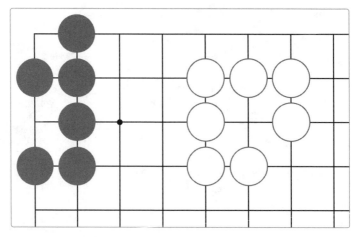

FIGURE 8-12: *On the left, a live chain; on the right, a dead chain*

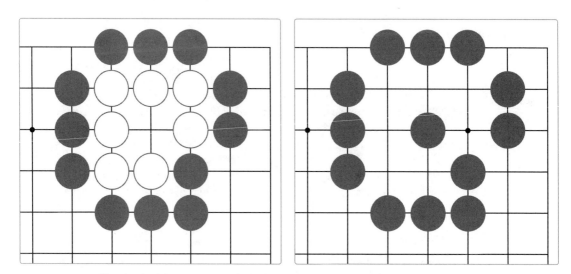

FIGURE 8-13: *The death of the one-eyed chain, before and after*

Game Play

The player using the dark pieces (pennies) goes first. A player can place a stone at any intersection on the board at any time, but it's customary (and strategically wise) to make your first moves in the corners of the board, near the stars. The two players alternate, placing one stone at a time, and removing stones as they are captured. On his or her turn, a player may either place a stone or pass (if he or she believes there are no useful moves to be made). Once the two players pass consecutively, the game is considered over.

To score the game:

Step 1   Remove any dead pieces that are still on the board; these are considered captured.

Step 2   If there are any neutral spaces on the board, the two players take turns filling them in with their own stones.

Step 3   Count up the number of liberties each player controls.

Step 4   Subtract the number of stones each player lost during the game. A shortcut is to simply fill in your opponent's territory with his captured pieces; his score is then the number of liberties remaining. Scores can be negative.

The highest score wins. Since dark always plays first, and thus has a tactical advantage, it's customary to grant light a few extra points, called *komi*. In tournaments, light gets 6.5 extra points to compensate for going second; in casual play, it is generally agreed that light wins all ties. Usually the weaker player is allowed to play dark. If the players are of very different skill levels, light can grant dark a number of extra handicap stones. These are placed on the stars (starting with the right corner star, as viewed by the dark player), in lieu of dark's first move.

Playing Tafl

This *Tafl* variant is based on *Tablut*, which was once popular in Lapland, and recorded by naturalist Carolus Linnaeus in 1732. Linnaeus did not share a language with his hosts; he determined the game's rules by directly observing players, and historians have grown to doubt some of Linnaeus's conclusions. The rules outlined here are a best guess based on Linnaeus's writings, scattered partial descriptions in historical documents, and a great deal of play testing and analysis.

Begin a game by setting up the board as in Figure 8-14, noting that the center piece (i.e., the king) is a nickel, not a dime.

One player controls the raiders (pennies) and the other the king (the nickel) and his men (the dimes). The king's goal is to reach any corner of the board; the raiders' goal is to capture him. Pieces are captured when they are sandwiched by attackers but can pass, or even rest, between two attackers without being captured, as illustrated in Figure 8-15.

The king and his men get the first move, and the players take turns thereafter. Each turn consists of moving one piece as many spaces as you like in a straight line (like a rook in chess).

The Xs are called bases. No one but the king can move through them or rest on them, but a piece can be captured by sandwiching it against the corner base. Once a raider has left his base, he cannot return. Likewise, no one but the king can pass through or rest on the throne at the center of the board. The king cannot be captured on his throne.

The game is over when the king escapes or is captured or immobilized.

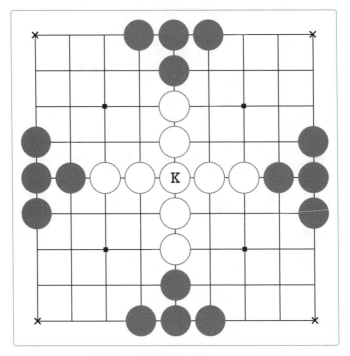

FIGURE 8-14: *Tafl board, initial positions*

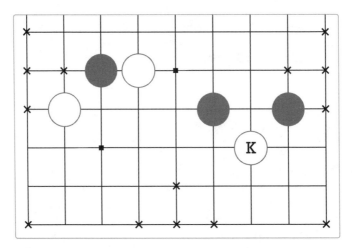

FIGURE 8-15: *On the left, a raider will be captured when the king's man moves up one space; on the right, the king can move up one space (or several) without being captured.*

Other Games

Obviously, a large number of games (including checkers, chess, and their variants) can be played on this board. Here are two lesser-known alternatives.

String Five

This is a horizontal precursor to Connect Four, shown in Figure 8-16. Two to four players (each with his or her own color pieces) take turns placing one piece at a time anywhere on the board. The first player to get five pieces in a row (diagonally, horizontally, or vertically) wins.

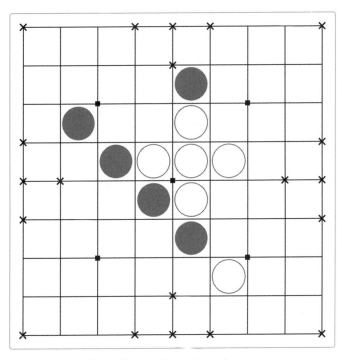

FIGURE 8-16: *String Five, midway through a two-person game*

This game's rules were printed on the back of my boyhood checkerboard, which cryptically titled the game Goban (which is the Japanese word for the Go board itself).

Fox and Geese

This is a highly simplified Tafl variant: Place four pennies (geese) on alternating end squares (beginning with the dark player's left corner) and one dime (the fox) on any of the four squares on the opposing edge not sharing a column with a penny (see Figure 8-17). Either player can go first, moving diagonally a single square. The geese want to corner and trap the fox, while the fox wants to make it to the opposing side (where the geese started). Geese can only move forward, but the fox can go any direction. No one can jump. The game is over when the fox is cornered or slips past the geese.

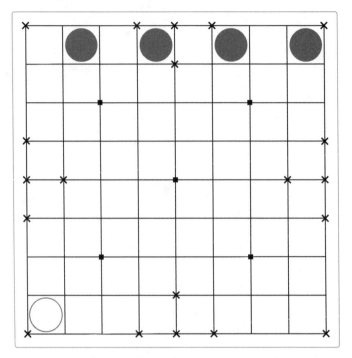

FIGURE 8-17: *Fox and Geese, initial positions (the fox is on one of the only two points on the board where a single goose can trap him; where is the other such point?)*

Resources

▶ *http://www.dragongoserver.net/*   The Dragon Go Server is one of many online Go communities. This one has useful forums and FAQs, a strong international membership, and a chat function; some seasoned players are willing to talk through their reasoning as they play, in order to give new players a leg up. I play there under the moniker *mcwee*.

▶ *http://www.aagenielsen.dk/*   This Danish page, maintained by Aage Nielsen, is available in English and hosts links and commentary on the history and play dynamics of the Tafl family of games, as well as Java versions of several Tafl variants.

PART II

Electro-Skiffle Band

With origins in the 1920s, skiffle is fast-paced, fun-time American music made on improvised instruments, often played by "juke" or "spasm" bands at rent parties (which were called *skiffles* in New Orleans). In the age-old artistic battle between musical virtuosity (epitomized by chamber music) and well-meaning energy (epitomized by punk), skiffle music errs on the side of the latter. While only some of these instruments, like the $10 Electric Guitar and X-Ray Drums, have legitimate skiffle roots, all of them rely on repurposing cheap and common parts in the service of rocking the house.

One invaluable tool for the neophyte instrument builder is a *chromatic tuner*. A tuner reports back what pitch it's hearing and is conventionally used to tune string instruments. (Beware of *guitar tuners* that only recognize the pitches commonly played on guitar; these are much less useful.) Having a chromatic tuner will greatly expand your ability to tune and play the $10 Electric Guitar (Project 13) and Cigar-Box Synthesizer (Project 17). Several software packages (like Apple's Garageband or the free Gibson Learn & Master Guitar Application for the iPhone and iPod Touch) include tuners, and there are many stand-alone software tuners available for free online (like the Seven String Tuner: *http://www.seventhstring.com/tuner/tuner.html*).

X-RAY TALKING DRUM

Building your own hand drums has traditionally meant a little bit of woodworking and a whole lot of stretching, tacking, and tanning of raw animal hides. Working hides is tricky and can be expensive (especially if you don't happen to hunt or live near a slaughterhouse that processes sheep and goats), and the results range from incredible to mediocre. In this project and the next, you'll build two drums from cheap, everyday supplies. The first is a simple *talking drum* whose pitch you can change as you play, and the second a somewhat less conventional *thunderdrum*.

Rumor has it that Cuban *bongoceros* often use old x-ray films to replace the heads of their bongos (especially on the smaller drum, called the *macho*). Although this sounds both obtuse and William Gibson-ish, x-ray films actually have much to commend them: They're big (large ones are around 14"×17", while the smaller films are 10"×12"), free, incredibly durable (the materials are intended to survive long-term archiving, even in less-than-ideal conditions), and can be pierced without tearing.

As far as scrounging supplies, some doctors' offices might give you over-exposed x-ray films, but laws making them liable for releasing patient information will make most offices reluctant to do so. A slightly more casual environment (like a chiropractor's office) might be helpful, but your best bet is a veterinarian. Remember to specifically ask for a blank or overexposed film; even dog doctors care a lot about their patients' privacy. If you happen to get an x-ray with a good image on it, consider cashing in on the sci-fi appeal by mounting a couple of LED lights inside the drum (maybe using the circuit from Project 2, the Switchbox).

FIGURE 9-1: *The finished X-Ray Talking Drum*

Tools

- a jigsaw or keyhole saw
- a utility knife
- a pair of spring clamps
- an electric drill and several bits, including a 1/8" bit
- a wood saw (For a complete discussion of the merits of various wood saws, check out "Crosscut Saw vs. Pull Saw" on page 10.)

- ▶ a tape measure
- ▶ a miter box

Supplies

- ▶ a large x-ray
- ▶ several yards of cotton clothesline
- ▶ a square 4-gallon bucket[1] (The top should measure around 9 1/2" along one edge.)
- ▶ four turnbuckles
- ▶ four 3/4" corner braces
- ▶ four 1" corner braces
- ▶ sixteen #8 1/2" wood screws
- ▶ sixteen #8 1" wood screws
- ▶ eight medium screw eyes (e.g., 7/8" long screw eyes with a 1/4" eye capable of bearing 11 pounds of pressure)
- ▶ 8' of 1"×1/2" trim wood

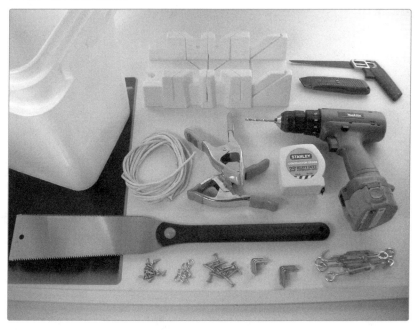

FIGURE 9-2: *Tools and supplies*

1. Cat litter is commonly sold in this sort of square 4-gallon bucket. Other free sources include bakeries, since many bulk ingredients (like the nutty, cinnamon-and-sugar schmeer used on sticky buns) are shipped in these. A square bucket is preferable to a common cylindrical bucket, as a square drumhead frame is much easier to craft than a circular one.

Building It

We'll start by building the drumhead, which is composed of two square wooden frames, each 1/2" wide and 1" deep. These nesting frames will hold our x-ray film tight, so it can be stretched taut against the bucket while still vibrating freely. One frame (the *outer frame*) has an external width of 12" and an internal width of 11". The other (predictably, the *inner frame*) has an external width of 11" and an internal width of 10". Making these requires using a *miter box*.

A miter box (shown in Figure 9-3) guides the saw so that you can accurately cut precise angles. There are lots of specialty miter boxes available with different angles, but even the most basic miter box has slots for cutting 90-degree and 45-degree angles. Framing the drumhead calls for 45-degree cuts. Since we are making a square frame, each side will have a 45-degree cut at either end, so that each piece of the frame is a skinny trapezoid with a long edge that is 1" longer than its short edge.

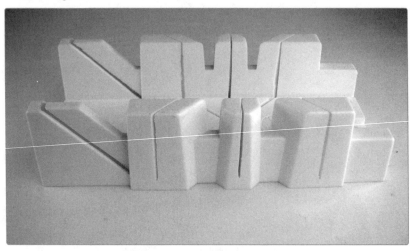

FIGURE 9-3: *A miter box*

Step 1   Using the miter box as a guide, cut four pieces of wood that are 12" long, with a 45-degree angle at either end (like the example at the top of Figure 9-4); these are for the outer frame. Then cut four similar pieces that are 11" long (like the example at the bottom of Figure 9-4) for the inner frame. Note that each piece has a 45-degree angle at either end and that the angles are not parallel.

    ✳ **NOTE:** Measure twice! Cut once! *Before you pull the saw, ask yourself, "Have I oriented this piece of wood properly? Am I cutting across the 1/2" face of the board, so that I can have a 1" deep frame?" It seems like I'm senselessly belaboring this point, but rest assured: If this is your first time, you are going to reverse one of those cuts and kick yourself. Cut the longer pieces first, since you can transform a screwed-up long piece into a workable short piece.*

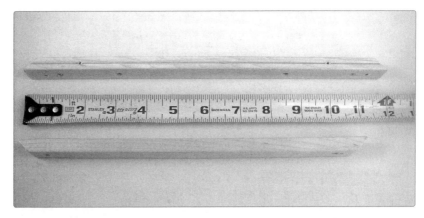

FIGURE 9-4: *Two pieces of the frame: The top piece has one 12"side and one 11"side, and the bottom piece has one 11"side and one 10"side.*

Step 2 Mock up the outer frame, then install the 1" corner braces around the outside of the frame using 1/2" screws. It's easy to accidentally split these thin strips of wood; to avoid splitting, carefully drill 1/8" guide holes for each screw before screwing it in.

Step 3 Now build the inner frame. This time you'll mount the 3/4" braces on the inside of the frame (as shown in Figure 9-5), securing them with 1/2" screws (again, drill guide holes for each screw in advance).

FIGURE 9-5: *Detail of an inner frame corner brace*

Step 4   Test to make sure that the inner frame fits snugly in the outer frame (as in Figure 9-6) and that the inner frame will easily fit around the lip of your bucket.

FIGURE 9-6: *The finished frames*

Step 5   Place the outer frame on the workbench, lay a large x-ray film over it, center the inner frame within the outer frame, and push hard, sandwiching the x-ray between the two. Once the inner and outer frames are flush, clamp them together as shown in Figure 9-7.

Step 6   Now that the frame is temporarily secure, drill a 1/8" hole through the outer frame, x-ray, and inner frame right next to an exterior corner brace. Drive a 1" screw through all three, securing the two frames and trapping the x-ray between them (illustrated in Figure 9-8). Repeat this on the other end of this side, then the opposite side and each of the adjacent sides. When you're done, you will have installed eight 1" screws.

Step 7   Remove the clamps, then measure and mark 3" in from each corner (Figure 9-9). These marks show the positions for the last eight 1" screws (which will serve as secondary securing screws).

Step 8   In order to keep as much strain as possible off of the screws that are piercing the x-ray, we need to make sure that the inner frame is as snug to the outer frame as possible. Flip the drumhead over and remove the interior corner braces (which are no longer necessary). Drill guide holes and install the last eight 1" securing screws

FIGURE 9-7: *The clamped frame*

FIGURE 9-8: *Securing the frames at the corner*

FIGURE 9-9: *Measuring for a secondary securing screw*

at the points you marked in Step 7. Finally, remove and re-drive the first set of 1"
securing screws (the ones right next to the exterior corner braces), so that the inner
and outer frame are drawn together as tightly as possible.

Step 9   Flip your drumhead face down and trim the x-ray film. You'll likely have a reasonably tight drumhead; hold the wooden frame and give the head a few fingertip
beats. This kind of simple, shallow drum (sometimes called a *lollipop drum* in kids'
music classes) is similar to an Irish *bodhrán* and pleasing in its own right. If your
drumhead doesn't sound at all drum-like at this stage, don't panic: the drumhead
ultimately gets its tension from being drawn taut against the lip of the bucket. None-
theless, since the x-ray film is so rigid, it's highly likely you'll have a serviceable
drum in hand at this step.

Step 10   Next, install mounting hardware. Find your slimmest drill bit, and use it to drill eight
holes on the underside of the outer frame, 2" from each corner (Figure 9-10). Screw
the eyes into these holes, being sure that they are fully seated and oriented so that the
eyes look down the edge of the frame, not out. Set aside the drumhead.

Step 11   Get out the 4-gallon bucket and flip it over. Draw a 4" square in the middle of the
bottom, drill a 1" hole in each corner of that square, and saw between the holes.
Then, drill a 1/8" hole in the middle of each edge of the bucket's bottom, as shown
in Figure 9-11. Fully extend your four turnbuckles and slide the hooked end of each
into its 1/8" hole.

Step 12   Stand the bucket up (the turnbuckles should sit snugly in the 1/8" holes, making this
a relatively painless operation). Place the drumhead on top of the bucket, face up.

FIGURE 9-10: *Drilling a guide hole for a screw eye*

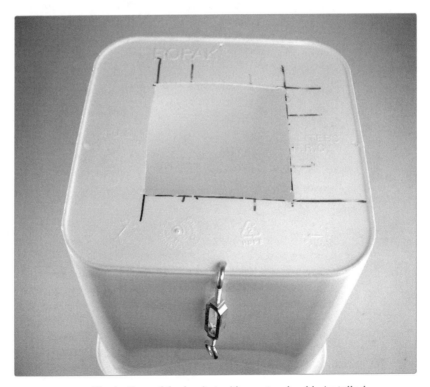

FIGURE 9-11: *The bottom of the bucket with one turnbuckle installed*

Run a 3 1/2' piece of clothesline in a loop from one screw eye, down to the eye on the turnbuckle, to the other screw eye, and back through the turnbuckle. Tie it off with a square knot, taking up as much slack as you can (Figure 9-12). Repeat on each side, then trim the excess cord.

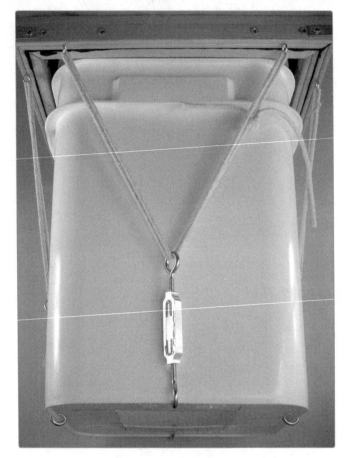

FIGURE 9-12: *Detail of the drum's suspension*

Step 13   To tune the drum, give one turnbuckle four clockwise half-turns, then do likewise with the opposite turnbuckle, then with one adjacent turnbuckle, and then with its opposite. Repeat this three or four times, until the head begins to become taut (e.g., the turnbuckles will no longer rattle against the body when you lightly tap the drumhead). Fine tune the drum by turning each turnbuckle one half-turn, working around the perimeter of the drum in a circle rather than by tightening opposites, until you get a tone you like. Too much tension will deaden the tone, and if you keep going, will deform the bucket. It could even begin to tear the drumhead within the frame, although that's unlikely if you are tightening the turnbuckles evenly.

Step 14 (optional) You can also add a piezo pickup (like the one in the next project, the Thunderdrum) to the X-Ray Talking Drum; here it's best to glue the pickup to the body of the drum, rather than the head. Distortion effects, especially a heavy-metal oriented stomp box like a BOSS Metal Zone, can be pretty wicked awesome on a drum.

Playing the X-Ray Talking Drum

The X-Ray Talking Drum can be played like any other hand drum. While some will find it most natural to hold it between the knees (like a set of bongos or an African *djembe*) or run a length of clothesline between the drum body and suspension and sling it over one's shoulder like Ricky Ricardo playing a *conga,* I prefer to tuck it under my left arm like a Middle Eastern *doumbek.* I then play it primarily with the fingertips on my right hand and use my left to mute the head, provide counterpoint, and pull on the suspension, shifting the drum's pitch so that it "talks."

Unlike most hand drums—especially those with natural hide heads—the X-Ray Talking Drum can take a lot of abuse, including being left in direct sunlight, a hot car, a damp basement, or out in the rain. You can even bang on it with drumsticks (which will cut right through a goatskin head) or mallets (like those used to play xylophone). A good mallet can be made by drilling a 5/32" hole into a high-bounce ball (e.g., the ones you get from a supermarket vending machine), filling the hole with glue, and inserting a piece of dowel, a chopstick, or a sharpened pencil.

If you've never played a hand drum before, here are two tips:

▶ Use a light touch—everyone bangs loudly at first, and it's hard to sound good while making a crazy damn racket. Focus on using your fingertips as a single unit, and hit the drum firmly with a loose wrist, so the fingers naturally bounce back, letting the drumhead resonate freely.

▶ Explore the drumhead for different tones. The center of the head will have the deepest tone, but it will also be fairly flat, because of the blocky shape of the X-Ray Talking Drum. The tone will get higher as you move out toward the edge, with the rim singing out as a high, ringing tone that's very responsive to "talking" by putting pressure on the suspension. Experiment with muting tones with your free hand or by letting your hand "deaden" the head rather than bounce back as you play.

10 THUNDERDRUM

Although there is much to commend durable x-ray film to neophyte drum crafters, perhaps its most notable quality is that it can be pierced without tearing, even when stretched. X-rays are thus ideal for this unconventional metal-bodied thunderdrum, which relies on a resonating spring mounted through its drumhead in order to produce its formidable rumble. We'll also install an acoustic pickup on this drum so that the thunder can be routed into effects and amplified.

FIGURE 10-1: *A finished Thunderdrum*

Tools

- ▶ work gloves
- ▶ a flathead screwdriver
- ▶ a can opener
- ▶ a flat piece of scrap wood (such as a chunk of 2"×4") wider than your metal can
- ▶ needle-nose pliers
- ▶ a thumbtack
- ▶ a standard soldering kit (See the appendix.)
- ▶ a small nail
- ▶ a hammer
- ▶ an electric drill with a 3/8" bit

Supplies

▶ a small x-ray (See Project 9, the X-Ray Talking Drum, for more information.)

▶ two #36 hose clamps (These are roughly 10" long and are used on hoses 1 13/16" to 2 3/4" in diameter.)

▶ a largish metal can, such as a 32-ounce coffee can or the large tomato or fruit cans used in restaurant kitchens

▶ an 18" screen door spring

▶ a piezo element, such as a 20 mm 6.5 kHz piezo buzzer element, Digi-Key part #102-1126-ND

▶ a 1/4" mono phone jack (a guitar jack)

▶ room-temperature vulcanizing rubber or silicone-based household glue

FIGURE 10-2: *Tools and supplies*

Building It

Step 1 Begin by opening the hose clamps and fitting their ends together to form a 20" steel hoop (Figure 10-3). Set this aside.

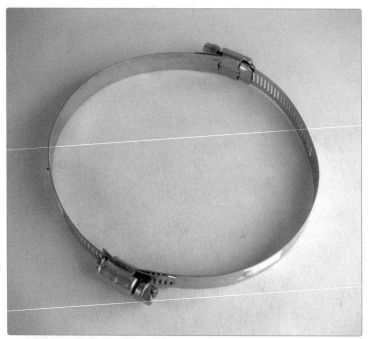

FIGURE 10-3: *The Thunderdrum's hoop of steel ("Hoop of Steel" is also a good name for your new electro-skiffle band)*

Step 2 Prepare the spring. The spring should be loose enough so that it can be dangled and jiggled in a manner that a kitten would love (the ideal goal is to be able to twirl it into a sloppy standing S-wave, as in Figure 10-4). An old, used screen door spring will likely already be this way.

A new spring will be too rigid to do this (and is likely stiff enough to balance upright on its end). If you must use a new spring, then don work gloves and gently stretch the spring out: work up and down the length, making it stretch a little farther than it likes. Be sure to keep the coils tight at one end (this will make it easier to mount it on the drumhead in Step 8).

Step 3 Use needle-nose pliers to open up the loop on the tighter end of the spring, making a hook (as in Figure 10-5). Set the prepared spring aside.

Step 4 Use the can opener to remove the bottom of the coffee can.

If you're sure you want to install a pickup on the inside of the drum, consider skipping ahead to Step 11 (drilling the hole) now, as it will be somewhat harder to do after you install the drumhead. See Step 10 for more information.

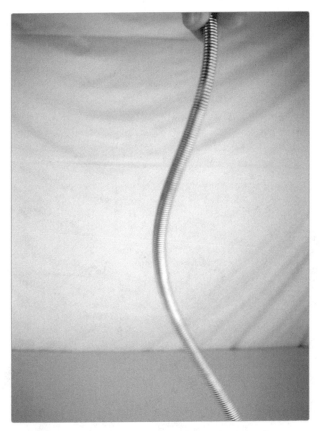

FIGURE 10-4: *Twirling a good Thunderdrum spring*

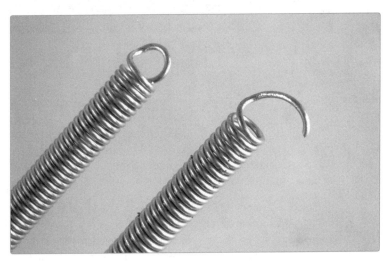

FIGURE 10-5: *The end of the spring before (left) and after (right) being opened into a hook*

Step 5   Lay the small x-ray over one end of the can and place the hoop of hose clamps on top of it, centered around the can's opening. Lay the piece of scrap wood over the hoop and press down, forcing the hoop to crumple the x-ray film around the mouth of the can. X-rays are very rigid and don't like this at all; it is much harder than you'd expect. Fortunately, x-rays are also shockingly durable, and the cylindrical steel wall of a food can is quite sturdy. If you can't get the x-ray to succumb using arm strength alone, try setting the can on the floor and pressing your knee on the scrap wood, driving the hoop around the can's wall, pinching the x-ray between the two. You want to get the hoop as far down the can as possible, ideally just behind the rolled steel rim of the can (Figure 10-6).

FIGURE 10-6: *The rolled steel rim of the can*

Step 6   Once the hoop is in place, keep your weight on the wood scrap and pull down on the edges of the x-ray to get the head as taut as possible (although tension is not a vital issue with this drum). Then start tightening the hose clamps. *Do not* take any weight off of the wood scrap until the clamps are tightened, as the x-ray and clamps will pop right off. A drum head under symmetrical tension will wear better, so try to tighten both sides of the clamp-hoop equally.

Step 7   Once you've removed the wood scrap, take a second to tug on the edges of the x-ray, then use the screwdriver handle to work the hoop down a little farther. Tighten the clamps again. Use scissors or a utility knife to trim off the excess x-ray, if you like (although it can be handy to keep it intact, so that you can periodically tug the head tighter).

Step 8   Pop a hole in the center of the drumhead with the thumbtack, making the smallest hole possible. From the outside of the drum, thread the hook on the spring's tight end into this hole (see Figure 10-7). Twist the spring so that two or three coils are inside the drum and the rest dangles out.

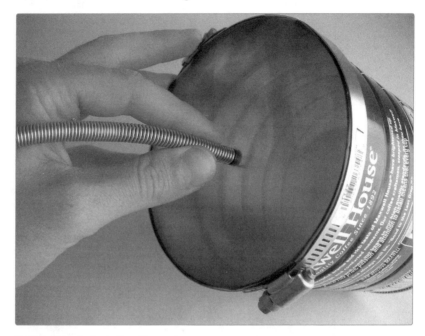

FIGURE 10-7: *Installing the spring*

Step 9   To build the acoustic pickup (Figure 10-8), solder the leads from your piezo element to your jack's lugs; it doesn't matter which wire goes to which lug.

Step 10   To test the pickup, turn the volume all the way down on your amp, connect your pickup, bring the volume up a few notches, and gently tap the brass disk. The piezo element is pretty efficient, so even light prods should produce major thunks and even feedback. Using a scrap of tape, experiment with different placements of the pickup on the inside and outside of the drumhead. You'll often get more bass boom on the outside and more high-end crackle on the inside. That said, it's easiest to install the pickup inside the drum—although be aware that drilling the side of the drum will deaden it a little bit. Flip ahead to "Playing the Thunderdrum" on page 111 and experiment with the drum a little before proceeding. Installing the pickup at this stage is a little more challenging but gives you an opportunity to weigh your options; if you're sure you want to add a pickup from the start, then consider doing Step 11—drilling the hole—at Step 4.

Pickup Primer Part One: The Piezo Pickup

All sound amplification works the same: an element picks up vibrations, translates them into a fluctuating electrical current, and sends these to an amplifier that (*surprise!*) amplifies them. The Thunderdrum uses the *acoustic "piezo" pickup* (also called a *contact mic*) shown in Figure 10-8. Piezo pickups are made from a *piezoelectric* element; *piezoelectric* substances generate an electric current in response to pressure (usually as the result of the physics of putting mechanical stress on a crystalline structure, like quartz); squeeze the element, get some voltage. Squeeze harder, get more. Most cheap piezo elements take the form of a brass disk coated on one side with a crystalline ceramic compound. Piezo pickups are great for realistically reproducing the sounds of acoustic instruments (like a violin or acoustic guitar), because the pickup directly translates the vibration of the instrument's body to electrical pulses. It's popular to crack open piezoelectric buzzers (like RadioShack part #273-059) and use those elements for all sorts of music amplification applications, but that is a bit pricey, risks damaging the element, and doesn't make the best pickup. Ordering online, you can have a more sensitive pickup at a quarter of the price (using, for example, the 20mm 6.5 kHz piezo buzzer element, Digi-Key part #102-1126-ND).

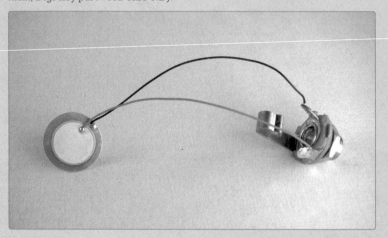

FIGURE 10-8: *The prepared acoustic pickup*

Step 11   To install the acoustic pickup, lay the drum on its side, pick a point roughly halfway along the wall, and use the hammer and nail to put a dimple in the metal (the spinning drill bit will want to skate all over the smooth metal, slip off the edge, and bite you; adding the dimple will make it much easier for the drill to bite into the metal). Drill a 3/8" hole in the can; you can see the results in Figure 10-9.

jack hole

FIGURE 10-9: *The drum, with jack hole*

Step 12   Unscrew the nut from your jack, pass it through the wall of the drum, and screw the nut back on. Then either tape the pickup to the inside of the head or glue it down with room temperature vulcanizing rubber or any silicone-based household glue.

Playing the Thunderdrum

The Thunderdrum is a pretty unconventional percussion instrument. To play it, hold the drum upside-down with the opening facing up, the head pointed at the floor, and the spring dangling down, as shown in Figure 10-10. Jiggling will give you a nice distant-thunder rumble, while flicking the spring (or rhythmically striking it with a stick) makes a booming crack. Grab the spring between thumb and index finger and run your thumbnail down the coils, as in the middle of Figure 10-10, for a very dramatic "washboard in the unpopular backwaters of a dead galaxy" sound.

Or you can use the fingers of your free hand to beat out patterns on the drumhead itself. The suggestions from the previous drum project still hold: Start with a light touch (focusing on using the fingertips) and explore the drumhead for different tones.

FIGURE 10-10: *Playing the Thunderdrum*

Resources

I've posted a video demonstration of the Thunderdrum online: *http://www .davideriknelson.com/sbsb/.*

11 THE ELECTRO-DIDGERIDOO

The mysterious didgeridoo is in a class of instruments called *labrosones* (so called because their sound is made by vibrating the lips), which includes reedless brass instruments like the trumpet and bugle. Labrosonic instruments are tubes modified to convert lip-based fart noises into music. A column of air within the tube, excited into a standing wave by the vibration of the player's lips, produces a note, which the player can alter by changing her lip vibrations. The lowest note a labrosone can sound is determined by the length of the tube; longer tubes give lower fundamental notes—the valves on a trumpet actually change the total length of the tube in order to increase the instrument's range.

Genuine didgeridoos are the only wind instruments crafted by animals for human use: They are made from eucalyptus trunks hollowed out by termites. After harvesting, these instruments enjoy little modification, apart from the addition of a beeswax mouthpiece and some surface decoration. Since artisans spend an inordinate amount of time wandering around inhospitable climates searching for eucalyptus trunks that the termites have gotten just right, genuine didgeridoos can be very expensive. Cheaper didges made from teak and bamboo are common, but in terms of tone, volume, and playability, you can build your own for just a few dollars and get as good—or better—results.

To get a sense of what you can do with a PVC didgeridoo, let's make a "30-second didge" by adding a simple duct tape mouthpiece to some PVC. Grab a 4' length of PVC plumbing.

✳ **WARNING:** *If you're cutting the PVC yourself* **wear a respirator and work outside,** *since the friction from the saw can heat the PVC enough for it to release gases; see Step 2 for a full discussion of the dangers of PVC fumes.*

Use your fingers to clear away any rough snaggles from the edges, and then wash off any grease, grime, or grit that's on the pipe. Take about 5" of duct tape and wrap it around the pipe so that half the width hangs off the end (as shown in Figure 11-2). Tuck the duct tape into the pipe and give it a good rub; warmth and pressure encourage adhesion.

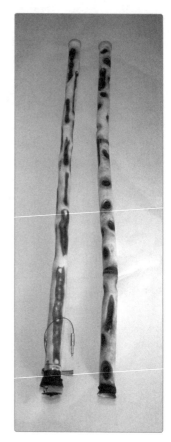

FIGURE 11-1: *Finished PVC didgeridoos (the one on the left has a pickup installed)*

FIGURE 11-2: *The duct tape mouthpiece before folding, after folding, and interior*

Now flip to "Playing the Didgeridoo" on page 126 and give your didge a few experimental toots. Although a straight PVC didgeridoo will make an acceptable sound, it's muffled and muddled, with few of the complex overtones that make the didgeridoo popular. Modifying the PVC didgeridoo—adding a proper beeswax mouthpiece, belling the end, and adding complexity to the interior of the didge—increases back pressure (making it easier to play a sustained note), brings out overtones, reduces the "PVC rattle," defines the tone, and makes it easier to shift up from the fundamental drone. Finally, adding a pickup means being able to process and filter the didgeridoo's sound—using software on your computer, store-bought guitar stomp boxes, or the effects and filters in later projects—and directly hook into an amplifier, PA system, or recording rig.

Tools

▶ a propane torch with "pencil flame" end (If you can get your hands on a heat gun, like those used to strip paint, you can use that; it will heat the PVC enough to be malleable with less risk of charring it.)

▶ a round-headed bolt, preferably one with a nickel- or dime-sized head

▶ a long-necked plastic funnel (Look in the auto supplies aisle of your hardware store; a wide-mouthed kitchen funnel won't work.)

▶ a beer bottle

▶ a respirator mask suitable for filtering organic solvent fumes

Supplies

▶ a 4' length of 1 1/4" diameter thin-walled PVC pipe[1] (Have it cut to length at the hardware store if possible.)

▶ duct tape

▶ beeswax (available from most health food/dietary supplement stores, organic grocers, or beekeepers)

▶ an old pair of cheap headphones

▶ a #24 hose clamp (i.e., one good for pipes 1 1/16" to 2" and roughly 6 1/2" long when laid flat)

▶ a 1/4" mono phone plug (i.e., a TS connector, like those on a guitar cable)

▶ a wire coat hanger or similar length of rigid wire

▶ glue suitable for working with metal and plastic

....
1. This assumes you intend to fully modify your didge by heating and twisting it. If you're not going to do any modifications beyond adding a mouthpiece, then you might be happier with 1 1/2" or even 2" diameter PVC. These are a little trickier to play, since the wide bore offers little resistance (making it harder to sustain a note) and the thick walls don't resonate very well. But the larger volume of air in the tube will offer a richer unmodified sound, and the thick walls lack the rattle characteristic of thinner pipes. In any case, you'll almost certainly be happier if you upgrade to the beeswax mouthpiece described in Step 12.

- ▶ clamps or binder clips
- ▶ a standard soldering kit (See the appendix.)
- ▶ (optional) all-purpose indoor/outdoor Krylon spray paint for decorating your finished didgeridoo

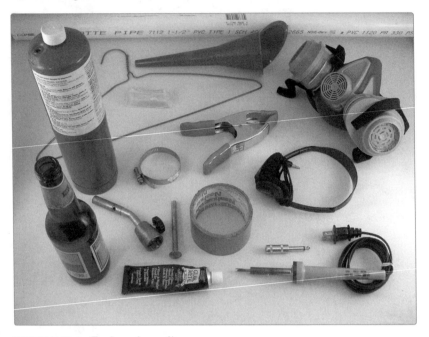

FIGURE 11-3: *Tools and supplies*

Building It

Step 1   Prepare your piece of PVC. If you need to cut it to length yourself, wear a respirator mask and safety goggles; shreds of PVC are very sharp, and the friction from the saw can release toxic fumes (see the first warning in Step 2 for more details). Even if you get your PVC precut, take a moment to clear any sharp burrs off of the cuts, and then clean the PVC with soap and water.

Step 2   First, you'll add a bell. Traditional eucalyptus didgeridoos are naturally flared like a trumpet, increasing both volume and clarity. In order to bell the end of your PVC didgeridoo, you'll need to heat it using a torch.

＊WARNING: *Never heat PVC indoors! Always wear a carbon-filter respirator capable of filtering organic chemicals while molding PVC! When heated, PVC releases chlorine and phosgene, a pair of WWI-vintage chemical weapons that are very bad for the lungs. A professional-grade respirator mask can be bought at any hardware store for about $30; don't end up in an iron lung.*

Head outside, don your mask, and spark up your blowtorch. Stand the torch up and hold one end of the PVC over it, rotating the tube in order to heat it evenly.

＊WARNING: *Be very careful with the blowtorch; the flame can be almost invisible on a sunny day, and it will give a severe burn in a fraction of a second. Also, a lot of very hot air will be channeled up the pipe, so refrain from pointing the open end into your face.*

FIRE DANGER!

Slowly heat the bottom lip of your didgeridoo (it will quickly toast and scorch like a marshmallow over a campfire). You'll find that the PVC is pliable once it's golden brown and will stay so for 10 or 15 seconds once the heat is removed.

Step 3 Slide your funnel into the pliable PVC, as shown in Figure 11-4, being careful not to burn yourself (the PVC holds heat well). Press the funnel firmly into place (twisting can help work it back a little further) and hold it for 30 seconds.

Remove the funnel and repeat, this time heating the bottom inch of the tube before sliding in the funnel and letting the PVC cool. Repeat again, until you've belled out the bottom 2" of your didgeridoo. For the final touch, reheat the bottom 1/2" of the bell and then press it down over the neck and shoulders of a beer bottle, flaring the bell. The inside of the bell should ultimately be just under 2 1/2" wide (as shown in Figure 11-5).

FIGURE 11-4: *Starting the bell*

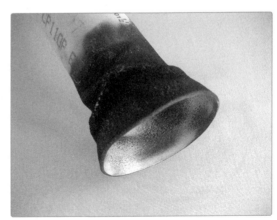

FIGURE 11-5: *The completed bell*

Back Pressure

It's much easier to sustain a tone—and thus accentuate overtones and form rhythmic patterns—when you are blowing against something (as every grade-schooler knows: contrast the puny lip-based fart noise to the grandeur of the crook-of-the-elbow butt-trumpet). Horn players sometimes call this *back pressure*. Straight PVC pipes are engineered to let fluids pass through them as easily as possible, which is great for plumbing a toilet, but terrible for making an instrument. A genuine eucalyptus didgeridoo is the result of the capricious will of tunneling ants, and is thus not at all a uniform tube.

Adding dimples to the PVC didgeridoo increases the back pressure and clarifies the tone, bringing out the characteristic rich overtones. The added dimples decrease the resonance (which is a shame) but in doing so also eliminate the tell-tale rasp of a straight piece of PVC. Figure 11-6 offers a comparison between the interior of a natural didgeridoo and a PVC didgeridoo that's been dimpled.

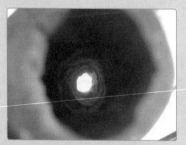 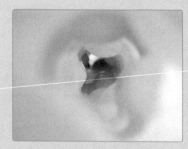

FIGURE 11-6: *The inside of a natural didgeridoo (left) and of a modified PVC didgeridoo (right)*

Step 4   To add a dimple, lay the didge on a fireproof surface (like a concrete driveway), and use the blowtorch to heat a nickel-sized area on the PVC for a few seconds (just until the spot has scorched). Carefully, but firmly, press down on that spot with a round-headed bolt, as in Figure 11-7. Hold for 20 seconds. Remove the bolt and let the PVC cool for another 20 seconds. (**Be careful**; both the bolt and PVC will retain a lot of heat.) Repeat this at least 30 times, working up and down the pipe on all sides. Be sure to leave the last couple inches of the mouthpiece end unmodified. If you mess up and make a dimple too deep or too close to the end, you can reheat the PVC, slide a broom handle into the tube, and push the dimple back out.

Step 5   You might also consider adding long dimples, like that shown in Figure 11-8: Use the torch to draw a 4" or 5" line running along the length of the didge, working back and forth so that it toasts uniformly. Set the torch safely aside, and quickly roll the sharp edge of the round-headed bolt down the line, pressing it firmly as you roll it. As you work up and down the line, gradually slow to a snail's pace, lingering for several seconds on each turn. Once the long dimple begins to harden, let it cool for a half minute, then start a new long dimple.

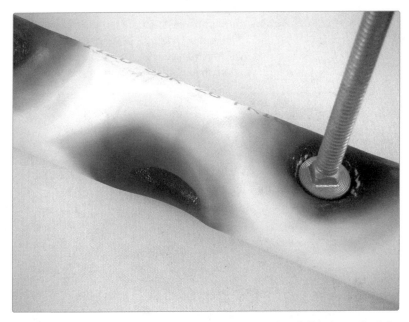

FIGURE 11-7: *Adding a new dimple; note the completed dimples to the left*

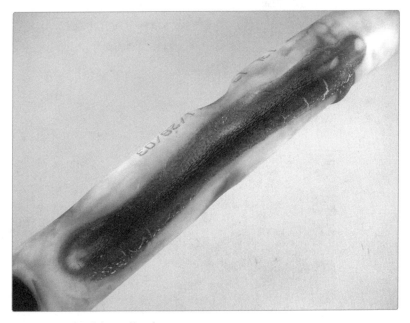

FIGURE 11-8: *A long dimple*

Step 6   Next, add minor kinks to complete the back pressure improvement regimen. Pick up the PVC by its mouthpiece end and hold it parallel to the ground. Pick a point roughly one third of the way down the length of the pipe. Gradually heat this point, rotating the pipe to heat the entire circumference evenly until the PVC begins to dip under its own weight (Figure 11-9). Keeping the PVC parallel to the ground, lower it until the mouthpiece end is roughly 1" from the ground, and let the belled end dip down and rest on your fireproof surface. Hold the didgeridoo steady in this position for a minute or two until the kink has fully hardened.

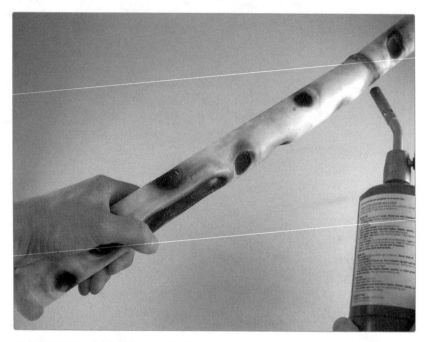

FIGURE 11-9: *Adding the first kink*

Step 7   Repeat, this time holding the didgeridoo by its belled end and running the kink the opposite direction (see the results in Figure 11-10).

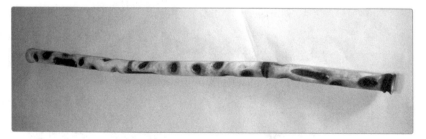

FIGURE 11-10: *A fully kinked didgeridoo; note that the kinks zig, then zag*

Step 8   Leave your finished didgeridoo outside for an hour or so to fully air out. Again, *phosgene and chlorine are poisonous gases that could irreparably damage your lungs*; minimize your exposure![2]

Since PVC is cheap, consider experimenting with making several didges at once. A good bell is almost mandatory, but there's a little magic to the dimples and bends; my favorite didge has no real kinks and is almost entirely twisted with long, drastic dimples. I've made others with tons of little dimples and very severe bends; all have interesting, distinct sounds.

If you aren't planning on building a pickup for your didgeridoo, then skip ahead to Step 12, and start preparing the beeswax for the mouthpiece while you wait for the didgeridoo to air out.

Step 9   To build a pickup for the didgeridoo, start by breaking up your headphones and tearing apart one earpiece, as in Figure 11-11. The goal is to expose the tiny speaker within.

FIGURE 11-11: *A gutted headphone earpiece*

---

2. Flick back to the bold warning at Step 2 for more information about chlorine and phosgene. To learn more about dying in a gas attack, please see Wilfred Owen's poem "Dulce Et Decorum Est."

Step 10   Snip off the speaker wires, keeping as much of the length as you can. Strip these, and solder one wire to each lug on your plug, as in Figure 11-12. It doesn't matter which wire goes to which lug, although if the speaker has terminals marked + and −, honor that by soldering the + to the tip of the plug and the − to the sleeve (for a full discussion of 1/4" plugs and jacks, see the appendix).

Step 11   Glue a straight 6" length of coat hanger to the edge of your speaker and clamp it in place (Figure 11-13). Allow the glue to set overnight.

Step 12   Meanwhile, add a beeswax mouthpiece to your didgeridoo. This will give you a better seal, a more comfortable fit, and a subtle hint of honey flavor. Start with a chunk of beeswax roughly half the size of your thumb (this is less than an ounce; beeswax can usually be purchased at health food or craft stores for less than $10 per pound). To soften the wax, place it in a sealable freezer bag and immerse the bag in a bowl of your hottest tap water for 15 minutes. Weigh it down with a rock or coffee mug; you may need to refresh the water several times before the beeswax starts to become malleable.

Step 13   Go outside and grab your new, freshly aired didgeridoo. A little soap and water will help clear away the grime, grit, and PVC soot. When the beeswax is warm, remove it from the bag and briskly roll it between your palms for a few minutes, making a pliable ball. Roll this into a "snake" roughly 4" long and half as thick as your pinky.

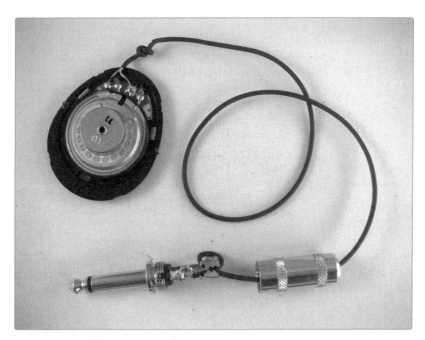

FIGURE 11-12: *The soldered plug*

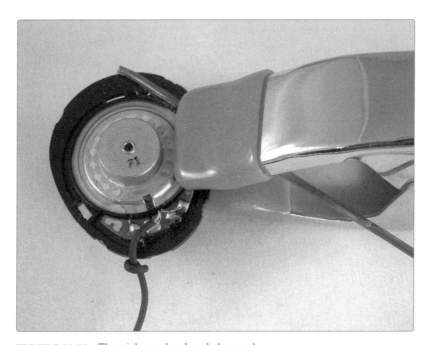

FIGURE 11-13: *The pickup, glued and clamped*

Curl the snake onto the end of the tube (as in Figure 11-14), then smooth it into place (as on the left of Figure 11-15). Since a traditional wooden didgeridoo generally has a wider internal diameter (around 2"), it's normal to use more wax, resulting in a bigger mouthpiece, often meticulously sculpted into a flat-topped volcano with an opening around 1 1/4" in diameter. The PVC didge already has an internal diameter of 1 1/4", so you'll only need to add enough beeswax to give a comfortable play and a good seal. Over time the mouthpiece will dry out and begin to flake off, at which time you should peel off the remaining wax and put on a new mouthpiece.

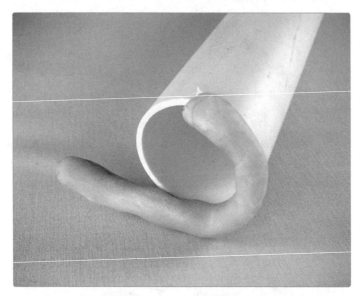

FIGURE 11-14: *Adding the beeswax mouthpiece*

FIGURE 11-15: *Our mouthpiece (left) and a traditional mouthpiece (right)*

Step 14   Once the glue has set on the pickup, bend the coat hanger roughly 90 degrees (as in Figure 11-16), so that when the pickup is laid on its back, both the coat hanger and the top of the speaker (the part that used to get pressed against your ear) point up. Knot the wire around the coat hanger; this will act as a strain relief, preventing an inadvertent tug from breaking the delicate connections.

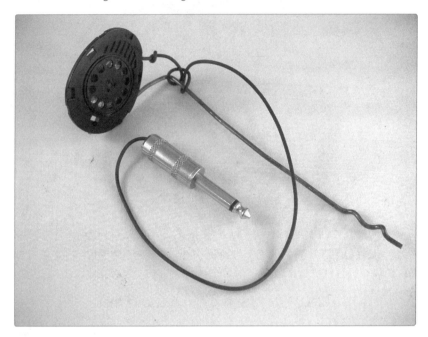

FIGURE 11-16: *The finished pickup*

Step 15   Use the hose clamp to mount the pickup just below the opening of the bell, as in Figure 11-17 (experiment with different positions and orientations to get the sound you like). You are now ready to plug into an amp, PA, soundboard, or any guitar effect; reverb units are neat, and digital delays are awesome—plug in to an old BOSS DD-3 digital delay, crank up the Feedback and Echo, set it to the longest delay, and start jamming out as a one-person didgeridoo orchestra.

Step 16   While, to some eyes, this finished didgeridoo has a post-industrial Mad Max chic, others might prefer to hide the scorched mess under a coat of paint. Now is the time for that. Most paints will not want to stick to PVC (although the rough treatment it's gotten from the torch will make it easier); try hearty spray paints like Rust-Oleum, or the all-purpose indoor/outdoor spray paint sold by Krylon.

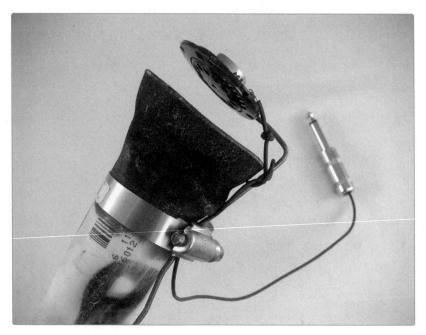

FIGURE 11-17: *A good position for our homemade limited-range mic pickup*

Playing the Didgeridoo

Start by making a few practice blows: Without the instrument, relax your jaw, loosen your lips, and blow, flapping your lips like a horse showing disapproval. Increase the pressure and tighten your lips until you've got an even-pitched fart noise or motorboat (this *bilabial trill* is pretty similar to a *Bronx cheer* or *blowing a raspberry*); it might help to pooch out your lower jaw a touch, so that your teeth are even (your lowers might even creep a little in front of your uppers). Once you are done laughing at yourself, press your lips firmly to your didgeridoo mouthpiece and repeat; you'll note that, as you vary the tension in your lips—even just slightly—you'll shift the didgeridoo's pitch. Your first goal is to sustain an even pitch, and you'll probably be able to do so after maybe 20 minutes of monkeying around. The next step is to shift to playing using the side of your mouth (thus taking advantage of the thinner edge of your lips, which you can articulate more finely). Shift your mouth so that one of the fleshy lobes of your lips is centered in the mouthpiece, and repeat your motorboat noises. You'll immediately notice that the signature didgeridoo overtones are clearer.

Other basic didgeridoo techniques include puffing and tightening your cheeks, working your cheeks and jaws as though you have a mouthful of water, and popping your tongue (try saying fast "*ta-ta-ta-ta-ta*"s or slow "*da da da da da*"s; harmonica players rely on similar tongue articulations). As you get the hang of these, experiment with growling and chattering in your throat as you play.

The gold standard of didge playing is *circular breathing*, which makes it possible to extend a note. This technique is common among many *aerophone* (brass and woodwind) players—Kenny G holds the record for sustaining a single, uninterrupted note: roughly 45 minutes. The jazz sax madman Rahsaan Roland Kirk is rumored to have once carried a single note for almost three hours during a live performance in the '70s. In order to circular breathe, fully extend your cheeks as you play, and then use them like a bagpipe bellows to keep air moving through your lips while you sip a little air in through your nose to replenish your lung supply. A good way to practice this technique it is to start out trying to circular breathe through the narrowest cocktail straw you can find. Work your way up to normal straws, and finally a large-bore milkshake straw. Don't get discouraged: Even taking these baby steps, it'll take a few months of didge playing—working those cheeks and making funny noises—to build up the strength to start getting a usable circular breath.

Apart from being an interesting aesthetic addition to your hippie-jam or avant-garde electronica repertoire, didgeridoo playing is also a very soothing meditative practice (at least for the player; mates and roommates tend to disagree) and a viable treatment for snoring and sleep apnea.

Resources

▶   "Didgeridoo Playing as Alternative Treatment for Obstructive Sleep Apnea Syndrome: Randomized Controlled Trial," Milo A. Puhan, Alex Suarez, et al. *http://www.bmj.com/cgi/content/full/332/7536/266* (accessed July 13, 2009).

▶   The didgeridoo modifications I've described (especially the dimpling and kinking) owe a huge debt to Steven L. Sachs; sadly, his didgeridoo website is no longer available online. I've archived portions at *http://www.davideriknelson.com/sbsb/.*

As you begin exploring the sonic pos-
sibilities of homemade pickups mounted
on didgeridoos (Project 11) and drums
(Projects 9 and 10) and winding your own
guitar pickups (Project 13), you might be a
little hesitant to plug these monstrosities into
your fully restored, vintage Vox tube amp.
You could buy a cheap battery-powered
amp (the RadioShack Mini Audio Amplifier,
part #277-1008, is pretty homely but a good
value at $15), but building your own is even
cheaper—less than $2 if you scrounge up
speakers and switches—and gives you good
practice working with somewhat delicate
components (like integrated circuits). The
following circuit is a classic mini-amp built
around the ultra-common, very affordable

LM386 *integrated circuit (IC)*; these sell for about a buck apiece, will drive any size speaker, and are hard to kill (but buy a few—we'll build our project so that you can easily swap in a new chip if you happen to jostle or fry one). For more info on ICs, see the appendix.

This project calls for an 8 ohm speaker (so called because the coil offers 8 ohms of resistance). This is the most common speaker used in consumer electronics, from goofy little baby toys to $3,000 component sound systems; pretty much any speaker you scrounge out of a $1 garage-sale stereo will be an 8 ohm speaker. If it isn't marked, you can test it with your multimeter (see the appendix for instructions).

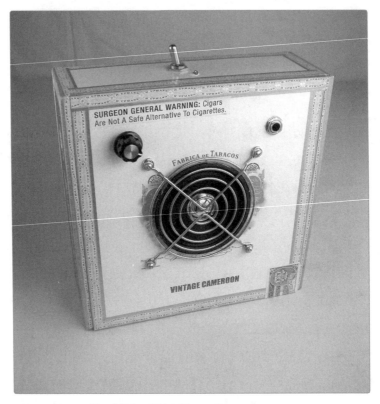

FIGURE 12-1: *The finished Dirt-Cheap Amp*

Tools

▶ a standard soldering kit (See the appendix.)

▶ an electric drill with a 3/8" or 1/2" bit

▶ (optional, depending on your enclosure) sandpaper and a keyhole saw

Supplies

▸ an LM386 op-amp (Many are available, including RadioShack part #276-1731 and Digi-Key part #LM386N-3-ND.)

▸ a red LED

▸ an 8-pin IC socket

▸ an 8 ohm speaker

▸ a 100 μF capacitor

▸ a 1/4" mono phone jack (a guitar jack)

▸ a 10k ohm variable resistor (Variable resistors are also called *potentiometers* or *pots*, and in this case you want an *audio taper*; see "Audio Tapers vs. Linear Tapers" on page 190.)

▸ a control knob cover, such as RadioShack part #274-415

▸ a 470 ohm resistor (coded with yellow-purple-brown stripes)

▸ a DPST toggle switch (This can be a little hard to find, but can easily be replaced with a DPDT switch like RadioShack part #275-666; it's pricey and far beefier than the project calls for but is also easy to install and looks great. For a full discussion of toggle switches, see "Types of Switches" on page 20.)

▸ a 9-volt battery clip

▸ a 9-volt battery

▸ 24-gauge insulated wire, either stranded or solid-core

▸ 22- or 24-gauge bare bus wire (This is uninsulated solid-core wire; the 22-gauge is slightly thicker than the 24-gauge and thus preferable.)

▸ whatever enclosure you choose (A cigar box is nice; hint hint.)

FIGURE 12-2: *Tools and supplies*

Building It

Step 1 The trick to working with ICs is that everything is numbered counterclockwise in reference to how the chip looks when viewed *from the top*, but you have to work on it *from the bottom*. Take out your LM386 op-amp and set it on a sheet of clean paper, with the IC's markings up and its little half-circle dimple to the left. The leg at the lower left is leg number 1. The next one to the right is 2, then 3, then 4, then the numbering wraps around: The leg at the upper right is number 5, its neighbor to the left is number 6, and so forth, as illustrated in Figure 12-3.

Step 2 Flip your chip over, so that its pins stick up like little legs (*dead-bug* style), and the little dimple is to the right. The legs are now numbered clockwise starting with the lower right, as shown in Figure 12-4.

FIGURE 12-3: *An adorable LM386, with legs numbered counterclockwise*

FIGURE 12-4: *The LM386 in dead-bug position*

Step 3 Label the legs in this new orientation, then set the chip aside, and replace it with your IC socket, also oriented dead-bug style, with legs up and aligned with your numbers. Look at the circuit diagram in Figure 12-5.

Step 4 Note that legs 1 and 8 of the IC socket are shorted to each other. Since these are right across from each other (the top and bottom legs furthest to the right), you can bend them in and solder them together. If the legs of your socket are too short to reach, you can use a little snip of bus wire to connect them (as in Figure 12-6) or even a length cut from a small paperclip.

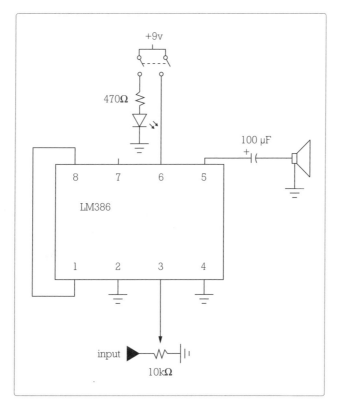

FIGURE 12-5: *The circuit diagram for the Dirt-Cheap Amp*

FIGURE 12-6: *Shorting pins 1 and 8 together*

Step 5   Now we'll start our *ground bus*—a single wire that will tie all of the ground connections (those represented by the little triangle made of three horizontal lines) to the negative terminal of the battery (which, for the purposes of the circuits in this book, is the ground). Snip a 2" length of bus wire. Bend down pins 2 and 4, then hold your piece of bus wire so that it runs the length of the socket, connecting pins 2 and 4 without making contact with any other pins (especially pins 1 and 8). Solder pin 2 to the bus, and then do likewise with pin 4; you should have 1" and some change of bus wire sticking out from the left end of the IC socket, like a little tail (see Figure 12-7). Set the IC socket aside for now.

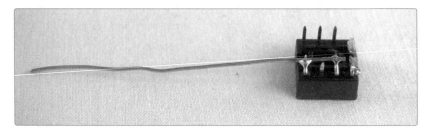

FIGURE 12-7: *The installed ground bus*

Step 6   Next, solder up some of the larger components. If your speaker doesn't already have wires attached to its lugs, then attach a length of insulated 24-gauge wire to each lug now.

Step 7   To build the power switch assembly shown in Figure 12-8, short together the two end lugs of the DPST switch, then connect the red wire from your battery clip to these end terminals and a length of insulated wire to one of the two middle lugs of the switch. (If you're using a DPDT switch, just ignore that spare pair of end lugs. For a full discussion of switches—with pictures!—flip back to "Types of Switches" on page 20.) Connect the resistor to the remaining middle lug of the switch, and then solder the resistor's other leg to the positive leg of the LED (that's the leg on the side opposite the flat spot on the LED's red plastic lens). Set the power switch assembly aside.

FIGURE 12-8: *The assembled power switch (with indicator LED)*

Step 8   Take a look at the 1/4" mono phone jack. This jack is also called a *TS connector*, because it has two lugs, one that will make a circuit with the *tip* of a plug when connected—this lug carries the audio signal—and the other that connects the *sleeve* of the plug to ground. (For a fully illustrated discussion of jacks and their lugs, see the appendix.) Solder one insulated wire to each lug; keep the tip wire under 6" (see Figure 12-9).

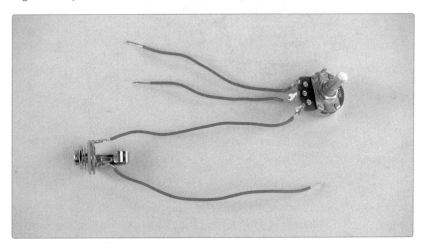

FIGURE 12-9: *The jack wired to the volume control—note that the pot's shaft has been trimmed*

Step 9   Solder the wire connected to the jack's tip to the first lug on the *variable resistor* (this kind of adjustable resistor is usually called a *potentiometer* or *pot*—there is a labeled diagram of pots and their lugs in the appendix). The first lug is furthest to the left when you look at the pot from the front with the lugs on top, like a crown. Solder lengths of insulated wire to each of the other two lugs on your pot; the wire attached to the middle lug should be under 6".

Step 10   Turn back to the IC socket and check the schematic again. Install the 100 μF electrolytic capacitor, keeping in mind that it is *polarized*: The leg that lines up with the stripe running down the side of the capacitor is *negative* and must ultimately connect to the ground. Solder the positive leg to pin 5 and the negative leg to one of the speaker wires (either is fine, although it's traditional to connect the capacitor to the red lead, as I have in Figure 12-10). Solder the other speaker wire to the ground bus. See how the negative leg of the capacitor is on the negative side of the circuit?

Step 11   Install the input. The wire attached to the central lug of the pot goes to pin 3. The remaining wire on the pot goes to the ground bus.

Step 12   Add power. Solder the dangling wire on the switch to pin 6, and then complete the circuit by soldering the final ground connection, connecting the black battery wire and the negative leg of the LED to the ground bus.

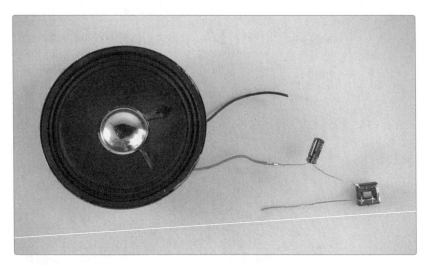

FIGURE 12-10: *The capacitor and speaker installed*

Step 13   Finally, install the chip. Flip the socket over so that pins 1 and 8 are to the left. Orient your chip so that its dimple is also to the left, carefully line up all 8 legs with their holes in the socket, and gently seat it with your thumb. The complete circuit is shown in Figure 12-11.

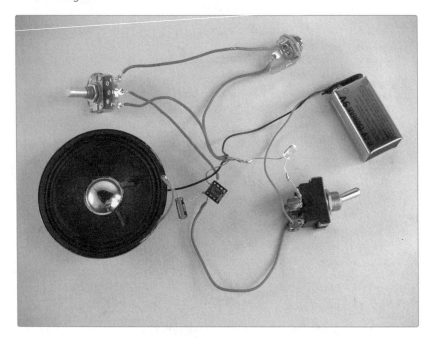

FIGURE 12-11: *The finished amp guts*

Step 14   Install the whole mess in your enclosure. In general, thinner wood (and even rigid plastic) resonates well. Both the jack and switch will fit nicely into 3/8" or 1/2" holes. Many speakers have mounting brackets around their edges, but Gorilla Glue will also hold a speaker snugly in place—make sure to drill some holes for the sound to pass through, or cut a hole and cover it with a screen to protect the speaker and help hold it in place (in Figure 12-1, I've used an old fan cover from a computer power supply).

Building the amp circuit without a circuit board (i.e., dead-bug style) results in something so light that it doesn't really need to be secured to the enclosure; the wires going to the hardware hold it up, like the suspension on a trampoline. If you want to secure it to the enclosure, you can do so with a dab of glue or strip of double-sided tape, although that will make it harder to repair. If you're concerned about the 9-volt battery rattling around and busting up the joint, you can likewise secure it with double-sided tape or with a handy 9-volt battery holder clip, as is shown in Figure 12-12 (RadioShack part #270-326).

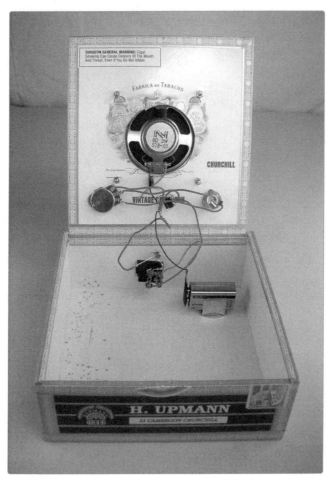

FIGURE 12-12: *The finished amp guts installed*

Tweaking the Amp

This little amp will work with almost any capacitor running between pin 5 and the speaker, from 1.5 µF to as high as 1500 µF; bass response is much better as you increase the value of the capacitor. If this design seems to put out too much bass for the speaker you want to use (thus causing unwanted distortion), try lowering the value to 47 µF. If the amp yowls and screeches, picks up local radio all by itself, or otherwise misbehaves (weird hissing, thumping, etc.), then add a *bypass* electrolytic capacitor (like a 4.7, 22, or 47 µF cap), soldering the positive lead to pin 7 of the LM386 and the negative lead to the ground.

By default, the *gain* (amplification) of the LM386 is set to 20 (i.e., the output voltage is 20 times higher than the input). To get the maximum gain of 200, bridge pins 1 and 8 with a 10 µF electrolytic capacitor instead of a piece of plain wire (the negative leg of the capacitor goes to pin 8).

Throughout the project you were asked to keep some leads as short as possible. As a rule, any wire carrying an audio signal should be less than 8" long, unless you use shielded wire (which we haven't)—I like to keep audio leads under 6", just to be on the safe side. This is to prevent interference from seeping into the circuit (simple amps are especially notorious for picking up local AM stations)—which brings us to a nice cheap-amp parlor trick.

The One-Component AM Radio

We're constantly awash in radio waves. AM radio encodes information (such as bloviating pundits and thirty-year-old Dolly Parton hits) by *modulating* the *amplitude*, or height, of these waves. The waves themselves are fairly energetic: If you string up a few hundred feet of thin wire—the kind you use to wind an electromagnet—solder it to the positive leg of an LED, and plant the other leg in the ground, the free-floating AM energy is often sufficient to drive the LED to a faint glow. So, why don't we hear AM radio every time we pick up a phone or turn on any amp? Fortunately, those big, fat AM waves (which have wavelengths thousands of feet long) spend as much time being positive as negative and thus average out to zero (as shown on the left side of Figure 12-13); from a speaker's perspective, this free-floating AM signal cancels itself out.

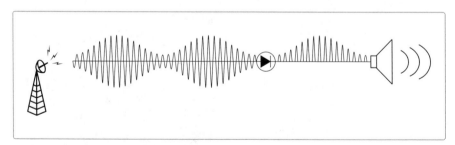

FIGURE 12-13: *AM broadcast and detection*

To make your Dirt-Cheap Amp into a simple AM radio, get a germanium diode (like a 1N34A) and a guitar cable. Plug the guitar cable into the amp, switch it on, and crank it up to 11. Now hold on to the positive lead of the diode, and touch the negative lead (the one marked with a stripe) to the tip of the cable. If there is a strong AM station in your area, you'll hear it through the amp. In this simple circuit, your body (which functions as a naturally occurring *tank circuit*) acts as the antenna; the diode—which is called a *detector* in this context and is represented by the diode symbol in the middle of Figure 12-13—acts as a *rectifier*, cutting out the bottom half of the wave. Since the signal no longer averages to zero (canceling itself out), the sound is detectable by our amplifier. *Fiat vox.*

A Frampton-Style Talk Box

Peter Frampton's signature hit is the 14-minute extended cut of "Do You Feel Like We Do?" on *Frampton Comes Alive!*. The song peaks with Frampton's famous "talking guitar" solo. You can easily emulate this sound by gluing a funnel over the speaker of your Dirt-Cheap Amp. Run a flexible plastic tube from the funnel into your mouth, and put your mouth close to a plain old microphone (I'm not making this up; this Rube Goldberg hack is how Frampton got the effect originally). Plug an instrument into the gimmicked amp, crank it up loud, play, and use your mouth to mold the sound.

Resources

- The Smokey Amp—an amp that fits in an old cigarette pack and is purported to be the best-selling guitar amp ever—is based on an LM386 circuit like the one you just built: *http://www.smokeyamps.com/*.
- For other ideas on using the LM386 Low Voltage Audio Power Amplifier (including three other audio amplifier designs), take a look at the National Semiconductor data sheet for the chip: *http://www.national.com/ds/LM/LM386.pdf*.

13 THE $10 ELECTRIC GUITAR

Conventional wisdom among luthiers (craftspeople who build and repair stringed instruments) is that 75 percent of an electric guitar's tone is defined by the pickups and strings, 15 percent by the quality of the neck, and 10 percent by "miscellaneous" factors (which include the entire body of the guitar, as well as hardware, bridge design and composition, electronics, etc.). In contrast to an acoustic guitar—whose body is almost wholly responsible for the instrument's timbre and volume—the shape, material, quality, and construction of an electric guitar's body has little bearing on its voice. To illustrate this point, the famous Roberto-Venn School of Luthiery in Phoenix, Arizona, keeps a vintage Fender guitar neck and pickups bolted to an old tool box; seasoned luthiers and pickers report that it sounds "basically like a Fender." The single-string electric guitar we're going to build in this project has a white maple neck (tough enough to make clean contact with the strings when you fret a note and dense enough to resonate nicely) and a hand-wound single-coil pickup, and it sounds reasonably like a '50s road-house guitar. Not too shabby for $10 in parts.

In the pre-electric era these single-string guitars were called *diddley bows*. They were likely brought to the United States by slaves from West Africa and are a cornerstone of blues guitar, especially Delta-style slide guitar. As folk instruments, diddley bows are traditionally made from just about any wood and wire that comes to hand. Delta bluesman Lonnie Pitchford used to make an ad hoc diddley bow by nailing a piece of wire to his porch (there's even a diddley bow built into his tombstone in Holmes County, Mississippi). Although you could use any old scrap of wood for the neck, hardwood (like maple) will be much easier to play. A steel guitar

FIGURE 13-1: *The finished $10 Electric Guitar*

string, backed by the pressure of your fingers, will easily cut grooves into soft wood like pine, making it hard to get good contact between the string and board and thus produce a clean note. Similarly, a wound guitar string is much easier on the fingers than a piece of baling wire.

Tools

▶ an electric drill with 1/2" and 3/16" bits

▶ 100-grit sandpaper

▶ a wood saw

▶ an electric sander or a sanding block (Maple is hard; if you have access to an electric sander, you'll want it for this project. If you don't have either of these, you can improvise a sanding block by wrapping your sandpaper around a soap bar–sized scrap of 2"×4".)

- ► a standard soldering kit (See the appendix.)
- ► (optional) a chromatic tuner

Supplies

- ► a 36" length of *finish grade* maple 1"×2" (Note that a 1"×2" technically measures 3/4" by 1 3/4"—for an explanation of this anomaly, read "About Board Sizes" on page 10.)
- ► a 3/8" hardwood dowel
- ► a few large kitchen matches or matchstick-sized hardwood scraps, approximately 1/8" thick and wide and roughly 2" long
- ► a 3/8" round-headed bolt
- ► a 3/8" washer
- ► a 3/8" wing nut
- ► a 2" long 3/16" eyebolt (also called a #10 eyebolt)
- ► two 3/16" washers (also called #10 washers)
- ► a 3/16" wing nut[1] (also called a #10 wing nut)
- ► cyanoacrylate glue (CA), such as Krazy Glue
- ► Gorilla Glue
- ► a playing card
- ► about 135' of 42-gauge enameled wire, often called pickup winding wire
- ► two small neodymium disk magnets (These are available in many hardware stores, often sold as "rare earth magnets" or "supermagnets"—I've used a pair of magnets 8 mm in diameter and 3 mm tall.)
- ► a chunk of beeswax roughly 1 1/2"×3" (an ounce or so by weight)
- ► 24-gauge stranded, insulated hook-up wire
- ► electrical tape
- ► a 1/4" mono phone jack (a guitar jack)
- ► a cookie tin or similar metal canister
- ► a steel ball–end acoustic guitar string, preferably a G (This is the third string on the guitar; light or medium weight is fine.)[2]

---

1. If you happen to have an old guitar tuning peg or if you can buy a single peg from your local guitar shop, then you can skip the 3/16" bolt, washers, and wing nut. Otherwise, we'll use these to build a tuning machine.

2. You can use an old string for this; guitarists usually break one of the two thinnest strings on the guitar but change all of the strings at once. If you live near a music store that offers lessons, it can be worthwhile to ask if they have any old strings lying around or would be willing to save them for you. Alternatively, shops often sell single strings at a reasonable price. In the worst case scenario, buy a full set of new strings and experiment.

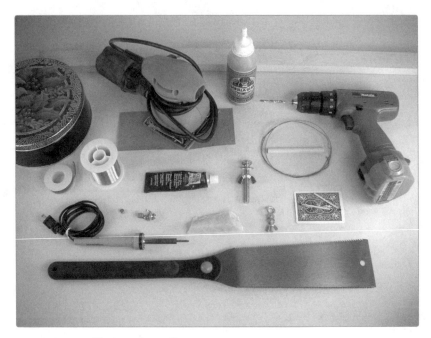

FIGURE 13-2: *Tools and supplies*

Building It

Step 1

The maple 1"×2" is going to be the neck of your diddley bow (Figure 13-3 is an anatomical diagram of a generic string instrument). Decide which 2" face looks nicest (and smoothest); this will be your fingerboard. Measure 2" from the end of your fingerboard and draw a line across the board. Now measure 25" down from this line, and draw a second line. Finally, measure 2" further down (or 27" down from the first line) and draw one more line. The first line marks the placement of your diddley bow's *nut* (on a stringed instrument, the nut is a slotted guide just below the tuning pegs; it holds the strings in place, keeping them the appropriate distance from the finger board to prevent rattle—usually called fret buzz). The second line marks the *saddle* (which holds the strings in place at the tail end of the instrument and transmits their vibrations to the body of the instrument). The third line marks the *bridge* (the point where the strings are anchored to the instrument's body). Run a wood saw over the saddle line two or three times, cutting in about 1/16" or 1/8". This will make it a little easier to seat the saddle later.

Step 2

Adding the position markers illustrated in Figure 13-4 will make the instrument more playable: Measuring from the nut line, put dots at 3 5/8", 5 7/8", 6 7/8", 8", 10 1/2", and 12". Doing this with a Sharpie will make them easier to see; burning them in (as described in Project 8, Small-Board Go/Tafl) is much classier. These dots (plus the open string) give you one full octave of the blues scale.

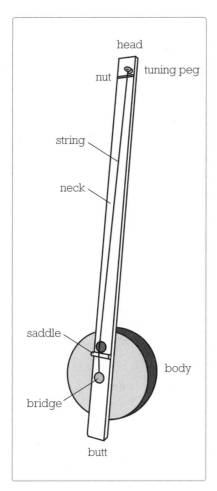

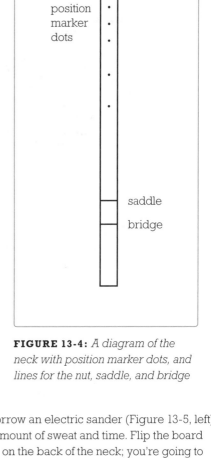

FIGURE 13-3: *The anatomy of a generic string instrument*

FIGURE 13-4: *A diagram of the neck with position marker dots, and lines for the nut, saddle, and bridge*

Step 3   Now sand the board. If at all possible, borrow an electric sander (Figure 13-5, left) for this step, as you'll save a significant amount of sweat and time. Flip the board over, and sand down the two long edges on the back of the neck; you're going to slide your hand against these a lot while playing, so you'll want to take the edge down significantly. Sanding the front two edges will make for more comfortable playing but is not vital. Also sand down the front top edge of the face (that's the area that corresponds to the lower-left edge of the neck in Figure 13-4, from the bridge line to the butt)—you'll end up resting your right forearm here as you strum.

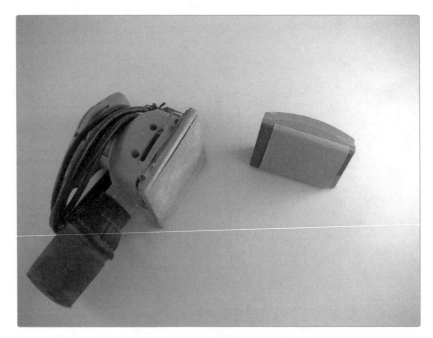

FIGURE 13-5: *An electric sander (left) and sanding block (right)*

Step 4   Flip the board face up, and place it so that the bridge mark is to your right; from this point forward, all instructions assume that you have the diddley bow oriented with the bridge to the right and nut to the left. We're going to drill the three holes illustrated in Figure 13-6:

▶   The tuning-peg hole: Drill a 3/16" hole 1/2" above the nut mark and 1/2" from the far edge of the board.

▶   The pickup-wire hole: Drill a 3/16" hole 1/2" to the left of the saddle line (i.e., the 3/16" hole is on the nut side of the saddle) and roughly 1/4" from the edge of the board closest to you.

▶   The bridge-bolt hole: Drill a centered 1/2" hole at the bridge line.

Step 5   Next, you'll install the tuning peg. Although the makeshift tuning peg described in Step 6 works fine (and stays in tune very well), it can be a little finicky at first; a guitar tuning peg will be easier to deal with. Replacement pegs can often be purchased for a few dollars at a guitar shop. Tuning pegs come in several flavors; two of the most common variants are shown in Figure 13-7. The simplest (and cheapest) pegs are *friction tuning pegs*; they are basically what we build in Step 6 and not really worth the extra money. Better are *geared tuning machines*, which come in *open* and *sealed* varieties; sealed are much more expensive, and the cost is not really justified in this application. Since tuning pegs come in different lengths, make sure the one you buy is long enough to pass through the neck of your diddley bow—a peg that has a shaft about 1" long (measuring from its base to the hole in the shaft) should be fine.

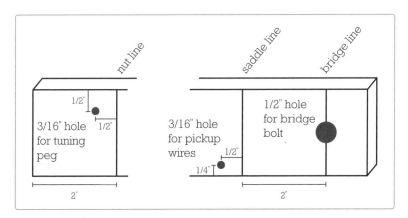

FIGURE 13-6: *The left diagram shows the position of the tuning-peg hole on the diddley bow's head; the right diagram shows the positions of the pickup-wire hole and bridge-bolt hole on the diddley bow's butt. Both diagrams are to scale.*

If you're using a store-bought tuning peg, then drill the final hole in Step 4 a touch larger—around 1/4"—and install the tuning peg, pushing it up from behind and securing it with its included screws. Since these screws are usually both tiny and cheap, use a small bit to drill guide holes for them; brute-forcing the screws into the hard maple will just strip them.

FIGURE 13-7: *A friction peg (left) and open-geared machine (right)*

Step 6 You can build your own friction tuning peg, shown in Figure 13-8, from a 3/16" eye-bolt, two 3/16" washers, and a 3/16" wing nut. Place one washer on the eyebolt, slide the bolt through the front of the 3/16" hole at the head of your diddley bow, add the second washer to the back, and spin on the wing nut.

FIGURE 13-8: *The homemade tuning peg installed, viewed from the back*

Step 7   Cut a 1 3/4" length from your hardwood dowel. This is the saddle.

Step 8   Set the neck aside, place the cookie tin bottom up on the workbench, and drill a 1/2" hole through the middle (this is where the bridge bolt will connect the neck to the resonator). Then drill a 3/8" hole into the side of the tin. This hole is for the guitar jack, so most players will want it to be on the instrument's tail; if you prefer, drill both holes in the bottom of the tin, which will be the face of the diddley bow's body. Line up the 1/2" hole in the neck with the 1/2" hole you just drilled in the tin. Using the neck as a template, drill a 3/16" hole in the tin that matches up with the 3/16" hole in the neck (the orientation of the three holes is shown in Figure 13-9). The pickup wires will ultimately pass through these holes and to the jack. Don't worry if these are a bit ragged; all the edges will be on the interior or covered by hardware later. If they are very rough, smooth them out with a few swipes from a tapered half-round file (see the appendix for details).

Step 9   Place the neck face up on top of the cookie tin, lining up the 1/2" holes. Slip the ball-end of your guitar string into the hole and then your 3/8" bolt. Flip the diddley bow over, slide the washer over the bolt so that it sandwiches the string against the inside of the cookie tin with its ball-end peeking out, then add the wing nut (as shown in Figure 13-10). Be sure that the pickup holes in the neck and cookie tin are lined up, and tighten the wing nut into place.

FIGURE 13-9: *The cookie tin, drilled to accommodate the bridge bolt (through the hole in the center of the silver bottom), pickup wires (through the small hole located at one o'clock), and the jack (which will be installed in the hole on the side of the tin)*

FIGURE 13-10: *Locking the string into place*

Step 10   Flip the diddley bow back over and thread the end of the guitar string through the eye of the tuning peg. Pull the string tight, then back it up, adding 1" of slack. Bring the free end of the string toward yourself (i.e., counterclockwise), loop it under the length of the string, then pull the end of the string up and back, crimping it where it crosses under (these three steps are demonstrated in Figure 13-11).

 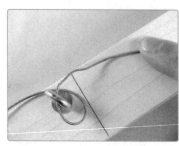 

FIGURE 13-11: *The three steps to properly stringing any steel-stringed instrument: (1) Give 1" of slack, (2) Pass the free end under, and (3) Kink it up*

Step 11   Begin to tighten the string with the tuning peg turning clockwise (Figure 13-12; if you're using a tuning machine, this may mean counterintuitively turning the knob counterclockwise). In order to accomplish this with the homemade peg, you'll need to twist the screw clockwise a turn, then hold it in place while you lock down the wing nut with your free hand. It's a little awkward at first.

FIGURE 13-12: *A properly wound string with floating matchstick nut*

Step 12   Once the slack is out of the string, slide the piece of dowel from Step 7 under the string and line it up with the saddle line. Then slide a matchstick under the string, and align it with the nut line (as in Figure 13-12). The matchstick may seem a little ridiculous, but it's a practical choice: Matches are made from aspen (which is soft but fairly strong) and are easy to replace. Any dainty scrap of wood put under the strain of a tuned guitar string is going to split eventually; just replace this "floating" nut whenever you re-string the diddley bow. (Actual guitar nuts are made from dense plastics, metal, or ox bone. Bone blanks can be bought at most guitar shops that sell replacement parts. If you want a permanent nut, buy such a blank, shape it with a file, and glue it into place.) A strung diddley bow is shown in Figure 13-13.

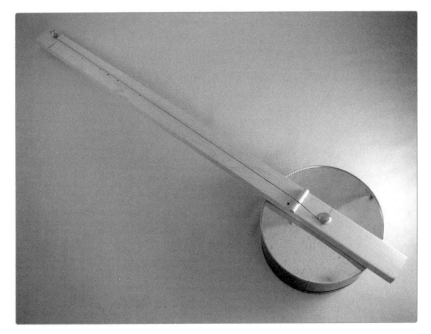

FIGURE 13-13: *A strung diddley bow*

Step 13   Tune the string up to G (or whatever pitch sounds good to you). The first G that you hit will actually be the G below the G on a guitar in standard tuning (i.e., the highest note on a bass guitar, two Gs below middle C). Since the lower tension will be easier to play initially, you might want to start here before tuning up to the standard G. The string will need to stretch somewhat, so expect to have to keep tuning the diddley bow back up to pitch for the first 10 or 15 minutes of playing around. You can speed this process up by tuning to your pitch, then pressing the middle of the string (near the last fret dot) all the way to the fingerboard, tuning back up, and repeating.

Either coil up the excess string or snip it off using wire snips. *Do not* use scissors or the diagonal cutters from your soldering kit! The hard steel of a guitar string will notch these delicate blades, ruining them.

Step 14   To start your pickup, cut two 1" diameter circles from the playing card, stack the two magnets, and Krazy Glue one circle to either side of the pair (making something like the body of a yo-yo, shown in Figure 13-14).

FIGURE 13-14: *The body of the pickup, ready for winding*

Pickup Primer Part Three: The Magnetic Pickup

Magnetic pickups are most commonly thought of as *guitar pickups* and consist of a very fine enameled wire coiled around a small, powerful magnet. As a steel guitar string vibrates near this pickup, it perturbs the standing field created by the magnet, causing current to flow through the coil. The guitar amp amplifies this tiny current into gnarly Eddie Van Halen two-finger tapping, mellow Wes Montgomery grooves, or blazing bluegrass riffs. Most "electric cigar-box guitar" designs floating around the Internet are amplified using a piezo pickup (like the one we built for the Thunderdrum in Project 10); this makes for a pretty miserable musical experience, as every bump and scrape on the fingerboard is amplified just as much as the notes being played. The $10 Electric Guitar uses a magnetic pickup so that all that gets amplified is the wail of the strings.

Step 15   You'll need to wrap roughly 1,500 windings of 42-gauge enameled wire around these magnets. This wire is only a little wider than a human hair and not quite as strong. When the glue on your playing-card-magnet yo-yo is dry, stick the magna-yo-yo to the side of your desk or a filing cabinet. Leaving 9" or 10" dangling, loop the wire once around the magnets (like winding a yo-yo), and then continue winding in this manner—*don't rush*; it's very easy to snap the winding wire (and then you'll need to start over). Once you get the hang of it, you can put 250–300 windings around the pickup in about 5 minutes. Carefully working in 5 minute intervals, it shouldn't take you more than 30 minutes to wind a pickup like the one shown in Figure 13-15.

FIGURE 13-15: *A freshly wound pickup*

1,500 windings will result in a nice clean pickup (no hum, little noise), but one that is also relatively low-level (or *cool*). If you need it to produce a *hotter* signal, simply add more windings (although keep in mind that hotter pickups are more prone to hum).

Step 16 When the pickup is wound, you'll want to add wires that will put up with more abuse than the 42-gauge winding wire. Cut two 8" lengths of 24-gauge insulated hook-up wire, strip the ends, and tin them (for details on soldering, see the appendix). Solder one of these wires to each of the two 42-gauge wires dangling out of your pickup (the enamel insulation on the 42-gauge wire will melt away under the soldering iron's heat, so you don't need to worry about stripping them, although you can do so using coarse sandpaper). Wrap a little piece of electrical tape around one of these solder joints so that the two don't short each other out. Solder the other ends of the insulated wires to the two lugs of your guitar jack (Figure 13-16); it doesn't matter which wire goes to which lug.

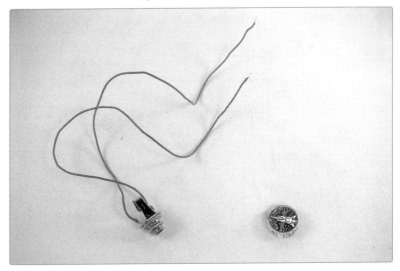

FIGURE 13-16: *Leads and jack attached, ready to test (note that the thin pickup wire is almost invisible when viewed from a foot away)*

Test your pickup by carefully plugging it into an amp and gently tapping on it. It should boing and clatter, and it will definitely thunk when you bring it close to a magnetic screw or nail. If the pickup works, go ahead to the next step. Otherwise, make sure your amp is working, then check the solder joints on your insulated leads and jack. If those look okay, then there is either a break or short in the pickup itself, and you'll need to pull off the 42-gauge wire and rewind the pickup. Once you have a working pickup, loop all of the trailing 42-gauge wire carefully around the pickup, followed by a loop or two of the insulated leads. Squirt a little Krazy Glue into the "yo-yo" to hold these wires in place, and set it somewhere to dry (preferably on top of waxed paper, so you don't end up gluing it to your table).

Step 17   Even a tightly wound pickup will boing and clatter whenever you touch it, since the minute shifts in the coils will generate a fluctuating current in the presence of the powerful magnets. In order to cut this noise, we need to *pot* the pickup, which means soaking it in molten wax to immobilize the coils. Place the beeswax in a clean glass jar, place the jar in a pot with a few inches of water, and place this over medium heat until it has just melted, then cut the flame.

> * **WARNING:** *Never leave beeswax unattended near a flame! A beeswax fire is a lot like a grease fire, so keep a box of baking soda on hand. If the beeswax catches fire, dump the baking soda over the flames to smother them. Do not douse them with water, as that will cause the burning wax to splash and spread the fire. If the beeswax smokes, it is too hot; cut the heat immediately.*

FIRE DANGER!

Dunk the pickup in the molten beeswax for 1 minute—tiny bubbles will drift to the surface as the wax soaks into the little crevices between the windings. Pull the pickup out and let it drain and cool for 30 seconds. Then dip it for another minute, let it drain for 30 seconds. After the third or fourth dip, you shouldn't see any more bubbles when you soak it. Leave it hanging over the lip of the jar to cool (Figure 13-17).

Step 18   Once the pickup has hardened, plug it into your testing amp. Tap it, and you'll notice that it's now quiet (although you'll still get a good racket when you drop a screw on it). To install it, desolder the guitar jack and thread the wires through the 3/16" hole in the neck, then through the 3/16" hole into the cookie tin. Resolder the jack, and mount it in the 3/8" hole in the tin, as in Figure 13-18.

Center the pickup on the neck, just to the left of the saddle (i.e., on the nut side of the saddle, as in Figure 13-19), and glue it down. Gorilla Glue is good for this; CA is not.

FIGURE 13-17: *A cooling pickup*

FIGURE 13-18: *The back of the finished $10 Electric Guitar*

FIGURE 13-19: *Detail of an installed pickup; the diddley bow's head is to the left and its butt to the right*

Playing the $10 Electric Guitar

Diddley bows are traditionally played with a slide (you can buy one at a guitar shop for a few bucks) but can be played just like any old guitar. Strum the open string, and you have a G; place your finger just above (i.e., to the nut-side of the first dot, as I'm doing in Figure 13-20), and you have B♭. If you *fret* (press down) just above the next dot you'll get a C, then a D♭, then a D, then an F, and finally another G, one octave higher than the open string—this is the basic blues scale (incidentally, the 12-bar blues is the basis of a lot of American rock music; you are now a White Stripe).

The diddley bow is fretless, so the *intonation* (the degree to which those dots precisely match where each pitch is located) is fairly forgiving; you can be a little sloppy about where you put your fingers and still sound good. Note that, as you increase the tension in the string, the intonation will get *sharper* (in other words, the desired note will be closer to being on top of, or even just below, its dot). Table 13-1 includes measurements for markings denoting two more scales you might want to add to your diddley bow's neck; most American folk music (such as "When the Saints Go Marching In") is in a *major scale*, and a lot of European folk music (such as "Hava Nagila") is in a *harmonic minor scale*. (To change the harmonic minor scale into the natural minor scale, use the second-to-last note from the blues scale rather than having the same second-to-last note as the major scale.)

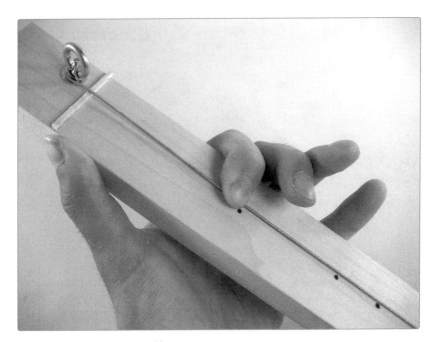

FIGURE 13-20: *Fretting a B♭*

TABLE 13-1: Markings for three useful scales

BLUES SCALE		MAJOR SCALE		HARMONIC MINOR SCALE	
inches from nut	note	inches from nut	note	inches from nut	note
open	G	open	G	open	G
3 5/8	B♭	2 5/8	A	2 5/8	A
5 7/8	C	5 1/8	B	3 5/8	B♭
6 7/8	D♭	5 7/8	C	5 7/8	C
8	D	8	D	8	D
		9 9/16	E	8 13/16	E♭
10 1/2	F	11 1/4	F♯	11 1/4	F♯
12	G	12	G	12	G

As you can see in Figure 13-22, I've added both the major and minor scales to my diddley bow by burning them into the top of the neck (the blues scale is burned into the front of the neck); the major is on the fretboard side, and the minor on the back side.

Modifying the $10 Electric Guitar

There's lots of room to customize and modify the $10 Electric Guitar. You can start by tuning to a different note; the markings will still be workable guides for the scales. You can also try different gauge strings; although the thinner, unwound guitar strings tend to sound flat (because there are no metal frets on the diddley bow's neck, it's hard to get a clear note fretting these thinner strings), the thicker wound guitar strings (the D, A, and low E string) all sound good.

The cookie tin functions as a very quiet resonator, giving the diddley bow enough volume so you can tune it and play it without an amp handy. The tin also makes it easier to rest the instrument on your lap while playing, and it gives the wires somewhere to go. You could omit the resonator altogether or replace it with a flat piece of wood, and this electric diddley bow would sound almost exactly the same. Conversely, if you want an all-acoustic diddley bow, try using a larger resonator (such as a large cigar box or a 5" deep piece from the bottom of a 5-gallon plastic bucket).

The pickup, bridge, and tuning peg are mounted so that you can easily add a second, lower-pitched string to the top of the neck (i.e., the side where your thumb rests when you're playing), a mirror image of the first string (Figure 13-21).[3] Use the next thicker string from the guitar (in this case you'd want the D string), and experiment with different tuning combinations. A good place to start is tuning the thinner string up to the G below middle C (the same as the G string on a guitar in standard tuning) and the thicker string to the G one octave lower. In this configuration, you can either fret both strings together to get a thicker sound for each note or leave the lower G string open as you strum so that it will function as a drone.

A slightly advanced technique is to have the two strings a *fourth* apart (i.e., if you're going by the book, the lower-pitched string is tuned to D and the higher to G; see Table 13-2 for other combos of fourths).

TABLE 13-2: Fourths

If the higher-pitched string is . . .	Then tune the lower-pitched string to . . .
G	D
A	E
B	F♯
C	G
D	A
E	B
F	C

---

3. In fact, the neck is wide enough that a clever and nimble-fingered crafter could likely bring this design up to full six-string functionality, provided he or she notched the saddle and nut in order to keep the highest and lowest strings in place or replaced the nut and saddle with comparably sized coarse-threaded bolts.

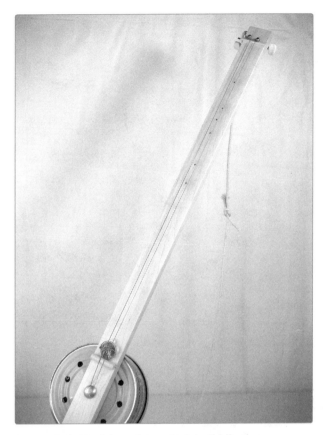

FIGURE 13-21: *A two-string electric diddley bow*

With the strings tuned a fourth apart in this manner, you can play an inverted power chord (i.e., one where the higher, rather than lower, note is the root) by just laying your finger across the strings (i.e., *barring* them, shown in Figure 13-22). In other words, on my diddley bow (which uses a G string for the higher-pitched string and a D for the optional, second, lower string), strumming the open strings plays a G power chord, placing my finger across both at the second dot plays a C power chord, barring at the fifth dot plays a D power chord, and barring at the last dot plays a G power chord one octave higher than the first. This is similar to playing in drop D tuning on a regular guitar; Kurt Cobain fans might think of this two-string electric diddley bow as a the *Nirvanatar.*

Finally, since the $10 Electric Guitar is fretless, there is a tremendous temptation to play a single-string model with a bow, like a junkyard cello. You can make a great, never-need-to-rosin fiddlestick from a piece of bicycle tire inner tube stretched over some scrap wood (see Figure 13-23). Most bike shops have scads of leaky tire inner tubes lying around and are more than happy to give them away rather than send them to a landfill.

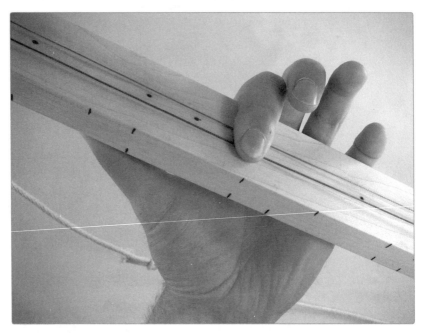

FIGURE 13-22: *Barring a power chord*

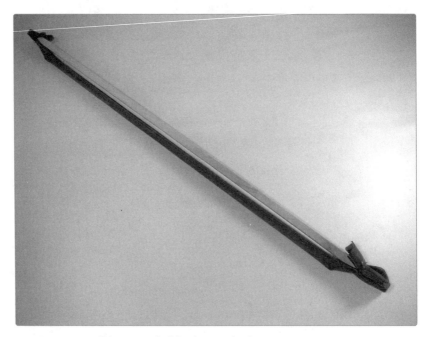

FIGURE 13-23: *A homemade bike inner tube bow*

Building Tip

The only pricey part of this project is the 42-gauge winding wire, which is usually sold in 1/2-pound spools (25,000 feet; these sell for around $30, although you can sometimes find a deal on eBay). It's pretty unusual to find 42-gauge wire in a guitar shop (even one that specializes in repairs) or electronics store. RadioShack, for example, doesn't carry anything thinner than 30-gauge wire, which isn't likely to work, as it's more than three times as thick as 42-gauge wire (flip to the appendix for a discussion of wire gauges, which can be a little deceptive). That said, you can go a bit thicker than 42-gauge: Folks have built this pickup with wires as thick as 38-gauge, although they needed to add significantly more windings. You can scrounge appropriately thin gauge wire from old relays, out of old TVs, or from older consumer electronics like plug-in hair clippers (42-gauge wire is popular in beefier electromagnets). However, if you don't know anything about TVs, **do not** open one up; those large capacitors can hold a deadly charge long after the set has been unplugged.

Resources

▶   Stewart-MacDonald is the go-to supplier for luthiers; you can find any guitar part here (including reasonably priced tuning machines and 42-gauge wire): *http://www.stewmac.com/*.

▶   I have a short $10 Electric Guitar blues tutorial video posted at *http://www .davideriknelson.com/sbsb*, where I also sell some kits and components, including 135' lengths of winding wire for making a pickup.

DIRT-CHEAP BOUTIQUE STOMP BOXES: THE SPRING REVERB

Guitarists hungry to craft their own sound often invest in boutique stomp boxes; these are handmade in limited quantities (even unique one-offs) and can cost hundreds of dollars. In the following projects you'll build three such effects—a reverb unit, a tremolo unit, and a fuzztone—for a grand total of about $20 (likely significantly less if you choose to mail order parts; RadioShack potentiometers and switches are pricey). All three effects rely on modern components to achieve classic sounds using old-school techniques.

The first of these effects is a simple reverb unit. Even with your eyes closed, you can easily tell if you are in a coat closet, bathroom, or gymnasium, because of how the space shapes *reverberations*: the short-duration, multiply-repeating echoes coming off the walls, floor, and ceiling. The Spring Reverb simulates the sound of playing in an actual space by amplifying your instrument's signal (using a version of the trusty Dirt-Cheap Amp, Project 12) and sending it through a spring. We mix the resulting signal (also called the *wet signal*), which is replete with reflected echoes generated by the sound bouncing up and down the spring, with the original, unaffected signal (i.e., the *dry signal*). This is how early amps, like the 1960s Fender Twin Reverb, added a simulated sense of space to the otherwise arid guitar.

FIGURE 14-1: *The finished Spring Reverb*

Tools

▶ a standard soldering kit (See the appendix.)

▶ cyanoacrylate adhesive (CA), such as Krazy Glue

▶ Gorilla Glue, foam-backed double-sided tape, or hardware to mount the reverb tank and circuit in its enclosure

▶ a ruler

▶ an electric drill with 1/4" and either 1/2" or 3/8" bits

▶ a utility or hobby knife

▶ pliers, preferably with built-in snips

Supplies

- two piezo elements, such as Digi-Key part #102-1126-ND or #478-4764-ND (Either is fine; I used one of each.)

- two small paper clips

- an LM386 op amp IC

- an 8-pin IC socket

- two 10k ohm variable resistors (i.e., *potentiometers* or *pots*, preferably *audio tapers*, not *linear tapers*; see "Audio Tapers vs. Linear Tapers" on page 190 for the distinction)

- two control knob covers (RadioShack part #274-415 is a good buy.)

- two 10k resistors (coded with brown-black-orange stripes)

- a 100 μF electrolytic capacitor

- an 8–1000 ohm audio output transformer, such as RadioShack part #273-1380

- a spring (light, thin gauge and roughly 3" or 4" long when at rest)

- two 1/4" mono phone jacks (guitar jacks)

- a 9-volt battery clip

- a 9-volt battery

- 24-gauge insulated hook-up wire

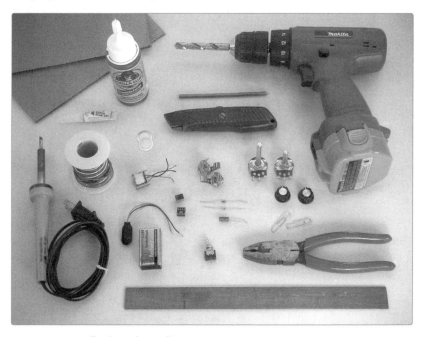

FIGURE 14-2: *Tools and supplies*

- a small SPST switch, such as RadioShack part #275-612

- pieces of sturdy corrugated cardboard or a small cardboard box around 6" long

- a largish, sturdy enclosure (A cigar box works well, since the reverb tank will take up a good deal of space.)

- (optional) 22- or 24-gauge bare bus wire

On Enclosures

At its simplest, an enclosure is the box you cram an electronics project into: drill a few holes; stuff in the batteries and wires; label your knobs, switches, and jacks with a Sharpie; and you're good to go. You can get cheap, sturdy electronic project enclosures at RadioShack, or go online to order the pro-grade die-cast enclosures and machined project boxes made by Velleman Incorporated and Hammond Manufacturing. Conversely, there are perfectly suitable ad hoc enclosures at the office supply store (look for the plastic storage boxes folks use to organize their pencils and paperclips) or craft supply store (many sell plastic organizers and plain wooden boxes in a variety of shapes and sizes). Even plastic food-storage boxes sold at the grocery will do in a pinch. If you're looking for something a bit more quaint, keep your eyes peeled for old cigar boxes, pencil boxes, candy or cookie tins, lunch boxes, or military surplus equipment cases and kits.

Considerations when choosing enclosures:

- Conductive or non-conductive? A conductive metal enclosure is great for a project like the Two-Transistor Fuzztone (Project 16), which works best when shielded from stray AM transmissions, and terrible for a project like the Marshmallow Muzzleloader (Project 24), where you are worried about an accidental shock.

- Do you have access to the tools needed to modify the enclosure? You'll need to add holes for jacks, switches, and pots; you can cut through an old plastic pencil box with a pocket knife but are going to have trouble piercing a steel ammo case with anything short of a drill press.

- Is the box big enough to accommodate the circuit, its battery, jacks (with plugs inserted!), or other hardware without causing short circuits?

- Will the box be able to withstand the intended abuse? A pretty little Chinese gift box makes a wicked cool Ticklebox (Project 7), but a terrible stomp box for gigging.

- Does it look frikkin' awesome?

Building It

Step 1

Unfold each paper clip to form a free-standing hook as shown in Figure 14-3. You might need pliers to shape these the way you like and will almost certainly want the snippers to trim them down. Place the piezos brass side up on your workbench, squirt a little puddle of CA into the middle of each one, and stand a hook in the puddle. Let these dry overnight.

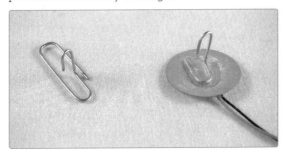

FIGURE 14-3: *A paper clip hook (left) and a prepared piezo element (right)*

Step 2

While your piezos are drying, you can build the rest of the circuit. As with the Cigar-Box Synthesizer (Project 17), this project includes a simple audio mixer (shown in Figure 14-4). To build it, solder one 10k resistor to the middle lug of each 10k potentiometer. Take a look at your enclosure, decide where you are going to mount these pots (flip ahead to Figure 14-11 for one possible layout), then cut four lengths of insulated wire long enough to reach the furthest corner of the enclosure; since these will carry audio signals, keep them under 8" long. Solder one wire to each of the 10k resistors and a wire to lug 1 of each pot. (Remember, the lugs are numbered from left to right looking at the pot from the front with the lugs on top; for clarification, check the appendix.) Then solder the two

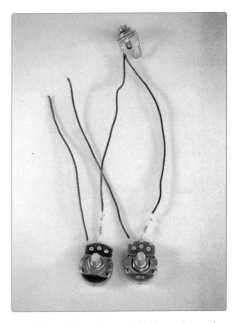

FIGURE 14-4: *The reverb's two-channel mixer*

resistor wires to the tip of the output jack (jack anatomy is discussed in the appendix, too). The third lug of each pot will ultimately be tied to the circuit's common ground.

Step 3   This circuit (Figure 14-5) is very simple, so we'll be building it *dead-bug* style (as we did in Project 12, the Dirt Cheap Amp), instead of mounting it on a circuit board. For an illustration of how the legs are numbered on this IC, check out Project 12 or flip to the appendix—and remember that the legs are numbered counterclockwise from the lower left as viewed from the top, but all soldering is done from underneath!

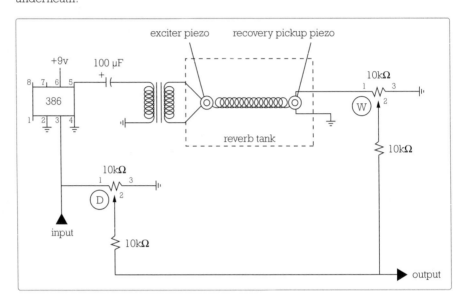

FIGURE 14-5: *The schematic for the Spring Reverb*

＊**NOTE:** *As in previous projects, it's strongly suggested that you use an IC socket to hold the LM386 chip. These chips can be damaged by static electricity or heat, so it's best to solder with the socket empty, even though the illustrations show the chip in place.*

Bend pins 2 and 4 under the socket and solder them together, then solder a length of insulated wire to pin 3 (this is the audio input, so keep it under 8"). Now solder another insulated wire to pin 6 and the other end of that wire to one lug of the SPST (this will be the power supply). Next solder a 100 µF capacitor to pin 5 (the leg with no stripe goes to the pin); this is the audio output. The circuit, thus far, is shown in Figure 14-6.

Step 4   Twist together the wire from pin 3 of the IC socket and the wire from lug 1 of either 10k pot. Solder these to the tip of the remaining jack; this is the input. Label this *pot D* (for dry signal).

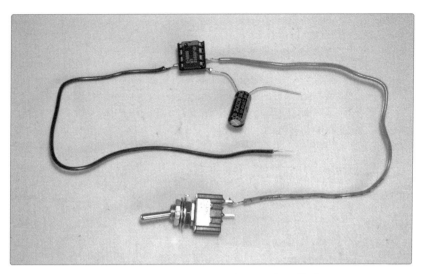

FIGURE 14-6: *The IC with input, power, and output installed*

Step 5   Once the glue is dry on the piezos, carefully solder one lead of one piezo to the wire connected to lug one of the other pot. Piezo leads are pretty delicate and a pain to solder back to the piezo element, so handle these carefully. This is your *recovery pickup* (it will pick up the echoey signal from the spring); label this *pot W* (for wet signal). Set the mixer/amp assembly aside.

Step 6   Look at the audio transformer; one side has two wires (if you are using the RadioShack model, they are white and red) and the other has three (blue, black, and green). Clip off the middle (black) lead, since you won't need it. Carefully strip the blue and green leads, and solder one to each of the leads on the remaining piezo. Insulate the solder points with electrical tape. This unit, shown in Figure 14-7, is your *exciter*; it drives the audio signal into the spring. Solder either of the remaining wires (red or white) on the audio transformer to the free leg on the 100 µF capacitor.

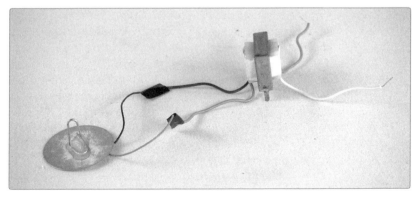

FIGURE 14-7: *The completed exciter*

Step 7   Solder the red wire on the battery clip to the open lug on the SPST switch.

Step 8   Next, you will run the ground wire. Since this will all be crammed in a box willy-nilly, you might want to use insulated wire. As in Project 17 (the Cigar Box Synthesizer), a shorter ground is often best here. Connect the ground lugs on both jacks, lug 3 on each pot, the remaining lead on the recovery pickup piezo, the remaining lead on the audio transformer (it will be either white or red), the black lead from the battery clip, and pins 2 and 4 on the IC socket (which you bent under the socket in Step 3). The Spring Reverb's finished guts are shown in Figure 14-8.

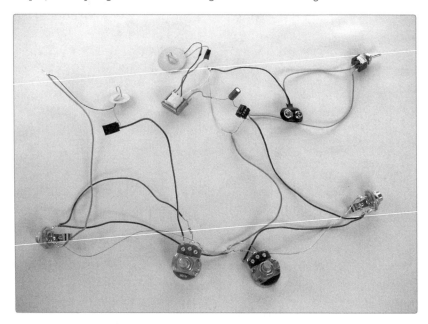

FIGURE 14-8: *The Spring Reverb's electronic guts thus far*

Step 9   Now it's time to test the unit. Turn both pots fully counterclockwise, plug an audio source (such as an old CD player) into the input, plug an amplifier (such as the Dirt-Cheap Amp from Project 12) into the output, add a battery to the Spring Reverb, and flip the power switch. If the Spring Reverb is *self-oscillating* (i.e., howling like a heart-broken dog) or picking up local AM radio, then try connecting a 4.7–47 µF capacitor from pin 7 of the LM386 IC to the ground (the leg of the capacitor marked with the thick stripe connects to the ground). Otherwise, turn on your audio source. Slowly turn the D pot clockwise; the audio signal from your radio (or whatever) should come out of the amp basically unchanged—this is called the dry signal. Turn the D pot all the way down (counterclockwise), and then slowly turn the W pot up; now you should hear your radio tinnily playing through the exciter piezo element. Gently nudge the other piezo element (the recovery pickup piezo); the amp should scrape and thunk loudly. Turn off the audio source and amp, turn both pots fully counterclockwise, and nudge the recovery pickup piezo again. If you hear scraping coming from the exciter piezo, then there is feedback within the circuit.

Try rewiring the ground to isolate the W and D pots (i.e., have the ground go back to the battery between the two). Failing all else, add a 1k resistor (brown-black-red) between the hot and ground lugs on the output, or interrupt the ground with a 1k resistor connected in series, especially on the recovery pickup's ground connection.

Once any intra-circuit feedback issues are resolved, switch the amp and audio source back on, turn the W pot fully clockwise, and hang the spring between the piezo elements, hammock style; you'll hear a sproingy, tinny version of the music. Experiment with stretching the elements apart to put some tension in the spring; now you should hear the music clearly (there won't be much bass) with lots of metallic echoes, like a radio playing inside a sealed 50-gallon steel drum at the bottom of a lifeless sea. This is the wet signal. Experiment with different amounts of tension until you find the one you like best, and measure the distance between the two piezo elements, as shown in Figure 14-9.

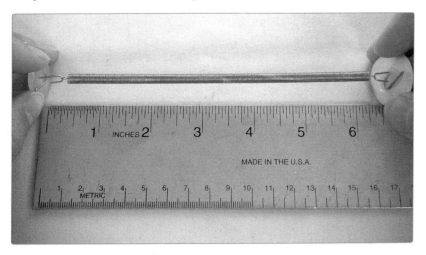

FIGURE 14-9: *Experimenting with tension in the spring*

Step 10   Now build your *reverb tank*. Turn off the amp, audio source, and Spring Reverb, and set it all aside. Take out the cardboard and build a box that is the same length as the distance you measured in Step 9 (the depth and width of the box are less important, as long as they are sufficient to keep the box from folding up under the spring's tension; it can be just an inch or two deep and wide, as shown in Figure 14-10). Use a nail or sharp pencil to poke a hole in either end of your box. Unhook the spring from the piezo elements, feed one hook through each hole, and remount the spring. This is your reverb tank. Test it again. Because of the girth of the exciter (we're stepping up the voltage to more than 100 volts; that piezo element would dance right off the table, given the chance) and the sensitivity of the recovery pickup, this circuit tends towards yowling feedback, with lighter springs being the most prone to problems. Adding that bypass capacitor between pin 7 and the ground (suggested in Step 9) might help with some feedback. Having a sound-absorbing reverb tank (i.e., made out of something that resonates poorly—such as sturdy corrugated cardboard—as opposed to something that resonates well, like thin, rigid plastic or a Stradivarius violin) isolated from the sides of the enclosure with double-sided foam tape is a good idea, as is keeping some distance between your amp and reverb unit (or placing the unit behind the cabinet of your amplifier). If all else fails, try packing some cotton gauze or polyfill (the stuffing used to stuff your Sock Squid in Project 3) around the reverb tank. If your amp doesn't have low- and high-pass filters, you might want to build a separate passive filter box or add them to the output of the unit, as judicious EQing can tame some feedback or yowling (for simple passive filtering circuits, see Figure 17-17 on page 213).

If, on the other hand, you are having no feedback problems and would like to beef up the reverb a bit, consider maxing out the amp's gain by adding a 10 μF capacitor between pins 1 and 8 (as described in Project 12, the Dirt-Cheap Amp).

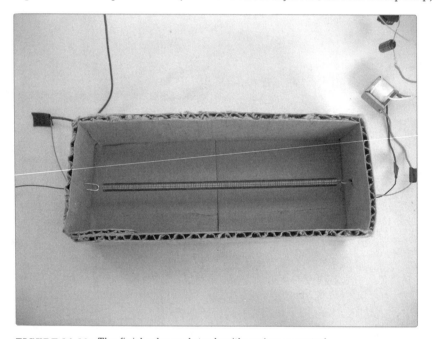

FIGURE 14-10: *The finished reverb tank with spring mounted*

Step 11   Now install this whole mess in the box of your choosing. Start by drilling a hole for the power switch (use the 1/4" bit) and then holes for the two jacks and two pots (3/8" or 1/2" bits usually work fine)—you'll note that in Figure 14-11, I've installed both jacks and pots on the front face of the box and the power switch on the right-hand side, but this is largely just a matter of personal preference. Before install-ing the jacks, switches, and reverb tank in the box, take a moment to wrap a little electrical tape around any troubling connections (points where it looks like wires might short out against each other). Then glue the reverb tank toward the back of the enclosure, bearing in mind that you'll have fewer feedback problems if there is dead air between the reverb tank and enclosure walls. Finally, install the jacks, pots, and switch with their included hardware. The lightweight amp circuit can float around, buoyed by the wires, but you'll want to glue the heavier transformer down (mine is on the right end of the reverb tank) and secure the battery with either double-sided foam tape or a holder clip (RadioShack part #270-326).

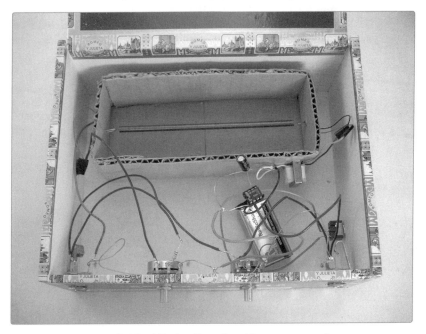

FIGURE 14-11: *The finished Spring Reverb, with guts exposed*

Step 12   Plug an instrument into the input, and run the output to your amp. Use the knobs to mix the straight, unmodified signal (the dry signal) with the ersatz reverb (the wet signal). This reverb responds best to higher pitches and faster attacks; try plucking strings as though you're playing slap bass. You can also thump the box to get zappy space-phaser *sproing!* sounds (early surf rock guitarists used to kick their reverb amps to get this effect).

Using the Spring Reverb

This Spring Reverb—like the next two effects projects—was designed with the $10 Electric Guitar (Project 13) in mind; in other words, it's built to work with a relatively low-level (or *cool*) input. To use the reverb with store-bought instruments or ones that have a line-level output (like synthesizers or drum machines), experiment with keeping the instrument's volume low or even adding a separate volume control to the reverb to attenuate the input. You can use something like the volume control at the bottom of the circuit diagram for the Dirt-Cheap Amp (Figure 12-5 on page 133).

You can also add a power indicator LED to this effect by replacing the SPST power switch with a DPST switch and adding the LED circuit from the Dirt-Cheap Amp (which you see at the top of the schematic in Figure 12-5 on page 133).

When using multiple effects, it is generally best to have the reverb unit last (i.e., just before the amp). I personally like to have the fuzztone first in the chain, followed by the tremolo, so that the tremolo can gate the fuzz. Others like to have the fuzztone after the tremolo and thus smooth the tremolo effect out.

Resources

▶ PAiA sells many reasonably priced effects kits (as well as kits for building modular synths and theremins), including an absolutely awesome reverb effect, Craig Anderton's Hot Springs Reverb Kit. See *http://www.paia.com/*.

▶ As with Projects 15 and 17, the Blinkie Tremolo and Cigar-Box Synthesizer, this project owes a great debt to Nicolas Collins's book, *Handmade Electronic Music*.

15 DIRT-CHEAP BOUTIQUE STOMP BOXES: THE BLINKIE TREMOLO

Tremolo is the rapid oscillation in volume that gives the guitar its shimmery sound in surf rock, rockabilly, and country music. Link Wray's guitar in his 1958 hit "Rumble" is a stand-out example of tremolo—required listening for anyone building a trem unit.

The heart of our Blinkie Tremolo effect is a homemade *optoisolator* (also called an optocoupler) made from an LED and a light-sensitive resistor. The photoresistor controls the volume of the audio signal; when the LED shines on the photoresistor, the resistance drops to near zero, and the audio comes through loud and clear. As the LED dims, the resistance climbs, and the sound fades. A timer circuit rhythmically pulses the LED, which pulses the volume, which gives your solo a throbbing retro drive. As with the Spring Reverb (Project 14), this trick is cribbed from early Fender amps.

Our Blinkie Tremolo has a remarkably clean output, since the optoisolator keeps the control circuit entirely separate from the audio signal, and *true bypass*, which means that deactivating the effect completely removes the modified sound from the signal without affecting the unmodified sound in any way.

FIGURE 15-1: *The finished Blinkie Tremolo*

Tools

▶ a standard soldering kit (See the appendix.)

▶ a ruler

▶ an electric drill with 1/4" and either 1/2" or 3/8" bits

▶ a utility knife

▶ (optional) Gorilla Glue, foam-backed double-sided tape, or hardware to mount the circuit in its enclosure

Supplies

▶ a 555 timer IC, such as RadioShack part #216-1718 (There are lots of 8-pin DIP 555 timer ICs out there, and they are all basically the same.)

▶ an 8-pin IC socket

▶ two red or orange LEDs

- a photoresistor, such as RadioShack part #276-1657 (also called a light dependent resistor, photoconductor, or CdS—cadmium sulfide—cell)
- a 22k ohm resistor (coded with red-red-orange stripes)
- two 470 ohm resistors (coded with yellow-purple-brown stripes)
- a 120k ohm resistor (coded with brown-red-yellow stripes)
- a 1.5 μF electrolytic capacitor
- a 100k ohm variable resistor, preferably a linear taper
- a control knob cover, such as RadioShack part #274-415
- two 1/4" mono phone jacks (guitar jacks)
- a printed circuit board (Any PCB, like RadioShack #276-148, will do, but #276-159 is especially handy here; it's the one shown in Figure 15-7.)
- a small, sturdy box to serve as the project enclosure (See "On Enclosures" on page 166.)
- a 9-volt battery clip
- a 9-volt battery
- 22- or 24-gauge bare bus wire
- 24-gauge insulated hook-up wire
- a DPDT switch, such as RadioShack part #275-666
- a small SPST switch, such as RadioShack part #275-612
- duct tape

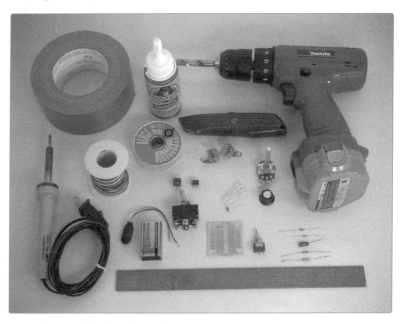

FIGURE 15-2: *Tools and supplies*

Building It

Step 1   Look at the schematic in Figure 15-3. We're going to start by building the optoisolator (located at the bottom of the schematic in the little dashed rectangle). In the old Fender amps, this unit was called a *vibrato bug*.

        Solder a 470 ohm resistor (yellow-purple-brown) to the base of one leg of the photoresistor. Then, place the photoresistor and one LED snout-to-snout. Cock out the negative leg of the LED (that is the one marked by the flattened side of the LED lens; see Figure 15-4) so that you'll recognize it later. Now wrap these two together with a strip of duct tape, sealing out as much light as possible.

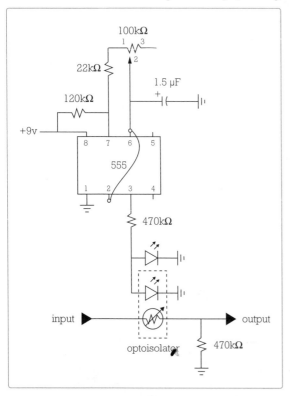

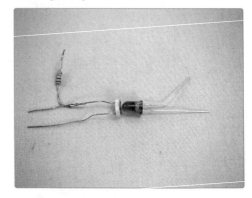

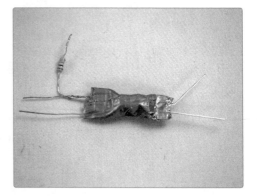

FIGURE 15-3: *Circuit diagram for the Blinkie Tremolo*

FIGURE 15-4: *The optoisolator before being sealed in duct tape (top) and after (bottom)*

Step 2   Now you'll prepare the external hardware: Both jacks, the small SPST switch, the DPDT switch, the 100k variable resistor, and the remaining LED (which is the indicator LED) will ultimately be mounted on the enclosure.

        Look at the bottom of the DPDT switch, holding it so that the six lugs are in two vertical rows. These are (from top to bottom) 1, 2, and 3 along the left, and 4, 5, and 6 along the right. Cut a short length of bare bus wire, and solder it between 1 and 6 (i.e., the upper-left and lower-right lugs; see Figure 15-5). Cut two lengths of insulated wire, strip them, and solder them to lugs 2 and 4 on the DPDT (the middle-left and top-right lugs; see Figure 15-5).

FIGURE 15-5: *The prepared DPDT switch. The insulated wire on the left is the effect send and the insulated wire on the right is the effect return. The audio input will ultimately be connected to lug 1 (which is shorted diagonally to lug 6), the audio output to lug 5, and lug 3 to ground.*

Vibrato vs. Tremolo

There's a lot of confusion about this in the guitar-head community: *Vibrato* is a subtle variation in pitch (e.g., the effect violinists create by quickly rocking their fretting fingers while bowing a note), while *tremolo* is a rapid variation in volume. Tremolo was the first built-in effect included in amplifiers (as early as the 1940s). Since honky-tonk and country musicians were the first to embrace electric amplification (because they had to play in such loud environments), they were also the first to embrace that shimmery tremolo sound, which is still strongly identified with these musical styles. When Leo Fender released his first amps featuring tremolo effects, he called this effect *vibrato* for unclear reasons (it's often suggested this was purposefully deceptive marketing, since no one offered a true vibrato effect at the time). Tellingly, during this same period Fender dubbed the *whammy bars* on his electric guitars *tremolo arms*, even though the device actually produces a vibrato effect. In Fender's defense, he was an engineer and radio repairman, not a musician, and was introduced to electric guitars by customers who brought in broken amps and pickups; it seems likely that he just confused the terms and never looked back, leaving generations of musicians to bicker.

Measure seven more lengths of insulated wire, strip them, and solder one to each tip lug on each jack, one to each leg of the indicator LED, one each to lugs 1 and 2 of the 100k potentiometer (if you're having trouble telling jack and pot lugs apart, flip to the appendix), and one to one of the two lugs on the SPST switch. Finally, solder the red battery lead to the other lug of the SPST switch. All of this wired-up hardware is shown in Figure 15-6.

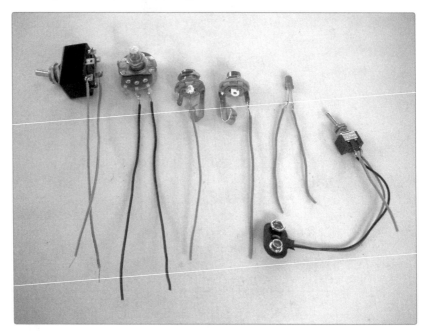

FIGURE 15-6: *The prepared hardware*

Step 3   The printed circuit board (PCB) we're using in this project is great for single-IC projects like this, because it gives us lots of room to bring multiple connections to each pin. Unfortunately, it can also be a bit confusing when viewed from the top (as you'll soon learn). Figure 15-7 shows the solder pads on the bottom of this board; hopefully, the PCB's utility is self-evident. As long as you follow the instructions and figures carefully, double-checking your work as you go, you'll be fine, even if this is your first soldering project.

✳ **NOTE:** *Keep in mind that it's best to use an IC socket and to solder with the socket empty, even though the illustrations show the chip in place.*

Mount the IC socket for the 555 timer on the circuit board. Snip a 2" length of insulated wire, fly it over the top of the chip from pin 2 to pin 6, and then solder it into place. As always, remember that pins are numbered counterclockwise, beginning with the lower-left pin; see the appendix for details. Note that, in Figure 15-8,

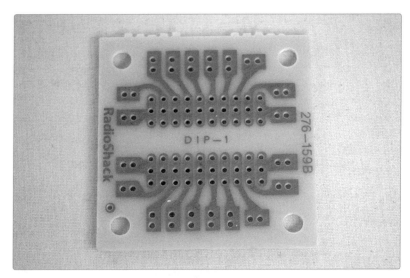

FIGURE 15-7: *The RadioShack #276-159 printed circuit board—my favorite PCB—viewed from the bottom*

we've offset the chip by one column of holes to the right; this is so we can use the left and right edges of the PCB for grounds.

If you are confident of your skills, you could solder this with the chip in place and use a short length of bare bus wire to connect pins 2 and 6, snugging it over the top of the IC.

FIGURE 15-8: *The jumper connecting pins 2 and 6*

Step 4   Solder the positive leg (the stripe-less one) of the 1.5 μF capacitor to pin 6, and run the other leg to the left-edge ground. Solder a 120k resistor (brown-red-yellow—it's the one crammed in the upper-left corner of the PCB shown in Figure 15-9) between pins 7 and 8, and one end of the 22k resistor (red-red-orange) to pin 7 (leave the other end pointing up in the air for now). Finally, solder a 470 ohm resistor (yellow-purple-brown) to pin 3 (likewise leaving its other leg hanging).

FIGURE 15-9: *The circuit board with resistors and capacitor in place; the 22k resistor is horizontal at the top, the 470 ohm resistor is horizontal at the bottom, and the 120k resistor is crammed into the upper-left corner, right next to the capacitor*

Step 5   Mount the optoisolator to the circuit board with the optoisolator's LED side toward the top of the PCB and its resistor side toward the bottom. Solder lug 4 of the DPDT switch (the upper right) to the output leg of the photoresistor (the one with the resistor hanging off of it) and the remaining insulated wire on the DPDT switch (lug 2) to the input leg, which is the only leg left on the photoresistor side of the optoisolator. (Don't worry about the dangling resistor—you'll solder that to the ground later.) In Figure 15-10, our optoisolator is straddling the middle of the PCB, just like the IC socket. The wire running from the PCB to the bottom of the picture is the effect send (connected to lug 2 of the DPDT switch, it brings the signal from your instrument into the effect via the input jack). The insulated wire to its right is the effect return, going to lug 4 of the switch, which sends the effected signal to the output jack (and presumably to your amplifier or other effects).

Step 6 Slip the 470 ohm resistor connected to pin 3 under the optoisolator (as noted in the caption to Figure 15-10), then solder it to both the positive leg of the optoisolator LED and the positive leg of the indicator LED (the other two LED legs will be tied to the ground later).

FIGURE 15-10: *Here is the installed optoisolator. The insulated wire at the top goes to the positive lead of the indicator LED; it connects to the positive lead on the optoisolator's LED and the 470 ohm resistor, which in turn runs under the optoisolator and connects to pin 3 of the IC socket, buffering both the indicator LED and the optoisolator LED. The two insulated wires running to the bottom-right corner of the PCB are the effect send and effect return; they connect to the DPDT switch.*

Step 7 Solder the wire attached to the tip of the input jack to lug 1 on the DPDT switch (that's the upper-left lug; it's connected diagonally to lug 6 on the lower right). Solder the output jack to lug 5 (the middle lug on the right side).

Step 8 Solder the middle lug of the 100k pot to pin 6 of the IC socket and the other wired lug to the dangling end of the 22k resistor attached to pin 7 of the socket. This pot controls the tremolo rate.

Step 9 Add power by soldering the wire from the SPST switch to pin 8. Then, carefully press the 555 time IC into its socket, being sure that the little dimple is to the left.

Step 10 Complete the ground by running a ground bus. Use bare bus wire to connect the ground lugs of both jacks with lug 3 of the DPDT switch, and then connect these to the common ground on either the left or right edge of the PCB. The negative (striped) leg of the electrolytic capacitor connects to the left-side ground, as do the black lead from the battery clip, the insulated wire going to the negative leg of the indicator LED, and pin 1 of the IC socket (jumper it to the ground using 1" or so of bare bus wire). Meanwhile, the dangling end of the 470 ohm resistor attached to the output of the optoisolator and the negative leg on the optoisolator's LED both go to the right-side bus. Finish this off by cutting a 3" length of insulated wire (preferably green), stripping both ends, and using it to connect the right- and left-side grounds. The finished Blinkie Tremolo circuitry is shown in Figure 15-11.

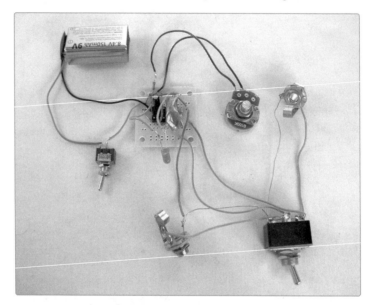

FIGURE 15-11: *The guts of the Blinkie Tremolo*

Step 11   Test it out: Connect an audio source to the input jack, an amp to the output jack, and a battery to the battery clip. Set the 100k pot (which controls the tremolo's rate) to the middle of its range, turn on the audio source (keep the volume low), turn on the amp, and flick the power switch. If the indicator LED is blinking, things are going well. Depending on the position of your DPDT switch, either you should hear the unmodified sound of your audio source or the audio should be cutting in and out in time with the blinking LED light.

If you're working under bright lights, you might want to put a little cardboard square over the optoisolator, as even small light leaks can make the difference between high and low volume less pronounced—this probably won't sound terrific, but you'll be able to tell it works. If the unit acts futzy (blinking at an irregular rate or working in fits and starts), then try adding a 0.01 µF capacitor (this is a little ceramic disk labeled *103*) from pin 5 of the IC to ground (it doesn't matter which leg goes toward the ground).

Remove the test audio source and add a guitar, synthesizer, or the $10 Electric Guitar (Project 13)—this unit is designed to work with a relatively cool input, like the pickup we built in Project 13; if you are using a "real" guitar or line-level instrument, like a synthesizer, experiment with keeping the volume pretty low. On the slower settings, the Blinkie Tremolo gives a driving, gated effect (a bit like a DJ doing a *transform*), and on the higher settings you get a shimmery, 1950s rockabilly country-western sound.

Step 12 Pack the whole mess into an enclosure. I've used a 5"×2.5"×2" RadioShack project enclosure (RadioShack part #270-1803); these sell for less than $4, are easy to work with common hand tools, and come with both a plain plastic lid and the classy brushed aluminum one you see in the figures. As you see in Figure 15-12, it's pretty snug in there (although you can secure the PCB to the bottom of the enclosure with double-sided tape, just to be sure).

A few build notes: As ever, a 1/2" or 3/8" bit is ideal for drilling holes for the jacks, pot, and DPDT switch, while a 1/4" bit is best for the power switch (mounted on the enclosure's side) and indicator LED (which is on the metal lid, right next to the rate-controlling potentiometer). When you're using a snug enclosure like this, you want to make sure that the jacks have enough clearance so that your instrument cable's plugs will fit all the way in without touching the PCB and causing a short circuit. I found the best location for the jacks is the right and left sides, about 2" from the "top" of the enclosure (where the power switch is mounted) and 3/4" from the back of the enclosure.

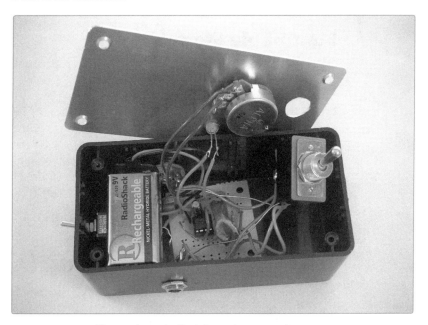

FIGURE 15-12: *The packaged effect, innards exposed*

Step 13 This effect, as shown in Figure 15-1, has fancier labels than the other projects; I made these using my word processor and the freely available TR-909 font. This TrueType font works on both PCs and Macs and is a loving re-creation of the font used by Roland on its early-1980s drum machines. Once I had the words laid out,

I printed them and took the paper mock-up to a copy shop, where they copied it onto a piece of plastic transparency (this cost about a dime). Then I carefully trimmed the label slightly *smaller* than the metal lid of the enclosure (which I'd already drilled), adhered the label to the face of the enclosure using clear contact paper, and cut out holes for the pot and indicator LED using a hobby knife.

Tweaking the Blinkie Tremolo

A good place to experiment with this design is the value of the output clamping resistor (that's the 470 ohm resistor from Step 1, which grounds the optoisolator output). As designed, the unit has a very pronounced tremolo. Using a higher value resistor—even as high as 10k—will result in a much more subtle effect. You could install a linear pot here and have a unit with a variable threshold (which will give the impression of variable depth).

As with the previous project, the Spring Reverb, the Blinkie Tremolo was designed with the $10 Electric Guitar (Project 13) in mind and thus works best on instruments with relatively cool outputs. It can be used with a "hotter" instrument or even a line-level output, if you keep the signal relatively low (using the instrument's volume control) or add an attenuating volume control (like the volume control used in the Dirt-Cheap Amp, Project 12) to the input of the tremolo unit itself.

Stompable Stomp Boxes

When you think of classic effects pedals, you likely imagine that little metal box with two knobs and a big, fat push-button stomp switch on top (hence the *stomp box*). Those push-on/push-off DPDT stomp switches are very hard to find and often pricey, so this project and the next use the hearty chromed DPDT switches from RadioShack. In practice, you can either use these effects in tabletop mode (flicking the switches by hand) or nudge them with your toe. If you are going to use these as stomp boxes, you'll want a heartier case than the simple, sturdy, affordable "project enclosures" sold at RadioShack. For the classic stomp box look, get a die-cast aluminum *small enclosure* or *project box* made by Velleman Incorporated or Hammond Manufacturing. (For more on choosing an enclosure, flip to "On Enclosures" on page 166.)

Resources

▶ As with several other projects in this section, if you've enjoyed building this tremolo, you'll love Nicolas Collins's book *Handmade Electronic Music.*

▶ If you're looking for the fancy (if pricey) stomp switches or enclosures, or kits for a whole slew of very cool (and often idiosyncratic) musical effects projects, check out Small Bear Electronics at *http://www.smallbearelec.com/.* As of this writing, the stomp switches are listed in the "Switches, Relays" section of the website's "Stock List."

16 DIRT-CHEAP BOUTIQUE STOMP BOXES: THE TWO-TRANSISTOR FUZZTONE

The last of our Dirt-Cheap Boutique Stomp Boxes is the Two-Transistor Fuzztone. This is a dirty, rudimentary amplifier, where one transistor overdrives another and the resulting signal is *asymmetrically clipped* by a set of diodes.[1] The result is a thick, aggressive, Hendrixesque tone with greatly increased sustain and sensitivity. This design is based on T. Escobedo's adaptation of Christian Holmberg's[2] venerable Bazz Fuss fuzztone box. Like any boutique effect worth its salt, both the Blinkie Tremolo from the previous project and the Two-Transistor Fuzztone

....

1. Think of an audio signal as a wave; the diodes in this circuit clip off the peaks and valleys of that wave, converting the smooth rolling hills of a natural s-curve into a series of mesas—sloppy square waves. The resulting sound, in various contexts, is called *distortion* or *fuzz*.

2. Holmberg is known throughout the Internet as "Hemmo P." He's made a huge number of simple, fun music circuit designs available online. His impact on the folk craft of mucking up guitar tone is immeasurable.

have *true bypass* switches, so you can bring the effects in and out of the effects chain without having to unplug everything, and with no signal degradation.

FIGURE 16-1: *The finished Two-Transistor Fuzztone*

Tools

▶   a standard soldering kit (See the appendix.)

▶   a ruler

▶   an electric drill with 1/4" and either 1/2" or 3/8" bits

▶   a utility knife

▶   one or two alligator clips

▶   (optional) Gorilla Glue, foam-backed double-sided tape, or hardware to mount the circuit in its enclosure

Supplies

▶   two 2N3904 transistors

▶   three 1N4148 silicon diodes

- a 1.5 µF electrolytic capacitor

- a 10 µF electrolytic capacitor

- two 10k resistors (coded with brown-black-orange stripes)

- a 100k variable resistor, preferably an audio taper

- a 5k linear taper variable resistor (*not* an audio taper)

- two control knob covers, such as RadioShack part #274-415

- two 1/4" mono phone jacks (guitar jacks)

- a small, sturdy box to serve as the project enclosure (Before choosing an enclosure, flip ahead to Step 13 or back to "On Enclosures" on page 166.)

- a 9-volt battery clip

- a 9-volt battery

- 22- or 24-gauge bare bus wire

- 24-gauge insulated hook-up wire

- a DPDT switch, such as RadioShack part #275-666

- a small SPST switch, such as RadioShack part #275-612

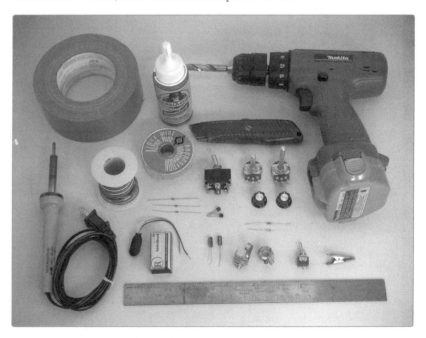

FIGURE 16-2: *Tools and supplies*

Building It

Step 1 This circuit, Figure 16-3, is another one that's simple enough to build *dead-bug* style. Start by joining the two transistors, as shown in the schematic (the diagram on the left illustrates how the legs in the schematic map to the legs on a real-life transistor).

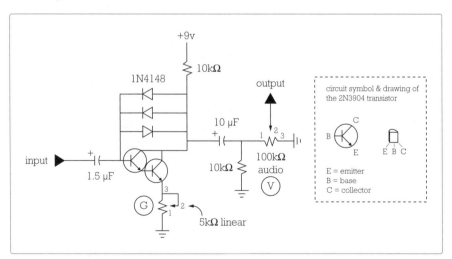

FIGURE 16-3: *The schematic for the Two-Transistor Fuzztone*

* NOTE: *Transistors are a little easier to damage with heat than other components we've used; as you solder them, attach an alligator clip between the solder point and the body of the component as in Figure 16-4; this will act as a* heat sink.

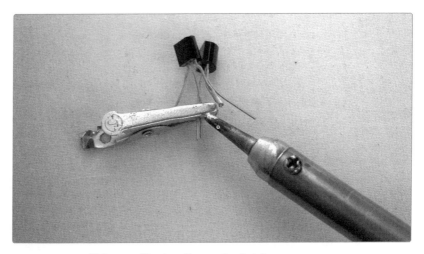

FIGURE 16-4: *Using an alligator clip as a heat sink*

Step 2   Put one transistor behind the other, like spooning lovers. Twist and solder together both transistors' *collectors*, then twist the rear transistor's *emitter* to the front transistor's *base*, solder these, and trim them down to 1/4" long. (This is shown in Figure 16-5; if the terms are confusing, refer to the inset on Figure 16-3. For more on what transistors actually do, flip to the appendix or to the Jitterbug's "How It Works" on page 270.) Notice that the final result is that the two now function as one big transistor with a single base, emitter, and collector. This configuration is called a *Darlington pair*; it was invented in 1953 by Sydney Darlington at Bell Labs as a way of addressing limitations in the quality and consistency of the earliest transistors. It's just a happy accident that his configuration can also be used to rock the house down.

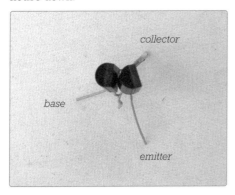

collector

base

emitter

FIGURE 16-5: *The joined transistors viewed from the top, with legs labeled*

Step 3   Next, build the *anti-parallel diode array*. This will provide the distortion. Diodes are also a little heat sensitive, so play it safe and use a heat sink. As is shown on the left side of Figure 16-6, solder the three diodes in parallel with the stripes (negative legs) of two pointing one direction and the stripe of the third pointing the other.

Step 4   Solder this diode array to the transistors so it connects the collector and base of the transistor pair; note that the side of the array with two negative legs should be toward the transistor pair's base.

You may want to consider using alligator clips to connect these to the circuit, rather than soldering them in now, so you can experiment. More diodes increase distortion but decrease the final volume. Symmetrical diodes (e.g., a total of four, two in each direction, as on the right side of Figure 16-6) will bring out metallic, clangy, gong-like overtones (a bit like a *ring modulator* effect—which makes sense, since a traditional ring modulator gets its sound by mixing two signals through just such an arrangement of diodes). This will be more pronounced if you accentuate the high end by swapping the 1.5 µF input capacitor in Step 9 with a much smaller value, like 0.022 µF. You can also use totally different types of diodes (like germanium diodes or even LEDs—they won't light up in this circuit, but they will add their own distinctive, tamer roar). You can even get away with just a single diode, connected with its positive leg to the collector and negative leg to the base.

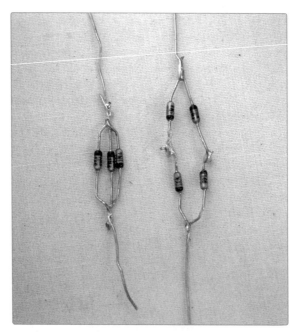

FIGURE 16-6: *Anti-parallel diodes; the array on the left is the one depicted in the schematic, while the one on the right is the ring modulator variation*

Step 5   Put together the hardware shown in Figure 16-7. As in the last effect, wire the DPDT switch with a length of bare bus wire between lugs 1 and 6 and insulated wire going to lugs 2 and 4 (see Figure 15-5 on page 179 for details). Cut five more lengths of insulated wire. Solder one wire to one lug of the small SPST switch, one wire to lug 3 of the 5k pot, and one wire to lug 1 of the 100k pot. Solder wires to the tips of each jack, and solder the red battery lead to the open lug of the SPST switch. Finally, solder a short length of bare bus wire between lugs 2 and 3 of the 5k pot. Label the 5k pot *G* (for gain) and the 100k pot *V* (for volume). (Check the appendix if you are confused by potentiometer and jack lugs.)

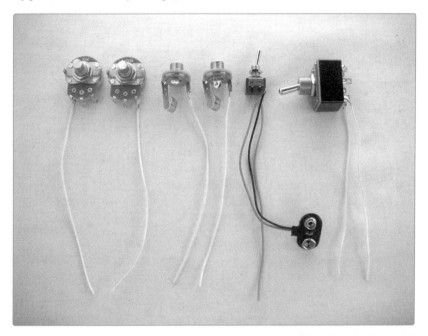

FIGURE 16-7: *Wired hardware; the potentiometer on the far left is the 5k "gain" pot, while its neighbor is the 100k "volume" pot*

Step 6   Twist together one leg of one 10k resistor (brown-black-orange), the positive (non-striped) leg of the 10 µF capacitor, and the collector on the transistor pair, and solder them. Then twist together the negative leg of the 10 µF capacitor, one leg of the other 10k resistor, and the wire connected to pot V, and solder all three together, as shown in Figure 16-8. The other leg of this second 10k resistor will be soldered to the common ground bus in Step 11, thus clamping the signal and helping weed out AM radio interference, which is a problem with this circuit, since it is essentially a high-gain amp with a bunch of diodes crammed into it. For more on AM radio, see Figure 12-13 and "The One-Component AM Radio" on page 138.

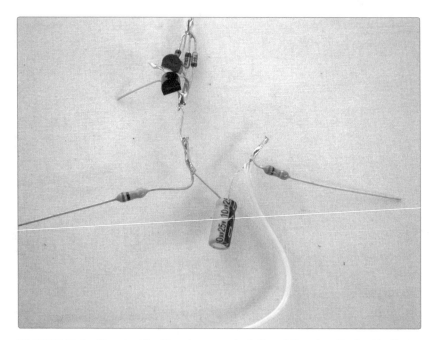

FIGURE 16-8: *The circuit with volume control; the white wire attached to the capacitor's right leg and going out of frame at the bottom of the figure connects to pot V*

Step 7   Solder the other leg of the first 10k resistor (that's the resistor connected to the positive leg of the 10 μF capacitor) to the insulated wire attached to the lug of the small SPST switch.

Step 8   Connect the insulated wire on pot G to the emitter of the transistor pair.

Step 9   Connect the negative leg of the 1.5 μF capacitor to the base of the transistor pair. (This is the input to the fuzztone; if you want a muddier tone, replace this capacitor with a larger electrolytic capacitor, like a 22 μF; to get more treble, use a smaller cap, like a 0.22 μF.)

Step 10   Connect the positive leg of the 1.5 μF capacitor to the wire that goes to lug 2 of the DPDT switch (Figure 16-9 shows the completed circuit). Now connect the input jack to lug 1 of the DPDT switch and the output jack to lug 5. Finally, connect the middle lug of pot V to lug 4 of the DPDT switch.

Step 11   Run the ground bus: Use bare wire to connect both jacks' ground lugs, the open lug on pot V, the open lug on pot G, the remaining leg of the 10k resistor attached to pot V, lug 3 of the DPDT switch, and the black lead of the battery clip.

FIGURE 16-9: *The circuit with power, gain, and input; the audio input is at the top (connected to the capacitor), the audio output at the right, the gain at the left, and the power at the bottom*

Step 12   Test it out: Spin pot G completely counterclockwise, set pot V to its midpoint, plug a "regular" guitar or the $10 Electric Guitar (Project 13) into the input jack and an amp into the output jack, connect a battery, and flick the power switch. Try both settings for the DPDT switch; when the DPDT is in one position, the instrument's volume will be markedly quieter (because the volume—controlled by pot V—is only at half-mast); that's the *activated* position. Leave the Fuzztone activated, and crank the volume knob (pot V) to full clockwise; the instrument should be about as loud as it would be with the effect deactivated. Start turning up the gain (pot G); the tone will first get subtly fuzzier and then much louder and more aggressively distorted. Use the volume knob to keep it at a tolerable loudness as you increase the gain; the overdriven distortion and increased sustain will remain, no matter how quiet you make the signal. As you play, you'll find that this fuzztone is highly responsive to your playing dynamics; you'll get more fuzz and bite if you pluck harder or use a pick.

Step 13   Cram it into a box à la Figure 16-10. It's a good idea to shield this effect by using a conductive enclosure (like this candy tin) and connecting the enclosure to the ground bus. As before, a 1/4" bit is good for drilling a hole for the power switch, while 1/2" or 3/8" bits are best for the DPDT switch, jacks, and potentiometers.

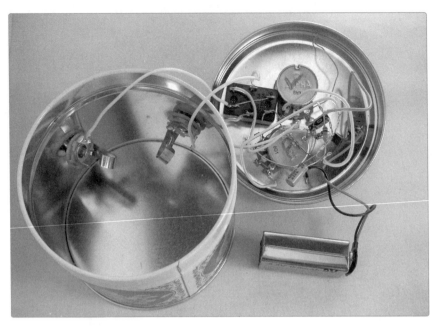

FIGURE 16-10: *The packaged Two-Transistor Fuzztone, guts revealed*

Using and Modifying the Two-Transistor Fuzztone

In contrast to the last two projects, this effect is just as good—if not even more impressive—when driven by instruments that output a "hotter" signal. Try it with the Cigar-Box Synthesizer (Project 17) or any old electric guitar you have handy—even consider using a preamp between your instrument and the Fuzztone; the hotter the signal coming in, the gnarlier the signal coming out.

Two simple modifications include changing the clipping diodes (as discussed in Step 4) and adding a power indicator LED by replacing the small SPST power switch with a DPST switch and adding the LED circuit from the Dirt-Cheap Amp (Project 12). Or, you might consider trading in the cheap RadioShack DPDT switch and candy tin case for a more impressive stomp box enclosure (as discussed in "On Enclosures" on page 166). A good place to find those heavy-duty enclosures and stomp switches is Small Bear Electronics (*http://www.smallbearelec.com/*). Alternatively, search online for a *small enclosure* or *project box* made by Velleman Incorporated or Hammond Manufacturing. Likewise, Small Bear always has the fat, iconic push-on/push-off DPDT stomp switches (look in the "Stock List" section of their website under "Switches, Relays").

Resources

- If you enjoyed these effects, then the next step is to get a copy of Craig Anderton's *Electronic Projects for Musicians* (which is the book that gets most amateur stomp-box tinkerers going) and its companion, *Do-It-Yourself Projects for Guitarists*, also by Anderton.

- PAiA sells many reasonably priced effects kits (as well as kits for building modular synths and theremins), including updated versions of several of the designs Anderton describes in his books. See *http://www.paia.com/*.

- As is the case with several electronic projects in this section, the Two-Transistor Fuzztone was inspired by T. Escobedo's circuit and instrument designs. Although Escobedo's excellent FolkUrban website is no longer online, I've archived several of his projects, including a whole slew of effects circuits like these, at *http://www.davideriknelson.com/sbsb/*. If you've built the projects in this book, then most of Escobedo's designs are well within your grasp.

17

CIGAR-BOX SYNTHESIZER

The Cigar-Box Synthesizer is an honest-to-God *analog monosynth*, not unlike the early synthesizers from Korg, Roland, and Robert Moog. Our simple little synthesizer is *analog* in that it abuses plain old integrated circuits into directly producing continuously variable musical notes and a *monosynth* because it makes one note at a time and thus can play melodies and bass lines but not chords. The Cigar-Box Synthesizer builds its thick tone by layering three octaves of each note and offers a musically useful range of about two-and-a-half octaves, with raw punky squeals above the high end and thunky mellow clicks below the low end. The resulting space-age theremin sound is harnessed with a dial-based pitch controller, which is much easier to master than the precise gestures of Leon Theremin and Clara Rockmore.

FIGURE 17-1: *The finished Cigar-Box Synthesizer*

The Cigar-Box Synthesizer is based on misusing two over-the-counter integrated circuits: a CD4093 Quad NAND Schmitt Trigger and a CD4040 12-Bit Binary/Ripple Counter. We're going to feed the first chip back on itself in order to make it function as an *oscillator*, producing a musically useful tone. If you're unfamiliar with the term oscillator, think of a metronome, which produces a click at regular intervals (remember that old-timey metronome with the pyramidal wooden case and oscillating pendulum click-click-clicking on Grandma's piano?). Run the metronome fast enough and your ear slurs those clicks together into a single burring tone. As the oscillator speeds up, the pitch of the tone increases.

The second chip functions as an *octave divider*; it will take the oscillator's tone and give back the same pitch one octave (or several octaves) lower. Since the oscillator is binary, it's actually producing a series of pulses, not a continuous tone. Slow them down and you hear them as discrete clicks. We feed that stream of pulses to the divider on its input, and at each output it generates one pulse for every two it receives, or one for every four, or one for every eight, and so on, thus producing ever-lower pitches exactly in tune with the input.

As with all ICs, references to the chips in this project assume you are looking at them from the top, with their dimples or half-circle notches to the left. In this position, the bottom left pin is number 1, the one to the immediate right is 2, then 3, all the way to the end of the row and wrapping around counterclockwise, as shown in Figure 17-2.

FIGURE 17-2: *The CD4093 (left) and CD4040 (right) ICs, with legs numbered*

Tools

▶ a standard soldering kit (See the appendix.)

▶ an electric drill with 3/8" and 1/2" bits

▶ Gorilla Glue

▶ coarse-grit sandpaper and a sanding block

▶ an amp, such as the Dirt-Cheap Amp built in Project 12

Supplies

▶ a CD4093 integrated circuit (Digi-Key stock #296-2068-5-ND), aka a Quad NAND Schmitt Trigger

▶ a CD4040 integrated circuit (Digi-Key stock #296-2048-5-ND), aka a 12-bit Binary/Ripple Counter[1]

▶ a 0.1 µF ceramic disk capacitor (These are usually marked *104*.)

▶ a 10 µF electrolytic capacitor

▶ a 100k ohm variable resistor, preferably linear tapers

▶ three 10k ohm variable resistors, preferably audio tapers, not linear tapers (See "Audio Tapers vs. Linear Tapers" on page 190 for details.)

▶ three 10k ohm resistors (coded with brown-black-orange stripes)

▶ a 1/4" mono phone jack (guitar jack)

▶ a length of coat hanger or similar stiff wire

----

1. There are plenty of CD4093 and CD4040s out there that will work fine; these are the cheapest at the time of writing. If you end up ordering something else, just be sure that it has a DIP layout and can tolerate being powered by 9 volts (most ICs in this family are fine with 5–20 volts).

- a playing card (or any fancy cardboard or thin plastic)
- a cylindrical control knob that fits over the shaft of your 100k ohm variable resistor, such as RadioShack part #274-403
- three more control knobs, either the same as above or something more stylish, such as RadioShack part #274-415
- a 9-volt battery clip
- a 9-volt battery
- a momentary push-button switch, such as a doorbell switch
- a cigar box or similar enclosure
- 24-gauge insulated hook-up wire (Stranded is better, and you might want to get several colors to help you keep connections straight.)
- 22- or 24-gauge bare bus wire
- a small printed circuit board, such as RadioShack #276-148
- double-sided foam tape
- (optional, but strongly recommended) a 14-pin IC socket and a 16-pin IC socket (You can substitute an 18- or 20-pin socket for the 16-pin one if it is easier to find; any of them will work fine.)

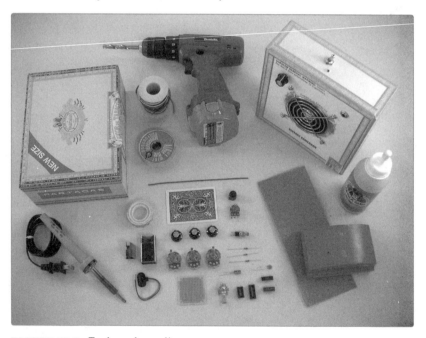

FIGURE 17-3: *Tools and supplies*

Building It

Step 1   Start with the pitch controller (shown in Figure 17-4), since that will need to dry overnight. Take a 5" length of coat hanger (or similar stiff wire), and curl one end so that it hooks snugly around the end of your cylindrical control knob. Cut a 1" circle of playing card; this will serve as a stylish knob cover. Put a penny-sized dollop of Gorilla Glue in the center of the playing-card circle. Press the top of the knob into the glue (forcing some out around its edges), and then hook the wire around it. Apply a little more glue to cover the wire (if needed), clean up any excess, and let this dry overnight. Remember that Gorilla Glue foams as it cures; an innocuous little smear can dry into a big foamy mess.

FIGURE 17-4: *Building the pitch controller arm*

Step 2   Now you'll install the ICs onto the printed circuit board (PCB). Take a look at the schematic in Figure 17-5.

    ✱ **NOTE:** *Although these ICs will put up with a fair amount of abuse, too much heat or a jolt of static will fry them. Using empty IC sockets and installing the chips in the final step is advised; for the sake of clarity, both the instructions and the illustrations show the chips in place.*

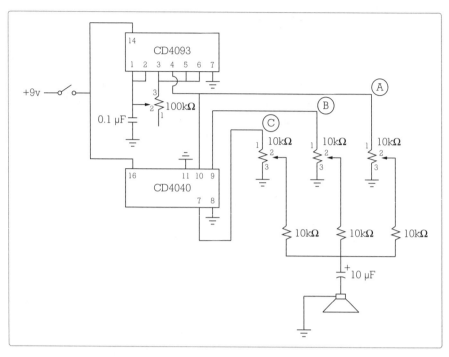

FIGURE 17-5: *The Cigar-Box Synthesizer circuit*

Step 3   Since these two chips are in the same family, they have similar layouts (even though the CD4093 only has 14 pins and the CD4040 has 16). Both get power on their final pin (upper-left corner), and both are tied to the ground by the last pin on their bottom row (that is, the one diagonal from the power pin: pin 7 on the CD4093 and pin 8 on the CD4040). Pin 11 on the CD4040 also ties to ground, so start by slipping the 14-pin socket for the CD4093 into the top of the circuit board (i.e., leaving two empty rows above it), and then adding the socket for the CD4040 four rows below (i.e., leaving three rows of empty holes between them; see Figure 17-6). Offset them so that pin 11 on the CD4040 (the lower chip) lines up with pin 7 of the CD4093. To ensure the sockets stay in place as you work, carefully flip the board now and bend down the corner pins on each IC socket.

* **NOTE:** *Remember that all of the pins are numbered from the top, but all of the soldering gets done from the bottom; once you flip the board over, the numbers will be reversed!*

Step 4   Start by soldering all of the *jumpers* (lengths of wire connecting pins on the ICs). Snip a 1" length of the bare bus wire, crimp it, and slide it into the first two holes corresponding with pins 1 and 2 of the CD4093 socket. Now flip the board over and solder this jumper to pins 1 and 2; be careful not to inadvertently create a solder bridge to any of the other legs of the socket. Solder similar jumpers between pins 3 and 5 on the CD4093 socket and another between pins 5 and 6. Then place a

FIGURE 17-6: *The socketed chips on the circuit board, viewed from the top (notice that the 16-pin CD4040 is in an 18-pin socket; the two empty slots are on the socket's right end)*

jumper from pin 7 of the CD4093 socket toward pin 11 of the CD4040 socket, leaving one empty hole between the jumper and pin 11 of the CD4093 socket; don't solder this jumper yet (you'll do that in Step 5). The installed jumpers are shown in Figure 17-7.

FIGURE 17-7: *Four jumpers installed*

Step 5 Cut a 1 1/2" length and a 2" length of insulated wire; strip and tin both ends of each (since this is for a ground connection, use green wire). Put one end of the 1 1/2" wire into the empty hole between pin 7 of the CD4093 socket and pin 11 of the CD4040 socket and the other into the first hole adjacent to pin 8 of the CD4040 socket. Solder the first end—the one that's between the two ICs—to both the uninsulated jumper you installed in Step 4 (which is one hole above the insulated wire) and pin 11 on the lower IC socket (which is one hole below the insulated wire). Then, solder the other end of the uninsulated jumper to pin 7 of the upper IC socket. Now put one end of the 2" wire in the next hole adjacent to pin 8 of the CD4040 socket; run the other end to the column of holes to the far left of the board (this will be your *common ground* for the circuit—check Figure 17-8 if you're confused). Solder together the two wires at pin 8, then solder them to pin 8; leave the common ground end alone for now, and set the board aside.

FIGURE 17-8: *The two socketed ICs with two "flying grounds" (the leftmost end of the horizontal ground line is not yet soldered)*

Step 6 Take out the 100k variable resistor (also called a *potentiometer* or *pot*). Cut two 9" lengths of insulated wire (for clarity, use a color other than green; since these are power connections, red is appropriate) and tin both ends. Solder one to the center lug and one to the third lug of the pot (potentiometer lugs are numbered from the left when viewing the pot from the front with lugs on top; check the diagram in the appendix if you're unsure which lug is which). If you'd ultimately prefer to have the Cigar-Box Synthesizer play lower notes as you turn the controller counterclockwise (which might feel a little more natural for folks with a piano background), then solder these wires to the middle and first lug, rather than middle and third.

Solder the wire attached to the center lug to pin 1 of the CD4093 socket and the other wire to pin 3 of the same socket. Depending on how you choose to package your Cigar-Box Synthesizer, these wires may need to be longer or shorter; since these connections are not part of the audio chain, making them longer won't be a problem. Any connection that *is* part of the audio chain will get noisier—and possibly begin to pick up AM radio—if it is much longer than 6". Keep this in mind when planning your packaging.

Step 7   Take the three 10k audio taper pots and 10k resistors. Cut six 5" lengths of wire (these will carry an audio signal, so choose a new color, like white). On each pot, solder a length of insulated wire to lug 1 (this is the input) and a resistor to lug 2 (the middle lug). Then solder a second wire to the remaining leg of each resistor, bring the loose ends of these three wires together, and solder them to the positive leg (the one that does not line up with the black stripe) on a 10 μF electrolytic capacitor; this is your output. (In Step 13 we'll wire the third lug on each to the ground.) Label these pots A, B, and C (you can write on the backs with a Sharpie). Congratulations—you've just built a passive mixer (shown in Figure 17-9); you can adapt this design to mix any audio signals (and, for example, make your Dirt-Cheap Amp, Project 12, into a 4-channel sound system).

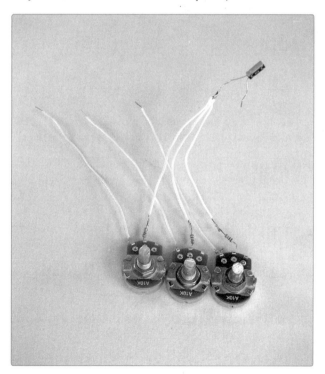

FIGURE 17-9: *The three 10k pots wired up as a simple mixer; note that the shafts have been cut down*

Step 8   Time to finish off the circuit board. Cut a 1 1/4" length of insulated wire (this wire will carry an audio signal, so use white). Strip and tin both ends. Slip one end into the second open hole adjacent to pin 4 of the CD4093 socket, and solder it to pin 4 (this can be a little tricky, since you don't want to short it to the jumper connecting pins 3 and 5). Slip the other end through the hole closest to pin 10 on the CD4040 socket, as shown in Figure 17-10, but don't solder it yet.

FIGURE 17-10: *The board thus far*

Step 9   Slip pot A's input wire into the next open hole at pin 10 of the CD4040 socket, and solder it and the wire from Step 8 to pin 10. Solder the input of pot B to pin 9 and the input of pot C to pin 7.

Step 10   Now you'll add power. Cut and strip two wires, one 1 1/2" long and the other several inches (neither will carry an audio signal, so keeping them short isn't vital; these are power connections, so red is a good color). Solder one end of the 1 1/2" wire to pin 16 (the upper-left corner pin) of the CD4040 (i.e., the lower) socket. Run the other end to pin 14 (also the upper left) of the CD4093 socket. Add one end of the longer wire to pin 14, and solder both wires to pin 14 of the CD4093 socket. Solder the other end of the longer wire to one terminal of your push-button switch.

Step 11   Strip the ends of your 9-volt battery clip, and solder the red lead to the remaining terminal on your push-button switch. Run the black lead from the clip to the common ground along the left edge of your circuit board (choose the open hole closest to the flying ground from Step 5).

Step 12   Connect one leg of the 0.1 µF ceramic capacitor to pin 1 of the CD4093 and the other to the common ground. Solder the leg to pin 1 (you'll solder the other leg to the common ground in Step 13). This capacitor sets the range for the pitch your oscillator will produce; you could use anything from 0.1 µF to 0.001 µF and still be mostly in the audible range; the larger the value of the capacitor, the lower the pitch.

Step 13   Next, begin installing the Cigar Box Synthesizer's guts (shown in Figure 17-11) in its enclosure. In order to minimize noise, we need to keep the ground connection through the mixer as short as possible. Start by mounting pots A, B, and C (from left to right in that order) on the side of the enclosure that will face you as you play (both pots and jacks usually need 1/2" or 3/8" holes); a little sanding will smooth any ragged edges. Many pots have a little protruding spike, used to anchor the pot to its enclosure and keep it steady through repeated tweaking (see Figure 17-12). When you install the pot, either drill a tiny hole to accommodate the anchor or use a pair of pliers to snap it off. Mount the output jack on the same face of the enclosure as the mixer.

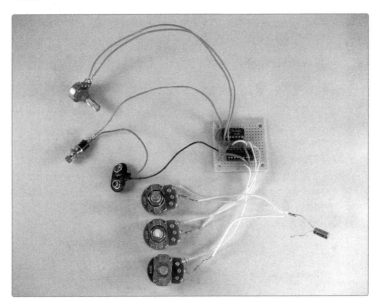

FIGURE 17-11: *The mostly finished guts*

FIGURE 17-12: *A close-up of a potentiometer's anchor*

To wire the ground for the pots, solder the end of your spool of bare bus wire to the sleeve of the jack (jack lugs are diagrammed in the appendix) and then to lug 3 of each pot, being careful not to short the ground against the other connections (it's fine for the ground wire to rest against the metal bodies of the pots). Finally, uncoil enough bus wire to reach the common ground on the left edge of the circuit board, snip the bus from the spool, slide the bus wire into the circuit board, and solder the common ground (you should have four wires there: the black lead from the battery, the remaining leg of your ceramic capacitor, the green wire from Step 5, and the bare bus line you just added).

Step 14   Finish the audio output by soldering the negative leg (the one lining up with the thick stripe) of the mixer's 10 µF electrolytic capacitor to the tip lug on the output jack (again, see the appendix for a detailed look at wiring a jack).

Step 15   To finish packaging the Cigar Box Synthesizer, drill two holes in the top of the box: one for the trigger switch and one for the pitch controller (see Figures 17-13 and 17-14)—a few swipes with the sandpaper will take out the splinters. Position the trigger in the upper-left corner, so it's clear of the pitch controller's arm. The most musically useful portion of the pitch controller's range of motion is the middle third, so place the hole for the tone-controller pot in the lower-right corner of the box top (as illustrated in Figure 17-14).

Once this pot is firmly mounted on the enclosure, twist its shaft so that it is turned fully clockwise or counterclockwise and can be twisted no further. Attach the tone-controller knob so that its wire extension arm points to the lower-right corner of the box (as shown in Figure 17-14).

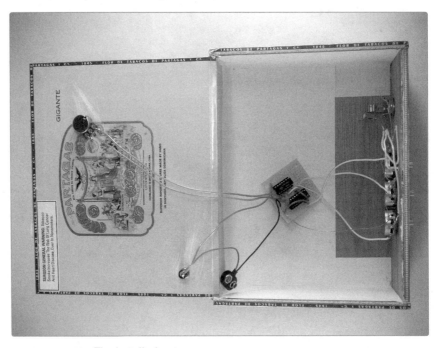

FIGURE 17-13: *The installed guts*

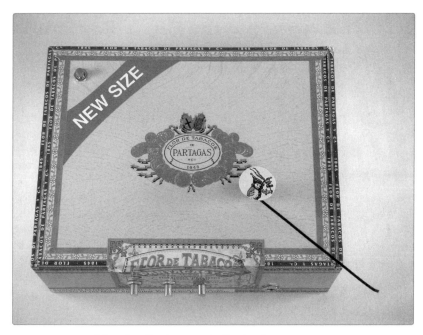

FIGURE 17-14: *Mounting the tone-controller knob*

Step 16 Finish off construction by using double-sided foam tape to secure the circuit board to the inside of the cigar box. Make sure all of the switches, pots, and jacks are secure, then add knobs to the mixer pots. It's also a good idea to use a little double-sided tape to hold the 9-volt battery in place (a metal clip–style 9-volt battery holder, like RadioShack part #270-326, is even better).

Step 17 The Cigar-Box Synthesizer is ready to play right now, although it's a touch more playable if you mark out the scale on the lid of the box. Get out your chromatic tuner, and pull the arm of your pitch controller around so that it just touches the edge of the box nearest you. Hit the trigger, and see what note you are near, then nudge the arm clockwise until you've got a solid *natural* (that is, neither sharp nor flat) note. Mark its position in pencil,[2] then keep nudging the arm clockwise, adding each subsequent natural note; they'll be very close at first and gradually space out to about 1" apart as the pitch gets lower. If you find that your pitch starts very low and gets higher as you turn clockwise, it's because, in Step 6, you soldered the second wire to lug 1 of the 100k pot instead of lug 3.

---

2. You'll want to do this in pencil because (1) it's easy to inadvertently nudge the knob cover out of alignment on the potentiometer shaft, thus knocking your tuning into disarray, and (2) analog circuits are notoriously unstable in the long term; as the capacitors age and the weather changes, so will this little Cigar-Box Synthesizer's tuning. Taping a strip of white paper to the top and marking the notes out there makes it easy to read and easy to update.

Expanding the Cigar-Box Synthesizer

As designed, this Cigar-Box Synthesizer only mixes two of the octaves that the CD4040 offers: The straight signal produced by the oscillator (the CD4093) is on pot A and is mixed with the tone one octave lower (pin 9 on the CD4040) and two octaves lower (pin 7 of the CD4040). Technically, each output on the CD4040 (pins 1 through 9, 11, and 12 through 15) is producing a fraction of the number of pulses that the chip receives on its input (pin 10). Pin 9, for example, puts out one pulse for every two that come in (thus producing a tone one octave below the input); pin 7 produces one pulse for every four that come in (i.e., two octaves below the input), and so on. Each of the remaining open pins on the CD4040 offers another signal, one octave lower than its predecessor (see the diagram in Figure 17-15). Most of the signals on the higher outputs are so slow that they register as "bonks" instead of continuous notes, but there is no reason you couldn't add them to your mix or have them go to separate outputs via either pots (like the mixer we built in Step 7) or switches. As a rule, any time you bring several audio signals together, you want to buffer each with a 10k ohm resistor (as we've done on the mixer in Step 7); so if you add switches in order to bring out the bonks on pins 2 and 3 (i.e., outputs Q5 and Q6), then put a 10k resistor on the output side of the switch, and solder it to the positive leg of the 10 μF capacitor on the existing mixer.

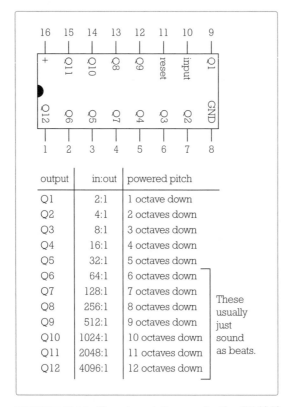

output	in:out	powered pitch
Q1	2:1	1 octave down
Q2	4:1	2 octaves down
Q3	8:1	3 octaves down
Q4	16:1	4 octaves down
Q5	32:1	5 octaves down
Q6	64:1	6 octaves down
Q7	128:1	7 octaves down
Q8	256:1	8 octaves down
Q9	512:1	9 octaves down
Q10	1024:1	10 octaves down
Q11	2048:1	11 octaves down
Q12	4096:1	12 octaves down

These usually just sound as beats.

FIGURE 17-15: *The pin-out diagram for the CD4040*

The CD4093 likewise hides additional secrets. Look at its logical diagram (Figure 17-16), and you'll see that its two sides are symmetrical. Rotate the chip 180 degrees, and you can build a whole separate synthesizer just like the first. Pretend pin 8 is 1, pin 9 is 2, and so on: Jumper pins 8 to 9 and 10 to 12 to 13, connect pin 8 to 10 with another 100k pot, ground pin 8 through a 0.1 µF capacitor, then run pin 11 to the tip of a jack, and—*BadaBoom Disco!*—you have two identical synthesizers for the price of one.

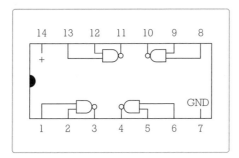

FIGURE 17-16: *Logic diagram of the CD4093 Dual-Quad inverter*

In order to shape the Cigar-Box Synthesizer's tone (some folks find the CD4093 oscillator's native square wave a little grating), you can add both *low-* and *high-pass filters* (there are circuit diagrams in Figure 17-17). The former filters out high tones and lets lower ones pass through, and the latter filters out low tones and lets high ones through—you are familiar with these as the treble and bass knobs on your stereo. They're simple and go on the audio output, just before the jack.

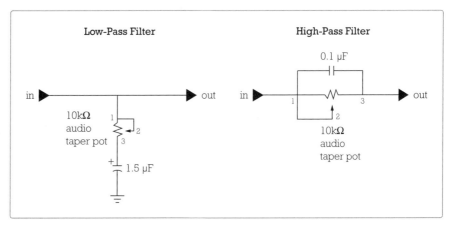

FIGURE 17-17: *A low-pass filter (left) and high-pass filter (right); yes, they look remarkably similar*

The low-pass filter will cut the high end, which manifests itself as the characteristic square-wave sound of an early '80s synthesizer: a reedy, fat squelch. I've used *very high* capacitor values, because the Cigar-Box Synthesizer has such an aggressive tone. These are based on classic guitar tone controls, where the caps are usually much smaller: between 0.01 μF and 0.05 μF for the low-pass filter and between 470 pF and 0.002 μF for the high-pass filters. If you decide to add low- and high-pass filters to other projects (like the Dirt-Cheap Amp in Project 12 or the $10 Electric Guitar in Project 13), you might be happier with lower values than those illustrated in Figure 17-17; start with a 0.1 μF ceramic disc capacitor (labeled *104*) in the low-pass filter.

Finally, you can get rid of the pitch controller pot altogether and replace it with either a homemade *ribbon controller* (à la T. Escobedo's synthstick; see "Resources" below) or your own body. For the latter, just remove the 100k pot, and mount a pair of brass knobs to the top of the box about 1" apart, making sure the knobs and their hardware aren't touching each other. Run a wire from pin 1 of the CD4093 to one of the knobs and another wire from pin 3 to the second knob. Grab both knobs in one hand; you won't feel the electricity, but your skin will act as a variable resistor: Touching the knobs gently will give you a low pitch that will steadily rise as you squeeze harder.

Resources

▶   If you enjoy this sort of low-tech, lo-fi electro music, get a copy of Nicolas Collins's *Handmade Electronic Music*, which is full of projects and great ideas for ways to tune up and freak out.

▶   This design—much like the effects earlier in this section—owes a great deal to the cornucopia of effects and musical instruments T. Escobedo shared on his FolkUrban website (including his synthstick, which uses a very cool and easy homemade ribbon controller). Sadly, Escobedo's site is no longer online, but I've archived some of his projects on this book's website: *http://www.davideriknelson.com/sbsb/*.

PART III

The Loco-motivated

From the humblest soda-straw spit-wad to the mightiest Nazi-crushing golem, there's an undeniable, universal human thrill to breathing a little life into otherwise inanimate objects. The projects in this section get things moving by a variety of novel means—harnessing steam, compressed air, tiny vibrators, FedEx envelopes, camera-flash-ignited breath spray, and esoteric physics. Dream of the future when all of these can be combined into one fantastic, terrifying project to end all projects.

18 CARDBOARD BOOMERANGS

Owing to the prevalence of untuned, Styrofoam toy-store boomerangs, generations of American children wrongly grow to believe that building and throwing boomerangs is very difficult. This flies in the face of reason: Using less-than-ideal materials, human beings have been building, throwing, and catching returning boomerangs for more than 11,600 years. The oldest boomerangs found thus far were recovered from the Wyrie Swamp in Australia—but boomerangs aren't unique to Australia. And despite the impressions you may have gotten from *Mad Max* and *Crocodile Dundee*, returning boomerangs were never used as weapons; they are, in fact, among humanity's longest-standing ways of showing off.

Boomerangs are absurdly easy to make—this is an ideal project to keep kids busy in a pinch. Learning to throw one is just a little tricky, but most of the trick is in properly *tuning* the boomerang. The easiest boomerangs for beginners to craft and throw are *quad-bladers*. This project includes two quad-blade designs. The first is a poster board *Fast-Catch Boomerang*. Fast-catch boomerangs usually have more than three wings and are characterized by a tight flight pattern and quick return. This design is ideal for indoor boomerang play and also good for *juggling* (catching and tossing two boomerangs in sequence so that one is aloft at all times). The second design is a slightly heartier cardboard *Cross-Stick Boomerang*, suitable for outdoor use. Cross-stick boomerangs, as the name suggests, are made from two separate wings connected at the hub, rather than being cut in a single piece.

Boomerang Hunting

Although returning boomerangs are crummy weapons—they're generally too light to kill anything and far too hard to aim—they are used for hunting birds. Hunters erect broad, low nets near large flocks and then approach from the other side. They throw boomerangs over the flock, which mistake the gyring toys for swooping birds of prey. The panicked flock flees low across the meadow and gets snared in the nets. Incidentally, bats can often be goaded into attacking tri-blade boomerangs, as the sound of the spinning blades can be similar in frequency to that of large moths' wings.

Many cultures, including Australian Aborigines, do use non-returning boomerangs for hunting. These heavier tools are more often (and less confusingly) called rabbit sticks, throw sticks, or, in Australia, *kylies*. They are heavy and have a biconvex airfoil—that is, both the top and bottom of the wing are curved; our Cardboard Boomerang wings, on the other hand, are only curved along the top, as are most conventional airplane wings. Thrown parallel to the ground with a spin, throw sticks are stable in flight and can go a long way, with the intent of crippling an animal's legs so that the hunter can capture and bludgeon it. The oldest known throw stick was discovered in Poland's Oblazowa Cave. Made from a split mammoth tusk, it was more than 20,300 years old.

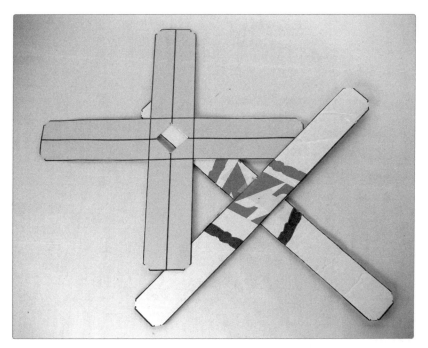

FIGURE 18-1: *The finished boomerangs: the indoor Fast-Catch Boomerang on the left, and the outdoor Cross-Stick Boomerang on the right*

Tools

▶ scissors or a hobby knife

▶ a ruler

▶ a pencil or pen

Supplies

▶ for the **Fast-Catch Boomerang**: poster board or similar lightweight cardboard (Large cereal, donut, or cake boxes are ideal, as are 24-pack beer cases.)

▶ for the **Cross-Stick Boomerang**: lightweight corrugated cardboard roughly 1/32" thick, e.g., a pizza box

▶ clear packing tape

FIGURE 18-2: *Tools and supplies*

Building the Fast-Catch Boomerang

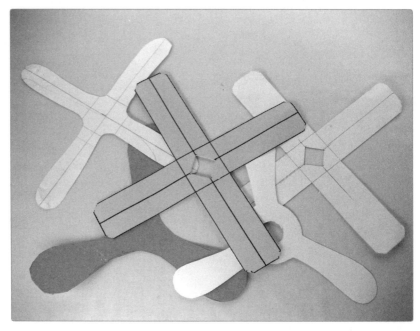

FIGURE 18-3: *Several cardboard Fast-Catch Boomerangs*

Step 1   Using a straight edge, draw a 1' by 1' plus sign on the poster board; these two strokes will serve as guidelines. They should be perpendicular but don't drive yourself nuts if the lines are a little skewed.

Step 2   Add 2" crossbars to the ends of each stroke, as in Figure 18-4. (In heraldry, this is called a *cross potent* and is the same as the central figure in a Crusaders' cross design.)

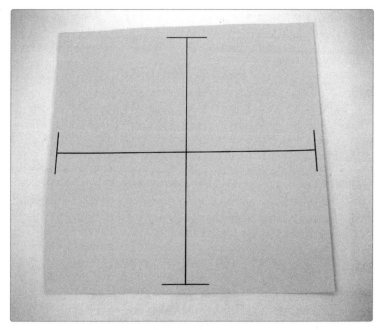

FIGURE 18-4: *The cross potent boomerang skeleton*

Step 3   Connect the 2" crossbars on either end of each stroke, resulting in a 1' plus sign with 2" thick arms. Cut out this giant plus sign (Figure 18-5).

Step 4   Trim off the corners of each blade: Measure and mark 1/4" on the side and top of the blade at each corner, and cut off the corner diagonally, as indicated in Figure 18-6.

Step 5   Now we're going to cut out the hub. Notice that the lines you added in Step 3 resulted in a 2" box at the center of the boomerang. Mark 1/4" along each of the original axes, measuring from the edge of this box towards the center of the boomerang, as illustrated in Figure 18-7. Connect these four points, and then cut out the cocked 1" by 1" square you've drawn.

FIGURE 18-5: *The blank for the Fast-Catch Boomerang*

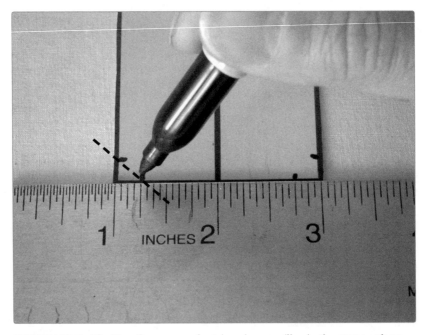

FIGURE 18-6: *Marking the corners for trimming; you'll snip the corner along the dashed line.*

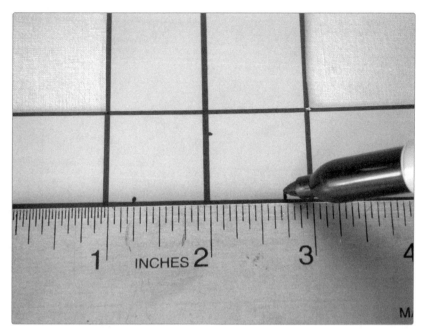

FIGURE 18-7: *Measuring for the hub cutout*

Step 6 Decide which side of the Fast-Catch Boomerang you want to think of as the "face" and mark it. If you throw right-handed, then viewing the Fast-Catch Boomerang face up, the left edge of each blade is its *leading edge*. (Imagine the Fast-Catch Boomerang on the right side of Figure 18-8 spinning counterclockwise, and it all makes sense.) Left-handed throwers will be spinning the Fast-Catch Boomerang clockwise, so their leading edges will be on the right side of each blade.

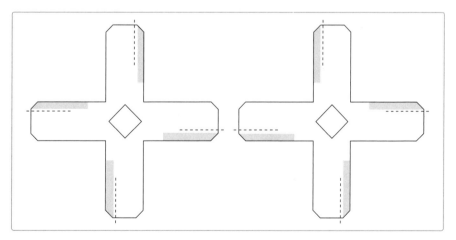

FIGURE 18-8: *The Fast-Catch Boomerang on the left shows the leading edge for left-handed throwers; the one on the right shows the leading edge for right-handed throwers. Leading edges are shaded, and quarter lines, described in Step 7, are dashed.*

Step 7   Holding the Fast-Catch Boomerang face up, use your thumbnail to gently crimp each blade at a point 1/2" behind the leading edge (i.e., crimp at the wing's *quarter line*—the dashed line in Figure 18-8), thus making a cheap and easy airfoil, as shown in Figure 18-9.

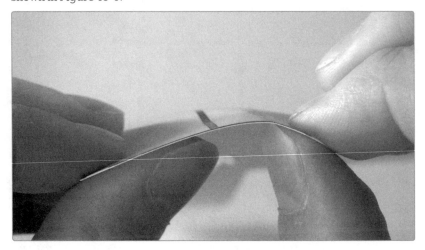

FIGURE 18-9: *Making an easy airfoil by crimping the blade, as viewed from the edge of one boomerang arm; the leading edge is to the right*

Step 8   Add a little initial *dihedral* to each wing by lifting the wing up several inches, as in Figure 18-10. Don't worry about trying to get the wing to curve; the very *slight* lift that remains after the cardboard relaxes is just fine.

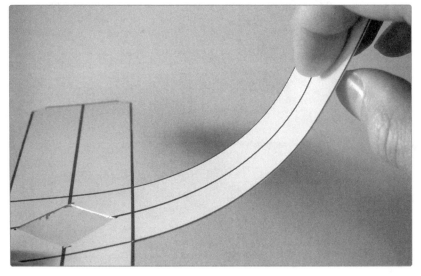

FIGURE 18-10: *Adding dihedral*

Done! Skip to the end of this project for instructions on tuning and throwing.

Building the Cross-Stick Boomerang

FIGURE 18-11: *Several Cross-Stick Boomerangs*

Step 1   The Cross-Stick Boomerang is even easier to make than the Fast-Catch Boomerang. Cut two 14" by 1 1/2" rectangles from the corrugated cardboard (Figure 18-12).

FIGURE 18-12: *The blanks for the Cross-Stick Boomerang*

Step 2   As with the Fast-Catch Boomerang, trim the corners of each stick at a 45-degree angle by marking 1/4" from the corner along both the side and top, and then snipping off that corner (see Figure 18-13).

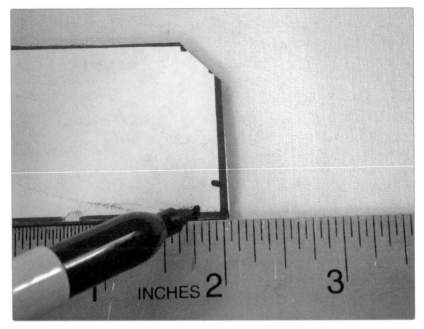

FIGURE 18-13: *Measuring and snipping a corner*

Step 3   Use strips of tape to secure the two blades, one strip front, one strip back. Try to center the arms and tape, as in Figure 18-14, but don't make yourself crazy: cardboard boomerangs are very forgiving flyers.

Step 4   As in Steps 6 and 7 for the Fast-Catch Boomerang, decide which side of the Cross-Stick Boomerang will be the face, and then crimp each wing at its quarter line. Remember, this is going to be different for right and left handers; see Figure 18-8. It's okay if the airfoil is hardly perceptible; aerodynamically, a little goes a long way.

Step 5   Add a touch of dihedral as explained in Step 8 of the Fast-Catch Boomerang.

Now you can move on to tuning and throwing.

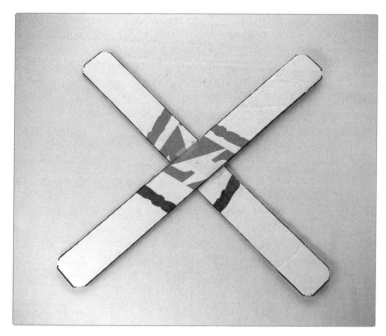

FIGURE 18-14: *The finished Cross-Stick Boomerang*

Throwing

To throw a boomerang, hold it in your throwing hand, pinching one wing near the tip (Figure 18-15).

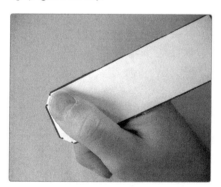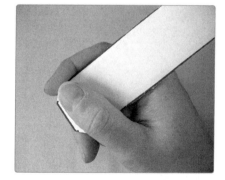

FIGURE 18-15: *Two good boomerang grips for beginners*

Cock your arm back so that the boomerang is vertical, with its face toward your head. Throw with a flick of the wrist, being sure to keep the boomerang vertical throughout your throw. Ideally, the Fast-Catch Boomerang will stay vertical and travel straight for a couple yards, then begin to curve to the left (for a right-handed thrower). It then *lays over* (leans into a more horizontal position) as it comes into its return curve, so that it ultimately is hovering horizontally in front of you, where you can easily catch it by sandwiching it between your horizontal hands. The Cross-Stick Boomerang tends to climb higher (10 or 12 feet from the ground, rather than the straight path of the Fast-Catch Boomerang) and go out further (perhaps 20 feet) before starting its return.

In very still air, you may find the boomerang is returning inconveniently far in front of you (following a path like a question mark). If this is the case, try throwing with some *layover*—angling the boomerang a few degrees away from your head, as illustrated in Figure 18-16. Since the boomerang naturally lays over as it goes into its return curve, throwing with some layover will put it into its turn sooner.

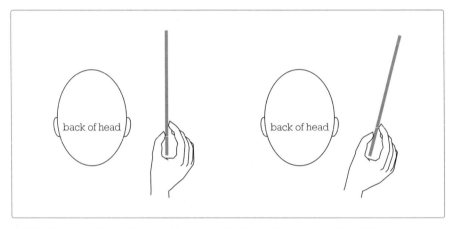

FIGURE 18-16: *Normal throwing position (left) and throwing with a little layover (right), as viewed from behind a right-handed thrower*

When throwing outside, throw a bit off-center of the wind. Aim about 45 degrees to the right of the wind if you're right-handed and likewise to the left if you're left-handed. As a rule, if there's more wind, you need less layover to get a good return.

Throwing and tuning go hand in hand. Once you've finished your boomerang, give it a few tosses, and then start tuning to get better performance.

Tuning

Here's the key to tuning: Tiny, almost imperceptible changes have a dramatic impact on the boomerang's behavior. Tune the wings one at a time, making a single change (e.g., adding a little dihedral or positive attack), give it a test toss, then tune some more.

There are three aspects to tuning: dihedral, positive attack, and weight:

▶ *Dihedral* is a curving of the wing so that it doesn't all lie along a single plane. Increasing dihedral makes the boomerang climb higher, follow a more circular path, and lay over sooner to finish with a long hover (which makes it easier to catch). Adding lots of dihedral makes these light Cardboard Boomerangs travel fast and tight. To add dihedral to a boomerang's wings, hold the boomerang by the hub with its face toward you, and pull the wing toward yourself (Figure 18-17).

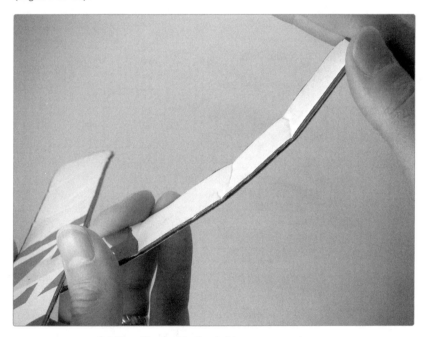

FIGURE 18-17: *Adding dihedral in the field*

▶ *Positive attack* is a twist along the length of the boomerang's wing, which slows the boomerang down, resulting in a flatter, rounder, lower flight path. To add positive attack, hold the boomerang by its hub with the boomerang's face up. Looking at the edge of the wing, twist it counterclockwise (for right-handed throwers) or clockwise (for left-handed throwers), lifting the leading edge of the blade (Figure 18-18).

FIGURE 18-18: *Adding positive attack for a right-handed thrower*

▶ Adding *weight* increases momentum, resulting in a longer, more elliptical flight. The easiest way to add weight to a boomerang is by taping pennies to one or more wings. The effect will be more pronounced as you put the weight further toward the tip. Add weight to one wing at a time. It's easiest to throw a weighted Cardboard Boomerang if the heaviest arm is directly opposite the one you are holding when you throw.

And, of course, if any of these behaviors are too pronounced, you can always decrease dihedral and attack. You can even try a negative dihedral or attack, which rarely work with these multi-bladers but can be useful with some more exotic store-bought boomerangs.

Store-Bought Boomerangs

All of this tuning and throwing advice holds true for any store-bought boomerang. Bear in mind that tuning a rigid wood or hard plastic boomerang might require heating the boomerang gently over a candle or low gas flame, adjusting the attack or dihedral to your liking, and then holding the wing under cold running water to "fix the tune."

A heavier boomerang is going to have quite a bit of momentum on its return flight, especially if it climbs high, which will result in a very fast, steep return. The rigid edge of a wood or plastic boomerang can make a mess of eyes, teeth, or soft mucous membranes. Thus, always wear pants when playing with a boomerang, and if you think you aren't going to make a catch—especially if the boomerang climbs high—then cover your eyes with your palms (which naturally results in the wrists shielding your nose and mouth) and turn away *fast*.

How It Works

A boomerang is basically a gyroscope made of wings and thus is subject to some quirky physics. Specifically, a boomerang benefits from *gyroscopic precession*, which is the tendency for a spinning mass to wobble when nudged, rather than falling over. Imagine a bicyclist riding no-handed: As she cruises down the street, she stays upright because the bike's wheels are a pair of gyroscopes, and their spinning gives them stability. If she wants to turn left, she leans left. Now, if this was a stationary wheel, nudging the top of it (as the rider does when she leans) would just knock it over. But since it's a gyroscope, adding an additional force to the top causes the gyroscope to turn perpendicular to its axis of spin (imagine a top and how it wobbles around its axis instead of just falling over), and the bike magically follows a big leftward looping path.

Since the boomerang is spinning, it's a gyroscope; this gives it stability in flight. Since the boomerang is a spinning set of wings, forces are acting on it unevenly (just as forces act unevenly on the spinning wheels of the bike when the rider leans). Although the boomerang, as a unit, has a single velocity, each wing has a different velocity relative to that, since the "top" wing is moving forward and the "bottom" moving backward as it spins. Slowly spin your boomerang on your desk while sliding it forward, and you'll see that the topmost wing is always moving forward and thus is moving a little faster than the unit's velocity, while the bottom wing is moving backward and thus subtracting its velocity from the velocity of the boomerang as a whole. Identical wings moving at different velocities exert different amounts of force, with the faster wing exerting more force. (This is why an airplane can't just tool along at 24 mph; you need some hustle to break free of gravity's ardent embrace.) So, there is a greater force acting on the top of the spinning boomerang than the bottom. This has the same effect as the bike rider leaning left, pulling the boomerang around in a circular path.

Boomerang Design

Now that you've dispelled the magical fog from the boomerang, it's time to design your own. A few tips:

▶   You want the hub to be lighter than the blades (since a gyroscope functions best when the bulk of its mass is on the outermost edges). It's best to narrow the blades as they approach the hub or cut a hole in the hub. This also prevents premature layover.

▶   Parabolic wing tips are better than flat.

▶   Different materials have different optimal lengths and widths, so experiment. In general, heavier materials mean narrower wings.

▶ Experiment with heavier, more rigid materials, such as the corrugated plastic used for political-campaign lawn signs. Sign-making shops often have scraps of interesting, dense plastics that are easy to work with hand tools. The throwing and tuning tips still apply; heed the warnings in "Store-Bought Boomerangs" on page 230 when throwing these!

Resources

▶ Download full-size stencils for a few smaller Fast-Catch Boomerangs in the boomerangs section of *http://www.davideriknelson.com/sbsb/*.

▶ I owe a huge debt to engineer and boomerang enthusiast Ted Bailey for these designs. Ted is a former United States Boomerang Association president, noted for revolutionizing boomerang design in the 1980s by adapting and miniaturizing NASA low-speed airfoil research. He has a lot of great boomerang info (and hordes of cool flying toys for sale) on his website *http://www.flight-toys.com/*.

19 POP CAN FLYER

The Pop Can Flyer is deceptively simple: Take a regular aluminum can, trim off the ends, and now you have an unlikely aircraft capable of eerily long, straight flights. While the building is straightforward, the physics of the craft are a bit trickier and pretty interesting. At the very least, the tools and supplies are almost universally available, and a few Pop Can Flyers can keep cranky nephews busy for at least an hour. As a bonus, this project includes instructions for making NASA's Finest Paper Airplane, which benefits from the same design properties as the Pop Can Flyer.

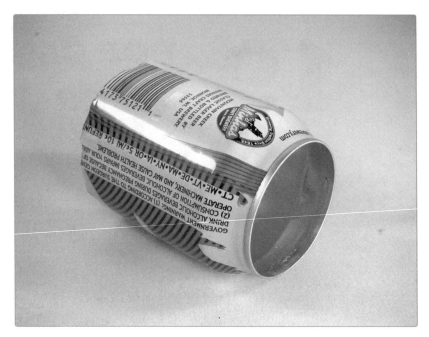

FIGURE 19-1: *The finished Pop Can Flyer*

Tools

▶ a utility knife

▶ a ruler or tape measure

▶ a can opener

▶ a Sharpie fine-point marker

Supplies

▶ a 12-ounce soda or beer can

Building It

Step 1   Thoroughly wash the can, then use a can opener to remove the top, leaving the rolled aluminum ring intact (Figure 19-3). Depending on your can opener, the top may come off more easily if you turn the can opener's crank backward.

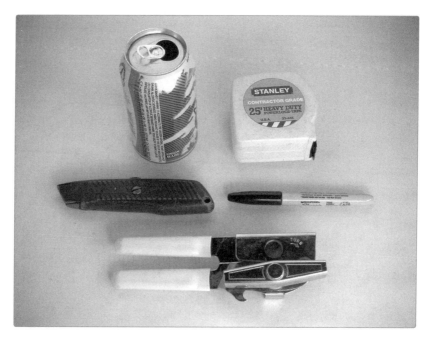

FIGURE 19-2: *Tools and supplies*

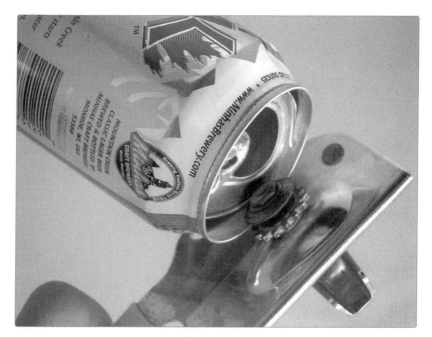

FIGURE 19-3: *Removing the top*

Step 2 Measure 2 1/2" down from the can's shoulder (Figure 19-4), marking this length at several points around the can's circumference.

FIGURE 19-4: *Marking the flyer; the "top" of the can is to the left*

Step 3 Use a utility knife to carefully cut away the bottom of the can, with the goal of keeping the flyer's body length uniform without slicing open your finger.

Step 4 Take your Pop Can Flyer for a test drive. Throw it like a football, with the can's top in front and plenty of spin.

Step 5 If you have lots of cans handy, experiment with different body lengths (2 1/2" from shoulder to cut gives good results; you can try going as short as 1 1/2" or as long as the full can). Shorter cans have greater in-flight stability but less stable overall paths (they tend to juke or weave unpredictably). Cans with different diameters (such as a big Foster's can or the pint-and-a-half tallboys from Labatt) will have different optimal lengths.

> **＊ WARNING:** *The trailing edge of the Pop Can Flyer might be sharp; this isn't baby's first football, and don't throw it at the cat.*

Step 6 Also try different trailing edges—dips and lobes, a jagged zig-zag, or even asymmetrical cuts—or adding one or more cutouts to the sides (Figure 19-5). To add a cutout, slip the flexible can over the end of a broom handle or mailing tube to support it as you cut (as shown in Figure 19-6). Work slowly—you don't want to crease the can or open a vein. Cutouts tend to decrease the flight distance, but keep it on a straighter path.

FIGURE 19-5: *Several alternative designs, homemade and store-bought; the flyer in the back right corner—a 1975 Milton Bradley Skyro—weighs just a few grams and will fly several hundred feet*

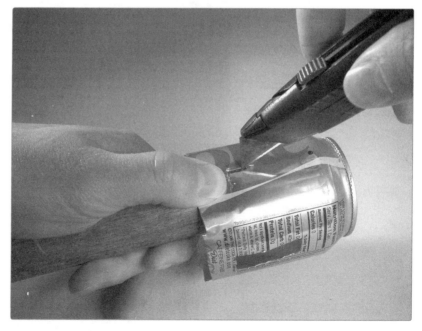

FIGURE 19-6: *Using a broom handle for support while adding a cutout*

How It Works

Why the Pop Can Flyer works is debated by engineers, physicists, and pilots (all of whom take very different views of flight to begin with), both within their respective fields and among each other. From an engineering perspective, flight is all about *boundary layer separation*. The boundary layer is the thin layer of air surrounding the body of an aircraft; because air is a viscous fluid, the boundary layer tends to want to "stick" to the aircraft. In order for a body to fly, you need the boundary layer to be part of a *laminar flow* of air around the vehicle. A laminar flow occurs when a fluid is moving in many parallel layers in the same direction, with no disturbance between the layers. The opposite of this is a *turbulent flow*, where various layers of air mix in many eddies and rough, chaotic lumps. As the air flows down a body, the boundary layer (which wants to stick with the curved side of the craft) will always eventually pull away from the main laminar flow of air, creating turbulence—a process called boundary layer separation. In the worst case, a pocket of stagnant air gets trapped against the body, acting like a lump of chewing gum stuck on the side of the craft.

Whenever it happens, the boundary layer separation acts as drag on the vehicle and destabilizes the flight. The leading lip of the Pop Can Flyer (being thicker than the rest of the can but with a circumference somewhat narrower than the body of the can) creates turbulence. This mixes the boundary layer with the surrounding air as it is about to pass over the can's length, so that the two layers more quickly form an efficient laminar flow. This more efficient flow delays boundary layer separation, so that turbulence occurs behind the can, rather than along its body. Try making a Pop Can Flyer with the full length of the can, and you'll see that it tumbles mid-flight, as though there is a gob of chewing gum stuck to it: mid-body turbulence is basically knocking it out of the air.

Bonus Project: NASA's Finest Paper Airplane

The queerest looking paper airplane (which we used to call a *UFO tube* as kids, and is now often called a *vortex ring*) benefits from the same physical properties as the Pop Can Flyer.

Tools

▶   (optional) a pen or marker

▶   (optional) packing or Scotch tape

Supplies

▶   a sheet of 8 1/2"×11" paper

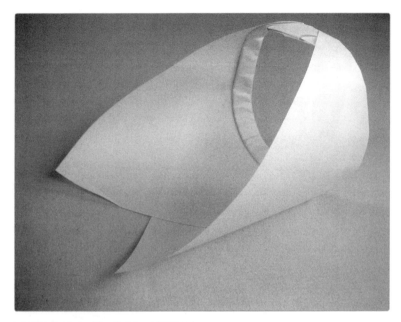

FIGURE 19-7: *The finished UFO tube*

Building It

To make a UFO Tube, follow these steps.

Step 1   Take an 8 1/2"×11" sheet of paper and fold it once diagonally (Figure 19-8).

FIGURE 19-8: *The first fold*

Step 2   Make a 1/2" fold along the length of this diagonal crease (Figure 19-9). Repeat this three times, for a total of four 1/2" folds. This will form the plane's leading edge. You may want to run the side of a pen or marker along the crease, making a nice sharp leading edge for your flyer.

FIGURE 19-9: *Adding the creases*

Step 3   Pinch the leading edge and run your fingers along it several times to curve the paper (Figure 19-10).

FIGURE 19-10: *Curving the leading edge*

Step 4   Tuck the ends of the creased leading edge into each other (Figure 19-11). If necessary, you can add a single staple or small strip of tape to hold them tight (you don't want to add much weight at this joint, as that leads to the flyer twisting and nose-diving soon after launch). It's best to tuck, if you can, so that you can adjust the diameter of the flyer in order to address launch problems.

FIGURE 19-11: *Tucking in the ends of the leading edge*

Step 5   To launch NASA's Finest Paper Airplane, either throw it like the Pop Can Flyer (remember to give it plenty of spin) or hold it between its two tail points (as shown in Figure 19-12) and toss it with a straight push from the elbow.

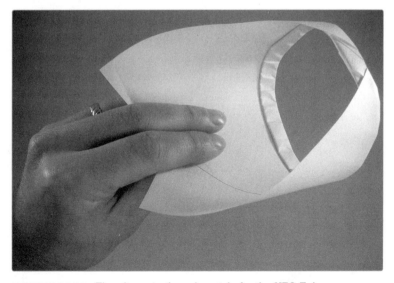

FIGURE 19-12: *The alternate throwing style for the UFO Tube*

QUICK-N-EASY WATER ROCKET

Although store-bought water rockets are an almost universal part of childhood (at least in suburban middle America, where I grew up), DIY water rockets are almost unheard of in the United States, despite being common in the United Kingdom. The key to the DIY water rocket is the ubiquitous plastic soda bottle. Often called *PET bottles* in the UK, these are basically made of polyester, just like your favorite pantsuit. Soda bottles can easily withstand 150 pounds of pressure per square inch—significantly more than a car or bike tire and more than enough to launch it into flight.

The following design dispenses with many of the issues surrounding valves, firing mechanisms, pressurization, and so on, because the unit is impossible to over-pressurize, thus eliminating the risk of a rocket explosion. It's quick and easy (no more than 5 minutes to construct) and, depending on the quality of your bike pump, can arc a bottle 30 feet at speeds safe enough to shoot at your pals or send a rocket soaring a hundred feet skyward.

FIGURE 20-1: *A finished Quick-n-Easy Water Rocket and launch tube*

Tools

▶   an electric drill with 1/4" and 3/8" bits

▶   a utility knife

▶   a ruler

▶   a pen

▶   a bike pump

Supplies

▶   a wine cork (A used cork is fine; if you're buying new, a #9 straight wine cork provides a good tight fit.)

▶   an old tire stem from a bike or car tire (See "Acquiring a Tire Stem" on page 245 for tips on easily getting a stem valve.)

- one or more 20-ounce water or soda bottles
- a section of tube wide enough to accommodate your bottles, such as a 3" cardboard mailing tube, or an oatmeal, potato chip, or snack can
- a thin dowel or garden stake
- duct tape

FIGURE 20-2: *Tools and supplies*

Building It

Step 1 If you're using a bike tire stem (shown at the right in Figure 20-3), cut away all of the surrounding rubber.

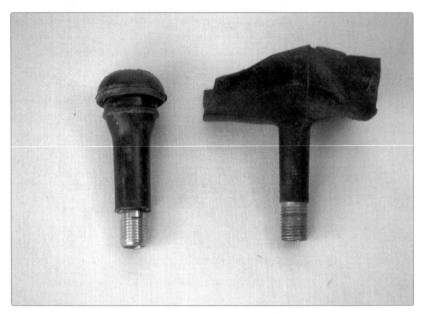

FIGURE 20-3: *A car tire stem (left) and bike tire stem (right); most of the inner tube has been cut away from the bike stem—you'll need to cut it all away to build your launch plug*

Step 2 To build your launch plug, cut the cork in half, and then drill a hole through the middle to accommodate the tire stem. Cork is a little trickier to work than other woods, since it tends to tear apart. Running the drill fast, start by drilling a 1/4" hole. If you're using a bike tire stem (which is a bit narrow), this should be fine (although you'll likely need to generously ream the hole or even bump up to the 19/64" bit[1]). For a car tire stem, switch to the 3/8" bit to expand the hole. In either case, the cork will offer a very snug fit (important for pressurizing the bottle). Test to see which end of your cork fits best into the bottle you have, and measure 1/8" from that end of the cork. Mark this "safe point" (which I'll explain later).

Step 3 Insert the threaded end of the tire stem into the safe point end of the cork, and push it through. Twisting as you go will help you work it into the cork. All of the brass threads should be pushed entirely through the cork, as shown in Figure 20-4. (You can use a utility knife to trim down the cork if it ends up being a little too long.)

---

1. As mathemagicians already realize, the 19/64" bit is about halfway between the 1/4" bit (which you can also think of as a 16/64" bit) and the 3/8" (aka 24/64") bit—so we are talking about a healthy reaming with the 1/4" bit.

FIGURE 20-4: *The completed launch plug (note the line marking the safe point)*

Step 4 Set your launch plug aside and build the launch tube. Cut a 7" length from the mailing tube and duct tape the garden stake to its side. (For a more permanent launch tube, consider using a piece of 3" diameter PVC and securing the stake with a pair of #44 hose clamps.)

Step 5 You're ready to launch! Head outside with your bottles, launch tube, launch plug, bike pump, and a jug of water. Stick the launch tube stake in the ground so that the tube is at a roughly 45-degree angle, with enough open room at the bottom for you to attach the bike pump.

Step 6 Fill the bottle 1/3 full with water, and then stick the launch plug in the mouth of the bottle, so that the threaded end of the valve stem sticks out. Insert the plug only as far as the safe point you marked in Step 2.

Step 7 Slide the rocket into the launch tube, connect the pump to the valve stem (Figure 20-5), and start pumping vigorously. After a dozen or so pumps (depending on the quality of your pump), the cork will *pop* and the rocket will go spraying across the yard, clearing at least 20 feet.

Water rockets launched with the plug inserted to the safe point and powered by normal hand-pumped bike pumps are pretty safe and suitable for a mortar-style *water rocket duel*: combatants work in teams—a gunner and a loader—situated at least 15 to 20 feet apart. Armed with a stockpile of empty bottles and water, the two teams blast away at each other until they grow bored or hungry. It's more fun than a squirt gun fight and less dangerous than a bottle rocket fight.

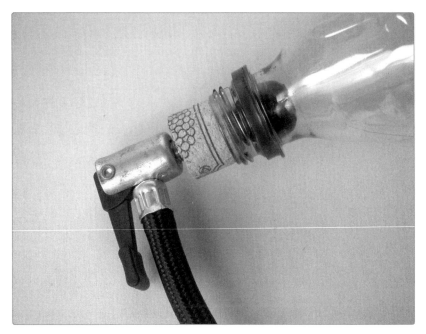

FIGURE 20-5: *Ready to launch!*

Building the Better Rocket

Because the force driving the rocket depends on the pressure of the water spewing out the back, you can improve flight time and distance in two ways: Increase the pressure in the bottle or make the water transfer momentum more efficiently.

Start by experimenting with driving the cork farther into the bottle and using different launch angles. A deeper cork requires more pressure to pop, so you can expect longer flights. The limiting factor here is your pump; any old pump will be able to launch a rocket whose plug is inserted only to the safe point, but as you drive the cork deeper, you'll need more pressure.

If you're using a very cheap bike pump, the back pressure can overwhelm the seals on the pump before the rocket launches. If the water is spraying out of the pump and onto your cuffs, it's safe to assume you won't see a lift-off with that setup. If you experience such a launch failure, grab hold of the pump's valve and the launch plug. Then, without leaning over the launch tube (you don't want to catch even a low-power water rocket in the face), reach down and grab the end of the bottle, jerking it off the cork. Water will spray everywhere.

Predictably, if a better hand pump gives better launches, then an electric compressor (shown in Figure 20-6) will be pretty awesome—higher, longer flights; shorter pressurization times; less effort; and more noise. That said, *do not shoot a rocket at your pal if you're using an air compressor!* Someone could lose an eye or a tooth.

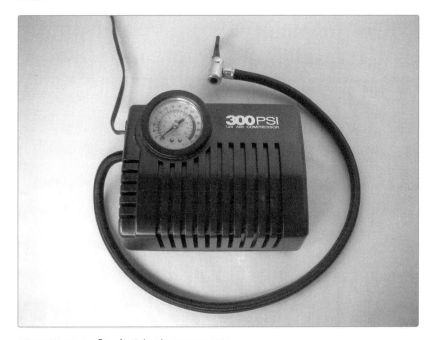

FIGURE 20-6: *An electric air compressor*

You can also experiment with making the water a more efficient *working mass* for accelerating your rocket. In terms of volume, this is a case of "less is more"; although having too little water means a disappointing thrust, too much water makes the rocket too heavy to overcome the weight of its own fuel. Denser propellant, on the other hand, will give you greater thrust (because it will transfer more momentum) without increasing *the burn time* (the amount of time it takes to vacate the heavy fuel, which is weighing down your rocket). You can make the water denser by adding dish soap or salt.

Of course, you can also improve the rockets themselves, as shown in Figure 20-7. The most obvious way is to move up to a larger size soda bottle. Regardless of bottle size, though, if you're interested in maximizing height, you can add a simple nose cone and stabilizing tail (the nose cone is cut from the top of an identical bottle and glued in place). Keep in mind that adding a tail may necessitate using a screw-on *valve stem extension* to connect the launch plug to the pump. Auto supply stores sell these extensions for less than $10; they can be handy if you need to check the pressure on a wheel with a fancy rim or if you want to top off your spare without unbolting it from its storage cubby.

FIGURE 20-7: *A pair of improved rockets with nose cones and tails (top), and a detail shot showing the cut-aways on the tail of the smaller rocket (bottom). Notice that the tail on the upper rocket is made from a Pop Can Flyer (Project 19) and attached with thin bamboo skewers and glue.*

* WARNING: *The Pop Can Flyer can be sharp, as can bamboo skewers; improved rockets aren't for lobbing at your pals on a hot summer afternoon.*

21 PUTT-PUTT BOAT

The annals of human locomotion are crowded with designs that work gracefully as models but prove to scale poorly; the Putt-Putt Boat is just such a vehicle. Sometimes called pop-pop boats, hot-air boats, or (most appropriately) flash steamers, the Putt-Putt Boat maneuvers around a bathtub or swimming pool under its own power with no moving parts, driven by a simple, valveless *flash boiler* made from a coil of copper tubing and a rudimentary alcohol burner.

Flash boilers are one of those technologies that seem ideal but never really work out. They are light, small, easily constructed, and don't need to be warmed up to produce a head of steam—all factors making them popular in early aircraft designs and nineteenth-century steam cars. Unfortunately, they also instantly overheat if they lose water pressure—not a big deal for a bathtub steamboat but a bit of a critical failure when you're flying above the Himalayas or steaming across the Mojave Desert.

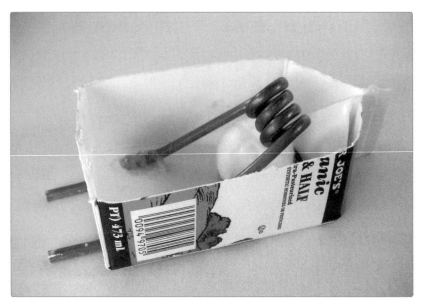

FIGURE 21-1: *The finished Putt-Putt Boat*

Tools

- ▸ a utility knife
- ▸ a small hacksaw
- ▸ an electric drill with a 1/2" bit
- ▸ a Sharpie fine-point marker
- ▸ a ruler or tape measure
- ▸ a sturdy curved surface, such as a broom handle, table leg, or beer bottle
- ▸ (optional) an awl (You can get by with a nail and a pencil.)
- ▸ (optional) a tapered half-round file or similar rat-tail file
- ▸ (optional) a large rubber band or masking tape

Supplies

- ▸ roughly 1 1/2' of 3/16" copper tube
- ▸ a 1-pint creamer carton (A quart or half-gallon milk carton works, too.)

- ▶ a small metal dish, such as a jar lid or empty lip balm container
- ▶ some cotton balls
- ▶ rubbing alcohol (This is usually 70 percent ethyl or isopropyl alcohol; any alcohol that is high enough proof to burn is fine.)
- ▶ a large piece of scrap wood and either several angle brackets or some smaller trim scraps and wood screws
- ▶ room temperature vulcanizing rubber or any similar silicone-based household glue
- ▶ (optional) a second metal dish to use as a *snuffer* for your alcohol burner

FIGURE 21-2: *Tools and supplies*

Building It

Step 1 Start by trimming your carton to size. Measure 1 1/2" from the back (the side opposite the pouring spout—see Figure 21-3) and make a dashed line down one side, around the bottom, and up the other side, roughly bisecting the carton along its length. Although it might seem like overkill, having the full line will make Step 2 much easier.

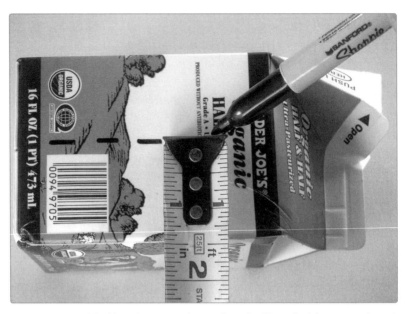

FIGURE 21-3: *Marking the carton for cutting; the "front" of the carton is at the top of the photo, the "back" is at the bottom, and the dashed line continues around the bottom of the carton (i.e., the left end) and along the other side*

Step 2 Use the utility knife to cut along the dotted line, then discard the front of the carton and set aside the remainder.

Step 3 Next, prepare to build the main body of the flash boiler, a 1/2" coil of copper tubing. Be forewarned that tubing—especially very narrow, thin-walled tubing like this—is prone to crimping when you bend it, especially if you do so freehand. Since water and steam need to flow unobstructed through the Putt-Putt Boat's engine, a crimped flash boiler won't do. There are several tricks to bending a pipe without crimping it. Many folks get good results by packing the tube with fine sand and taping up the ends; the sand functions as a mandrel, giving support to the inner walls of the tube, so that it bends without kinking. I prefer using a simple homemade jig, which immobilizes the *bitter end* (that is, the end you aren't working) as you pull the working end around, thus preventing crimping. As you see in Figure 21-4, this jig can be as simple as a piece of hearty scrap wood and a couple of old angle brackets.

To make a jig, start by driving the 1/2" bit into the wood and then removing it from the drill—this will serve as the bending guide for the 1/2" coil. Lay your piece of straight copper tube next to the guide, parallel with the edge of the board, and trace one edge (Figure 21-5).

Remove the tube, install one angle bracket along the line, then replace the tube so that a little more than 6" is below the bending guide (this is the tube's bitter end). Carefully snug the other angle bracket into place, locking the tube to the board. Be careful not to crush the tube! You don't need to worry about getting the brackets neatly lined up, as long as they run parallel to each other and immobilize the tube.

FIGURE 21-4: *Here are two versions of the simple pipe-bending jig. The one on the left is made from a pair of shelf brackets and uses a 1/2" drill bit as the bending guide; it makes a counterclockwise coil. The jig on the right is scrap wood, with a Sharpie marker slid through a 1/2" hole in the board as a bending guide, and makes a clockwise coil. Both work great.*

FIGURE 21-5: *Drawing a guide line on a jig*

Step 4   After checking to be sure that the bitter end of the tube is secured, slowly and firmly pull the working end around the guide. You want to add three full turns and then a half turn so that both the intake and exhaust are on the same side of the coil. It's easiest if you let the turns coil up the guide and then press them all together to tighten the coil after you've made the last half turn (as shown at the bottom of Figure 21-6). To test the coil for obstructing crimps, take a sip of water into your mouth, then blow it through the tube; if you get squirted in the face, then all is well. Set the coil aside.

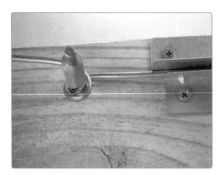

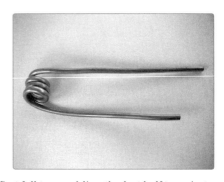

FIGURE 21-6: *From upper left: adding the first full turn; adding the last half turn; just prior to tightening the coil; the finished flash boiler coil*

Step 5   Take the halved carton (now the hull of the boat), and mark two points approximately 1/2" from the rear of the hull and 1/2" in from each side. If you have an awl, use it to pop two holes in the bottom of the boat roughly the same diameter as your exhaust and intake tailpipes (see Figure 21-7). Otherwise, use a sharp nail to start the holes and a sharpened pencil to enlarge them.

Step 6   Check the fit of the boiler in your boat. The coils constitute the bulk of the boat's weight, especially when the burner is in place under them. Usually, you'll want about 3" of tube (measured from the top of the coil) inside the boat, and you'll want the coil centered in the hull. It's okay if a lot of tube hangs out the back; we'll trim that in Step 8. When you find a good fit, use a Sharpie to mark the tube where it meets the floor of the hull.

FIGURE 21-7: *Adding the holes*

Step 7   Now you'll bend the tailpipes so that they can be secured to the bottom of the hull, keeping the coil above the burner and directly in the flame. Remove the coil from the hull of the boat, and lay the tailpipes over your sturdy curved surface. Slowly apply pressure so that they bend near your marks (see Figure 21-8; it's pretty easy to avoid crimping at this stage, although it doesn't hurt to blow another sip of water through the boiler after you've bent the tailpipes, just to be sure your tube remains unobstructed).

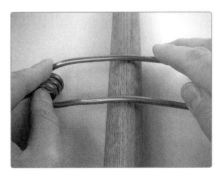 

FIGURE 21-8: *Bending the tailpipes (left) and a finished boiler coil (right); the tailpipes are bent around 20 degrees (although close is good enough)*

Step 8   Reinstall the coil so that the bends in the tailpipes are at the holes in the hull and the tailpipes stick out the back of the boat. Measuring from the back of the boat, mark 1" along each tailpipe (as shown in Figure 21-9). Remove the coil, and gently lock the tailpipe into the jig from Step 3 (or a modified version of it—you don't have to worry about crimping at this stage, just make sure to secure the tube while you saw; if you own a table vise, that's just as good). Carefully cut the tailpipe at the mark with a hacksaw. (Since the tube is so thin, you may be tempted to trim it with tin snips; *don't try it!* It's way too easy to crimp the tube closed with snips.) Repeat with the other tailpipe. Both cuts will be a little rough, so you will probably want to deburr each tailpipe using a rounded file (although skipping this step won't impede the boat's operation).

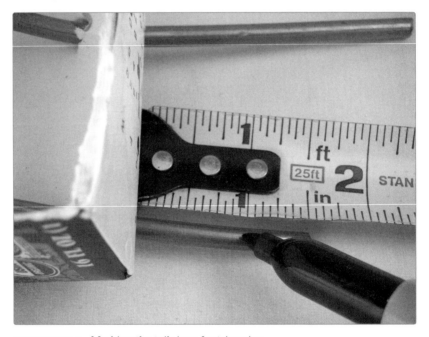

FIGURE 21-9: *Marking the tailpipes for trimming*

Step 9   Finally, install the boiler coil. Again, thread the tailpipes through the holes in the bottom of the hull, making sure the bends are even with the holes. Flip the boat over, and glue the tailpipes to the bottom of the boat, making a point to smear a good bit of glue into the holes in the hull, sealing them (Figure 21-10). Let the glue dry overnight—a strip of masking tape or large rubber band around the hull and tailpipes will hold everything in place as it sets.

Step 10   Once the glue is completely dry, you're ready for your first voyage. As the bathtub is filling, prime the flash boiler. In order for the engine to work, it needs to start out completely filled with water. This can be accomplished by pouring water into the tube from a small cup (flexible plastic shot glass, like the kind that comes with a bottle of cough syrup, works okay), possibly facilitated with a tiny funnel. But

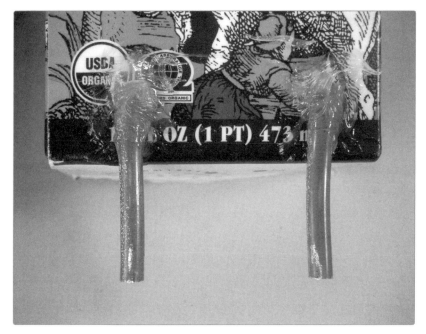

FIGURE 21-10: *Gluing the tailpipes*

the easiest way to prime the engine is to fill your mouth with water, hold the tube between your lips, and blow until water burbles out the other end. Once the engine is primed, set the boat in the tub without dumping the water out of the primed engine. Soak a cotton ball with rubbing alcohol, place the cotton ball in the metal dish, slide the dish under the coil, and light her up. In a few seconds, the boat will begin scooting around the tub.

✻ **WARNING:** *It can be a touch tricky to blow out an alcohol-soaked cotton ball, so you might want to keep another metal dish handy to snuff the burner. Note that the burner's metal base and the copper coil can easily get hot enough to brand you and that the water coming out of the boat's exhaust is boiling. This is not a bath-time tub toy for baby!*

How It Works

The narrow copper coil of the flash boiler holds a miniscule volume of water, so the heat of the alcohol burner almost instantaneously *flashes* it to steam. The expanding steam forces water out of one of the two tailpipes. Because the tube is completely full of water and sealed, fresh cold water is simultaneously drawn in through the other tailpipe. This new water then flashes to steam, expands, and bursts out through the exhaust, drawing more fresh cold water in its wake, and so on. The boat putters forward—gaining speed and momentum—until the burner goes out. Since the coil is symmetrical, either tailpipe can function as the intake or exhaust on a given voyage; that's for the vagaries of chance and thermodynamics to determine.

You might wonder how it is that the boat moves forward at all, since the intake is drawing in the same volume of fluid as the exhaust expels, at the same speed. At first glance, it seems like the forces should balance and the boat go nowhere (or, possibly, spin about its tail). The trick is that the exhaust, focused by the straight tailpipe, is coming out in a jet stream, while the intake is drawing in water from the broad, hemispherical region surrounding its opening. The forceful, directional exhaust stream overpowers the unfocused intake stream and thus propels the boat forward. Let this be a lesson to you.

22 JITTERBUG: YOUR FIRST ROBOT

Once upon a time, robots were either the fantastic, fully functional artificial humans of popular fiction (e.g., C3PO, the Terminator, Robby the Robot, Johnny 5) or the mundane workhorses of industry (e.g., discorporate robotic arms riveting Ford frames and powder-coating jet turbines). In either case, they were the expensive territory of PhDs and film producers. Fortunately, in the last two decades there's been a surge in small, cheap, robust little robots: *BEAM robotics.*[1]

BEAM enthusiasts focus on designing small robots without general microprocessors. Instead of analyzing their surroundings and incoming stimuli (like higher-order animals), BEAM robots behave like simple

---

1. This acronym is somewhat disputed, but according to Mark Tilden, who purportedly coined the term in 1990, it stands for *Biology, Electronics, Aesthetics, and Mechanics.*

multicellular organisms: Stimuli (like light, vibrations, or noise) directly trigger simple circuits that control actions, without the need for any sort of higher signal processing or self-reflection—like a reflex arc. BEAM designs often repurpose and recycle technological detritus and use novel power sources.

The Jitterbug is a very, very simple battery-powered photophobic robot. Much like a cockroach, it scurries around when a light is shined on it, coming to rest when it once again stumbles into darkness's loving embrace.

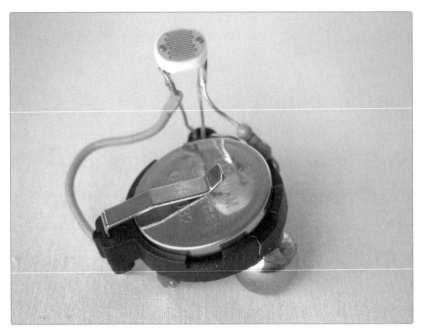

FIGURE 22-1: *A finished Jitterbug*

Tools

▶ a standard soldering kit (See the appendix.)

▶ room temperature vulcanizing rubber or any silicone-based household glue

Supplies

▶ a photoresistor, such as RadioShack part #276-1657

▶ a 2N3904 transistor

▶ a 4.7k ohm resistor (coded with yellow-purple-red stripes)

▶ one vibrator motor (This can be scrounged from a cell phone or pager or purchased new at RadioShack—part #273-107.)

- a 3-volt CR2032 button cell battery
- a CR2032 battery clip, such as RadioShack part #270-009
- 24-gauge insulated hook-up wire (unnecessary if your battery clip and motor have leads)
- two 5/8" ball bearings

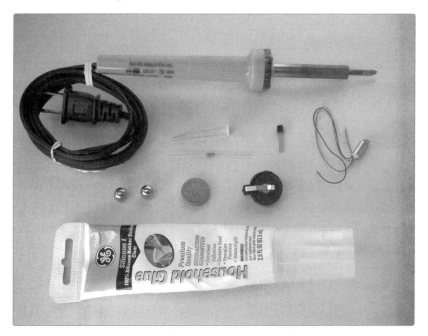

FIGURE 22-2: *Tools and supplies*

Save a Cell Phone, Save a Life

Do not break up a functional cell phone just for the $4 motor! US cell phone carriers are required to complete 911 calls from any functional cell phone, even if the phone has no service contract. You can donate functional cell phones to women's shelters or homeless-outreach programs, which will put them in the hands of folks that can really benefit from a wireless 911 hotline. When scrounging for vibrator motors, look for old pagers and smartphones. These almost always have a vibrate function, and it's often easy to scrounge up a dead one, since smartphone touchscreens and keypads are delicate, and pagers are useless to begin with.

Building It

Step 1   If you've elected to scrounge a motor from a broken cell phone or pager, start by making sure that your broken phone or pager has a vibrate function; if so, there will be a tiny, sprightly motor inside with a small weight mounted eccentrically on its shaft (see Figure 22-3 for examples). No vibrate means no motor. Having established that your phone or pager can vibrate, remove the lithium battery, and take out as many screws as you can find. Then use a screwdriver to pry open the plastic housing (there will usually be a single long seam running around the phone's edge).

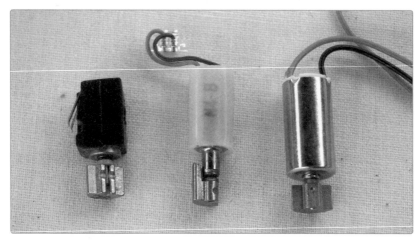

FIGURE 22-3: *Two scrounged vibrating motors (left) and a store-bought vibrator motor (right)*

Lithium Is Awesome and Dangerous!

Almost all cell phones use lithium batteries. Lithium is an *alkali metal*; you'll find it in the first column of the periodic table, right below hydrogen. When any of the alkali metals contact water, they boot the flammable hydrogen from the H_2O and latch onto the oxygen themselves (forming a salt). Snapping the hydrogen off of the oxygen is an *exothermic* reaction, which means that it releases heat—occasionally enough heat to ignite the hydrogen on its way out. (Since lithium is the least energetic alkali metal, it might not generate enough heat to light the hydrogen. The next two metals down the column—sodium and potassium—almost invariably spark off the hydrogen as they skitter and squeal across the water's surface). A fleck of lithium on sweaty skin or in the eye will burn you very badly very quickly. On a humid day, moisture from the air can be sufficient to start exposed lithium burning spontaneously. Lesson: You do not want to inadvertently crack open a lithium battery.

Now that the motor is revealed, as in Figure 22-4, you may find that it is epoxied or otherwise permanently affixed to the circuit board. Fortunately, these are usually mounted near the board's edge. Use needle-nose pliers to snap that edge off the board and be done with it. If you're having trouble finding the motor, check the inside of the case (where they are sometimes located in smartphones).

FIGURE 22-4: *An opened cell phone (the vibrator motor is circled), and a close-up of a cell phone motor in situ*

Step 2   This project is small enough to be entirely mounted on the plastic base of the battery clip itself. Flip the battery clip over; if it has two little plastic spikes on it (intended to help secure the clip to a circuit board; this size battery is often used to provide backup power to the CMOS clocks in older desktop computers), then snip these off with the diagonal cutters from your soldering kit. If your battery clip came with leads attached, snip off the black (i.e., negative or ground) lead. (Make sure to leave enough of the negative terminal's metal leg intact so that you can solder connections to the ground later.) Conversely, if your battery clip has no leads, then you'll want to add one to the positive terminal. Measure a 2" length of wire, strip and tin both ends, and solder one end to the positive battery terminal (this is the one that connects to the metal tongue that curls over the top of the battery holder).

Step 3   If you bought a motor at the store and it came wired with long leads, you can shorten these to about 1" (you'll make them even shorter later). Don't worry if your motor has no leads; you can solder directly to the terminals in Steps 7 and 8.

Step 4   Once the battery clip is prepared, smear the bottom with room temperature vulcanizing rubber or any silicone-based household glue, and place the motor across the base's diameter so that one of the motor's terminals is about 1/4" from the negative battery terminal (we'll call this the motor's negative terminal henceforward, even though the terminals are basically interchangeable). Be careful not to let the glue foul up the motor's spinning weight or shaft.

Place one ball bearing on each side of the motor, making sure that neither of the bearings obstructs the motor's spinning weight or makes contact with a battery terminal or motor terminal. Note that, as in Figure 22-5, ideally the ball bearings are not straight across from each other but grouped a bit toward the tail end of the motor so they form a triangle with the battery clip's positive terminal; the Jitterbug will ultimately scoot around using the two bearings and the positive terminal as skids. Set the base aside and let the glue dry overnight.

FIGURE 22-5: *The prepared base (the thicker wire jutting out to the right is connected to the positive battery terminal)*

Step 5   Meanwhile, build the Jitterbug's brain. As you can see from the circuit diagram in Figure 22-6, this is a very simple circuit, and we're going to endeavor to keep it as light and compact as possible. This means orienting the components in a slightly unorthodox manner. First, trim down the legs on the photoresistor to about 1/4". Now hold the transistor with its legs up and flat face away from you, and solder one leg from the photoresistor and one leg from the 4.7k resistor to the transistor's middle leg (which is its base—check out Figure 22-7 and remember that the transistor's flat face is resting on the table). Remember that transistors can be a little temperature sensitive; if you aren't sure that you can work quickly, consider using a heat sink (described in the appendix and illustrated in Figure 16-4 on page 191).

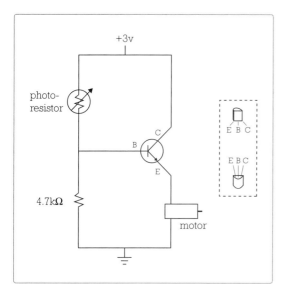

FIGURE 22-6: *The circuit diagram for the Jitter-bug (left) and diagrams of the 2N3904 transistor both in its "normal" orientation (right top) and as we use it here (right bottom)*

FIGURE 22-7: *Here is the transistor with both resistors soldered to its base (the center leg). The connections to the collector—the transistor leg on the far right—are not soldered yet.*

Step 6   Solder the other leg of the photoresistor and the positive (red) battery lead to the transistor's right leg (which is its collector), as shown in Figure 22-8. This step can be completed even if the glue is still tacky, but everything after this will have to wait until the glue is dry.

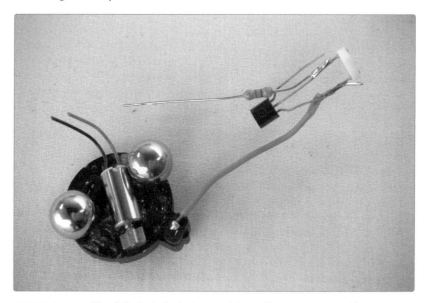

FIGURE 22-8: *The fully installed photoresistor, with power connection*

Step 7   Once the glue is completely dry, carefully bend down the transistor's remaining leg (the emitter) so it can be soldered to the motor's positive terminal (the one farthest from the negative battery terminal; see Step 4). Solder the emitter to the motor's positive terminal. Ideally, the body of the transistor will be more or less even with the edge of the battery clip's plastic base, as seen in Figure 22-9.

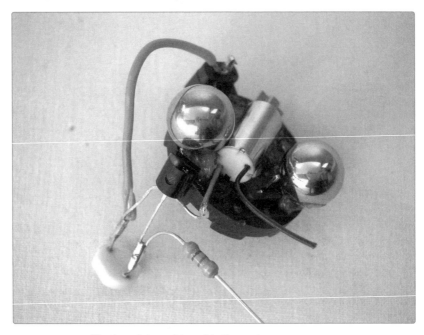

FIGURE 22-9: *The transistor soldered to the motor*

Step 8   Bend the negative battery terminal over, then bend the remaining leg of the 4.7k resistor down and around so that it connects to the negative motor terminal and slips beneath the negative terminal on the bent battery clip (see Figure 22-10). Solder this leg to both, slide in the battery, and your Jitterbug is ready to run.

Step 9   The wires from the resistor and transistor to the motor should be stiff enough to support themselves and the Jitterbug's photoresistor "eye." If you're worried about long-term stability, then use a toothpick to smear a healthy glob of glue on the transistor's face, and affix it to the edge of the battery clip's base (see Figure 22-11).

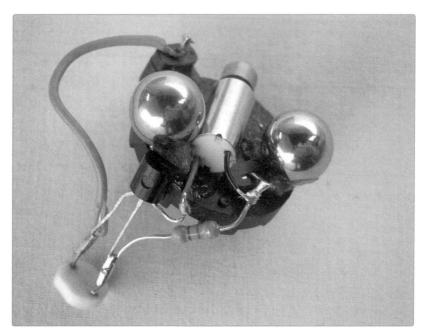

FIGURE 22-10: *The resistor connecting the motor to ground and completing the Jitterbug's brain circuit*

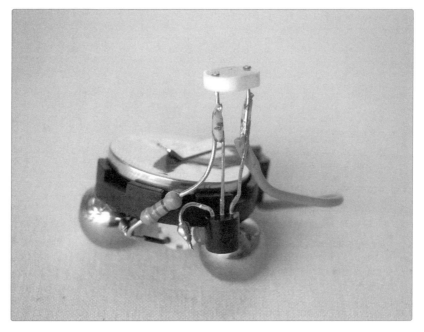

FIGURE 22-11: *The back of the finished Jitterbug, showing the configuration of the brain's resistor, transistor, and photoresistor*

How It Works

A transistor can either be used to amplify a signal (we used this very same transistor—the utilitarian 2N3904—as an amplifier in the Two-Transistor Fuzztone, Project 16) or to switch a signal. Here, we use it as a switch—although it might make more sense to think of it as a valve (like a bathroom faucet), rather than a bedroom light switch. If the transistor is a valve, then its base is the handle on that valve, and the battery's current is the hand waiting to turn that handle. In darkness, the photoresistor puts up a lot of resistance, and little to no current can reach the base. When the photoresistor is illuminated, its resistance decreases, and when the resistance drops beneath a certain threshold, enough voltage passes to the transistor's base to crack that valve open. The transistor permits some current to trickle from the collector into the emitter, which feeds the motor. The Jitterbug then quakes and palpitates. As more light shines on the photoresistor, more current reaches the base, which cranks the transistor open further, letting more current pour into the motor, which rattles even more furiously. This is all proportional, so if you like, you can double the fun by cramming two 3-volt CR2032 batteries into the battery clip (just be sure to stack them so their positive sides are up). The Jitterbug will shimmy and buzz until it stumbles into soothing darkness again, or until you cut the light.

Modifying the Jitterbug

If you want a photophilic Jitterbug (that is, one that gets the shakes in the dark instead of jittering out of the light), then just swap the positions of the 4.7k resistor and photoresistor in the schematic in Figure 22-6. If you want to play with the Jitterbug's photo-responsiveness in either configuration, try using different resistors in place of the 4.7k resistor. For a truly advanced Jitterbug, double up on the motors, resistors, and transistors, and build two brains (one to control each motor independently). Since the transistor gradually lets more power go to the motor as the photoresistor senses more light, it's possible, if you rig up the body carefully, to make the bug exhibit meaningful positive (or negative) phototaxis. Or, consider a major shift in the Jitterbug's basic body: Use a normal 3-volt motor instead of a vibrator motor, glue a toy car's rim and tire to the shaft, and build a zippy little Monowheeliebug.

Reverse Sumo Racing

If you build a pair of Jitterbugs, you can bet on them: Draw a circle on the table, shine a bright light on the circle, and wager on who escapes first or who stays in longest. If you prefer games of skill to those of chance, dig up a couple of cheap laser pointers, dim the lights, and see who can get their bug to escape the circle first by training the tiny prick of light on the maddeningly small photoresistor surface.

Resources

▶ This Jitterbug's brain is based on a circuit found in Forrest M. Mims III's *Getting Started in Electronics*. Sold in most RadioShack stores for decades, this book inspired most electro-tinkerers of my generation—more on Mims and his books in the appendix.

▶ If this project is for you, then go and get a copy of *JunkBots, Bugbots, and Bots on Wheels: Building Simple Robots with BEAM Technology* by David Hrynkiw and Mark Tilden. Tilden is the father of BEAM robotics, and the book is filled with awesome projects.

▶ Back before BEAM—with its ethos of *small, cheap, and easy*—the amateur roboticists' Bible was *Robot Builder's Bonanza* by Gordon McComb and Myke Predko. Recent editions of this book have added lots of new advances (such as LEGO MINDSTORMS) and kept the classics (extensive discussions of BASIC Stamp and other microcontrollers and detailed instructions for big, heavy, rugged robots built of steel and lumber).

▶ If the programmable robotics kits made by LEGO are your thing, then check out Laurens Valk's *LEGO MINDSTORMS NXT 2.0 Discovery Book*.

▶ *Solarbotics* is the go-to spot for BEAM robotics kits, supplies, and info; see *http://www.solarbotics.com/*.

23 FEDEX KITES

Cultures around the world have enjoyed kites as toys and curiosities for almost 3,000 years, but it was the Victorians who sought to exploit their full potential (and are responsible for the two styles of kite we'll be building; Figure 23-1). Eager men in bowler hats and sleeve garters hoped to harness the power of kites to pull sleighs, channel electricity, mount telegraph lines and wireless aerials, and haul scientific equipment, wary assistants, and low-ranking military scouts skyward. It was an age of wonders—and spectacular failures.

The key to kite design is finding materials that are light enough to support a manageable-sized kite but sturdy enough to weather the occasional hard landings and less-than-ideal conditions: Heavy winds, damp grass, and blown sea mist can quickly spoil paper kite sails. The two kites in this project (Figure 23-2) combine traditional, rugged bamboo frames (used in China for millennia) with cheap, nearly indestructible Tyvek sails (which are impervious to water and resist running rips).

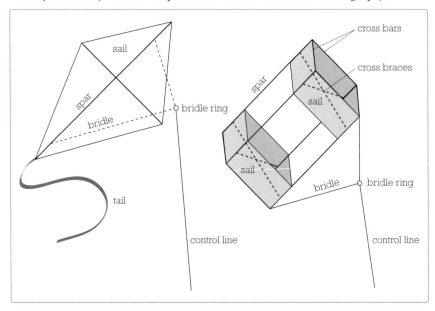

FIGURE 23-1: *The anatomy of a diamond kite (left) and a box kite (right)*

FIGURE 23-2: *The Box Kite (left) and Diamond Kite (right)*

Tools

- a wood saw
- a yardstick or tape measure
- a utility knife
- scissors
- (optional) duct tape (ugly but great for field repairs)

Supplies for the Diamond Kite

- two 4' bamboo garden stakes (Choose stakes that are sturdy, straight, unsplintered, and uniform in thickness.)
- five 10"×13" Tyvek mailing envelopes (which are actually 10 1/4" by 12 3/4", excluding the flap)
- a spool of kite string
- clear packing tape
- 9' of plastic caution tape
- (optional) cotton string slightly heavier than kite string
- (optional) a 1/2" diameter split ring, such as the ring used on a keychain
- (optional) a fishing swivel

Supplies for the Box Kite

- nine 4' bamboo garden stakes (sturdy, unsplintered, straight stakes of uniform thickness)
- six 10"×13" Tyvek mailing envelopes
- a spool of kite string
- clear packing tape
- cotton string slightly heavier than kite string
- (optional) 5' of plastic caution tape
- (optional) a 1/2" diameter split ring
- (optional) a fishing swivel

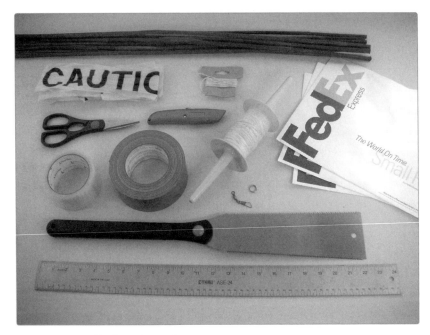

FIGURE 23-3: *Tools and supplies*

Building the Diamond Kite

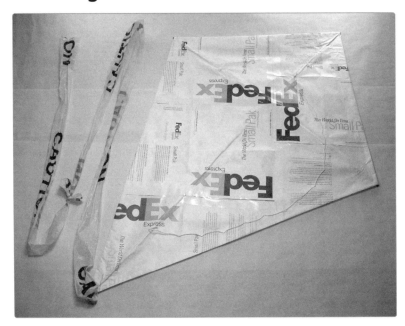

FIGURE 23-4: *The finished Diamond Kite*

Step 1   Begin by preparing the kite's sail. Trim off the self-adhesive flap from the first envelope. Cut the folded seam along one 13" edge and the 10" edge. Lay the envelope
flat to create a roughly 20" by 13" rectangle (Figure 23-5).

FIGURE 23-5: *A prepared envelope*

Step 2   Repeat Step 1 for the other four envelopes.

Step 3   Lay out the envelopes as shown in Figure 23-6. If you want your kite to advertise
the fine services of FedEx, UPS, or United Postal Service Priority Mail, then position the envelopes with the corporate logos facing up. If you prefer a white kite, turn
the plain sides up. You can decorate your kite using permanent markers. Because
Tyvek takes ink really well but packing tape does not, this is the time to decorate
the kite if you are going to draw a design.[1]

Step 4   Use strips of packing tape to join the rectangles into one large sheet, and then set
aside the large sheet.

Step 5   Trim one of the two bamboo stakes to 33" (leave the other at its full 4' length).

---

1. If you stick with plain white now and want to decorate later, you can get pretty cool results by decoupag-
ing colorful tissue to the kite using white glue thinned with water.

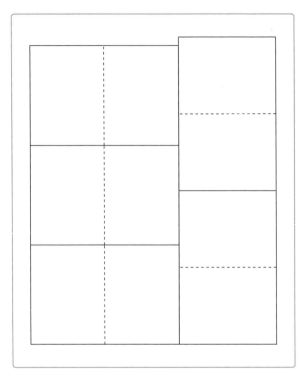

FIGURE 23-6: *Lay out the five envelopes, face up, into one big sheet. Notice that the upper-right corner sticks up a bit; leave it this way (we'll trim later, but need the extra room in the next few steps).*

Step 6 Cross the two stakes, or *spars*, as shown in Figure 23-7, so that the short cross bar is centered and 15" from the tip of the long spar, and then tie a snippet of string around this intersection. (This is optional, but it makes it easier to maneuver the spars; the string keeps them more-or-less aligned for the next step.)

Step 7 Lay out the large Tyvek sheet so that the packing tape is facing away from you and the extra bit of Tyvek is in the upper-right corner and jutting off to the right. Place the spars on top of the sheet, as shown in Figure 23-8.

Step 8 Use long strips of packing tape to attach the frame directly to the sail; be sure to leave 2" at the end of each spar untaped.

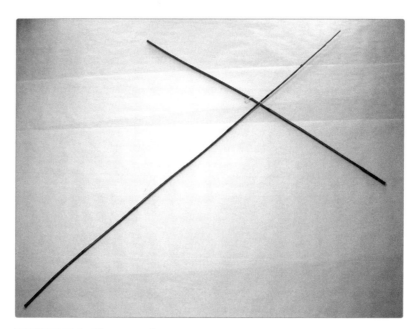

FIGURE 23-7: *The crossed spars*

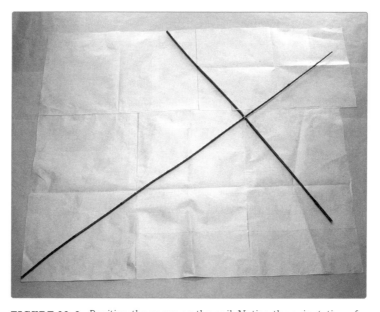

FIGURE 23-8: *Position the spars on the sail. Notice the orientation of the sail and spar; it's a tight fit. The bottom of the long spar and left end of the short spar should touch the edges of the Tyvek.*

Step 9	To reinforce the edge, tie the string to the end of any spar, and then run the string to the next adjacent spar, looping it several times around the spar and overlapping the string on itself (as shown in Figure 23-9). Run the string from spar to spar until you are back at the start. These lines should be taut without deforming the kite (which should be a symmetrical diamond); you can adjust them for maximum tension and symmetry. The combination of the almost untearable Tyvek sail, the flexible bamboo frame, and the fluid reinforcement of the string, will cause the wind to bend the kite into something similar to an Eddy bow kite[2]—a remarkably stable and easy-to-launch design. Eddy bows are the gold standard in simple recreational kites. This kite has the advantages of the Eddy bow without your having to invest a lot of time in tailoring a neatly curved sail.

FIGURE 23-9: *Detail of the string wrapping at the end of a spar (back side at left; sail side at right)*

Step 10	Use long strips of tape to secure the string around the edges of the sail. A taut sail will spill air evenly off its edges and will be more stable in flight, so be sure to keep the sail as taut as possible. (Realize that you are taping envelopes to string; it's not going to be taut as a drum head.) Leave a 1/2" section of the bottom of the long spar clear of tape.

Step 11	After the string is taped down, cut away the excess sail, leaving a 1/2" margin around the entire diamond, as shown in Figure 23-10. (This margin might be a little rough, but don't sweat it.)

Step 12	Snip off the margin at each vertex of the diamond sail (Figure 23-11) to create four flaps along the edges (similar to the envelope flaps you removed in Step 1) that you can fold over the string along the kite's edges.

---

2. Invented in the 1890s by William Abner Eddy, the *Diamond Eddy Kite* is stable in flight even though it has no tail. A journalist and accountant with the *New York Herald*, Eddy was also a passionate amateur meteorologist (as was the fashion at the time), with his heart set on launching heavy photographic and meteorological equipment into the atmosphere. He found that by bowing the face of the diamond kite, the kite could forgo a tail. With no tail to tangle in the control lines, he could run several kites in a "train," increasing overall lift and elevating his gear thousands of feet into the air.

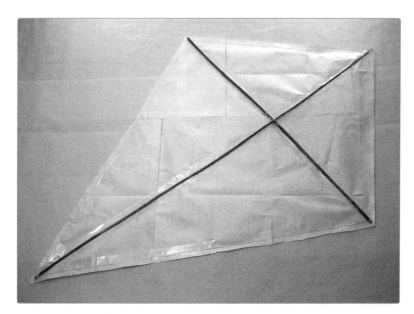

FIGURE 23-10: *The trimmed sail*

FIGURE 23-11: *Detail of a snipped-off diamond vertex*

Step 13   Fold each flap over the string, creasing it as close as possible to the string rein-forcement. (You can run the side of a marker down these creases to make them nice and sharp.) Tape the flaps down.

Step 14   Now you'll add the bridle. Flip the kite over so that the exposed spars are under-neath, measure 10" from the top and the bottom of the long spar, and mark these points on the face of the kite.

Step 15   Use the tip of the utility knife, scissors, or a nail to poke holes through the sail on either side of the long spar.

Step 16   Cut a 44" length of string for the bridle. (I don't advise using kite string; heavier string will hold up better, especially if you're omitting the 1/2" split ring.) Feed one end through the top set of holes, tie it to the spar, and then feed the other end to the bottom set of holes and tie it to the spar.

Step 17   (Optional) You can add the bridle ring now (see "Adding the Bridle Ring" on page 289) or wait until your first kite-flying excursion.

Step 18   Now for the tail, which adds stability by dragging down the bottom of the kite and shifting the center of the kite's weight toward the bottom of the diamond. (Think of a canoe, which is most stable when the weight is close to the bottom; stand up, and the boat gets very shaky.) A 9' caution tape tail might be overkill, but it looks pretty, even in a crash (especially if you get caught in a bad crosswind and start looping). You can trim it down—or add to it—at your discretion. To connect the tail, make a 1 1/2" cut into one end of the strip of caution tape. Then tie it around the open section at the bottom of the long spar, as shown in Figure 23-12. (If you don't have caution tape, you can tie together a few narrow newspaper bags or even use strips cut from a garbage bag. Since this plastic is so lightweight, you'll need to use a full 9' or more to stabilize your kite, depending on conditions. You can maximize the length of such a bag tail—and thus the drag it exerts—by splitting the bags along both long edges before tying them together.)

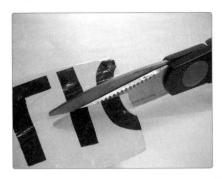 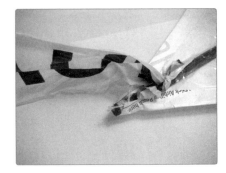

FIGURE 23-12: *Snip the caution-tape tail and tie it on.*

You're ready to fly! Skip to "Flying Tips" on page 288 for details.

Building the Box Kite

FIGURE 23-13: *The finished Box Kite*

Step 1   Once again, begin by constructing the sails. Split three 10"×13" envelopes down both 13" sides, resulting in three strips, each 10" wide by 26" long, plus the self-adhesive flaps (leave the flaps intact; see Figure 23-14).

FIGURE 23-14: *The 10"×13" envelope, cut and unfolded to a 10" by 26" piece of Tyvek*

Step 2   Use the self-adhesive flaps to connect the three envelopes in a single 78" long strip, as shown in Figure 23-15. Do the same with three more envelopes, and then set the two sails aside.

FIGURE 23-15: *A sail made of three Tyvek envelopes*

Step 3   Now to build the frame, which is more complex than the Diamond Kite's simple crossed spars. Select the four straightest pieces of bamboo. Cut each to 36" long. These will be used for the long spars along the kite's sides.

Step 4   Next cut four 21" pieces of bamboo to be used as cross braces.

Step 5   Finally, cut eight 15" lengths of bamboo; these will be used to frame the top and bottom sails of the kite. Set them aside for now.

Step 6   To build the frame, lay two of the 36" long bamboo pieces parallel to each other on your work table, and set two of the 21" cross braces 5" from either end—see Figure 23-16. These are the kite's spars and cross braces.

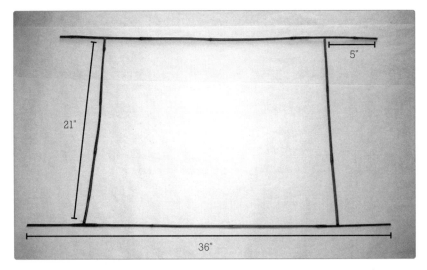

FIGURE 23-16: *Lay out the 36" bamboo spars (top and bottom) and 21" cross braces (left and right).*

Step 7   To create a taut sail, you'll need to keep the cross braces from butting up against the long spars, rather than crossing them—this makes building the frame a bit tricky. Make sure that the cross braces are placed squarely 5" from either end of the spar, and then use a 1/2" wide strip of packing tape to secure them temporarily (Figure 23-17).

FIGURE 23-17: *Secure the cross braces with tape.*

Step 8   Using the thicker string (not the kite string), wrap each joint, as shown in Figure 23-18. (Don't worry about exactly emulating the wrapping shown in the figure; anything stable will be fine).

FIGURE 23-18: *Wrap the cross braces' joints with string.*

Step 9   When you're finished, you'll have a sturdy two-rung "ladder." Build a second ladder with the other two 36" spars and 21" cross braces.

Step 10   Thread one half of the frame into the other, as shown in Figure 23-19. (Don't worry; the bamboo is flexible.) The 21" braces of each ladder cross in the middle, as shown in the figure. Wrap the intersection with thick cotton string. Repeat this on the other end of the kite. You want these to be basically centered and perpendicular.

FIGURE 23-19: *The top cross braces secured with string*

Step 11   To finish the kite's frame, use the 15" pieces of bamboo to frame the four rectangular faces of the kite. The easiest way to accomplish this is shown in Figure 23-20. First lay out a strip of packing tape, sticky side up, and make a T on top of the tape using two 15" cross bars as the horizontal arms and the long 36" spar as the vertical (note the gap between the ends of the 15" spars).

Step 12   Fold the tape over the joint, and then bend the joint so the two 15" cross bars are perpendicular to each other, as shown at the far right of Figure 23-20.

Step 13   Repeat this on all four sides of the top and bottom of the kite. Figure 23-21 shows the finished frame.

Step 14   Now attach the sails. Stand the kite on its end and use the self-adhesive flap on one of the two long strips of Tyvek to secure it to one of the 36" vertical spars. (You'll need to snip a slit in the flap to accommodate the cross brace.)

FIGURE 23-20: *Secure the cross bars with packing tape and bend them in place.*

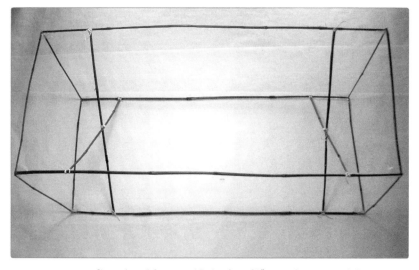

FIGURE 23-21: *Completed frame with the four 21" cross braces and the eight 15" top and bottom cross bars in place*

Step 15 Wrap the Tyvek around the kite so that one edge is flush with the bamboo cross bars. Trim off the excess sail, and use packing tape to secure the end.

Step 16 Run a length of string just inside the other edge of the Tyvek, looping the string around each vertical spar, as in Figure 23-22. Because this string is meant to reinforce the "inside" edge of the sail (preventing in-flight flapping), you need to make this line taut without deforming the kite.

Step 17 Tie off the string. Use long strips of packing tape to secure the top edge of the sail to the bamboo cross bars and the bottom edge of the sail to the reinforcing string.

Step 18 Flip the kite and repeat Steps 14–17 to attach the second sail to the kite.

Step 19 Now connect the bridle. Attach a 48" length of string to the top and bottom of one of the spars, as is shown in the kite anatomy diagram, Figure 23-1. You might need to poke a hole through some tape and the sail to attach the string; that's okay.

FIGURE 23-22: *Close-up of the reinforcing string on the inside edge of the sail looping around a long spar*

Step 20   (optional) Attach the bridle ring to the bridle. See "Adding the Bridle Ring" on page 289.

Step 21   (optional) Box kites rarely need tails, but if you're having trouble keeping the kite stable in flight, you can try attaching a small tail (4' or 5' long) to the bottom of the bridle, where it ties to the spar. (The box kite is symmetrical, so "bottom" is a little arbitrary; as Figure 23-1 illustrates, whichever end of the kite has the longer length of bridle will be lower in flight.)

Flying Tips

Although we often think of kite flying seasons as the spring and summer, in most of North America autumn is the best time to fly: the winds are a consistent speed and tend not to change direction abruptly. The beach is a great place for kite flying all year long, since the wind is steady, strong, and doesn't often change directions. Although the Diamond Kite can cope excellently with fickle breezes, the heavier Box Kite can be difficult to get up in gusty, intermittent winds.

The box kite was developed by skybound Australians, and a large box kite can produce a terrific amount of lift. A good gust, and a sturdy kite, can easily snap a lesser kite string (and thin cotton kite string can give you a nasty cut as it runs through your fingers). Consider wearing biking gloves when you're flying in high winds and upgrading to a spool of 90-pound test nylon kite string.

After you've purchased a new spool of kite string, it's a good idea to unwind the whole thing and make sure that the line is secured to the spool. The end of the string is often held in place with a scrap of tape or nothing at all; this can be a nasty surprise on an otherwise beautiful day. As you rewind the line, you can use a black marker to mark off every ten feet; once the kite is up and flying, you're going to start to wonder how high it is.

Adding the Bridle Ring

You can tie the control line (your big spool of kite string) directly to the kite's bridle, but this can make changing bridle angles a hassle—and bridle adjustments can be important, because you often need to fine-tune to accommodate various wind conditions. Even worse, string-on-string rubbing creates a lot of friction and can cut the line. Most kite makers elect to connect the control line to the bridle with a *bridle ring* (the optional 1/2" split ring from the supplies list). To connect the bridle ring to the bridle (illustrated in Figure 23-23):

Step 1   Pass a bit of bridle through the ring.

Step 2   Loop the bridle over the ring.

Step 3   Carefully tighten the loop so that it forms a *cow hitch* (also called a *lark's head*) around the ring.

FIGURE 23-23: *Three steps to connecting a bridle ring: (1) pass through the ring, (2) loop over, (3) tighten.*

You can then connect the control line onto the bridle ring however you choose. Doing so with a large fishing swivel, like the one shown in Figure 23-24, will keep the line from twisting if the kite loops and also make it easier to switch kites in the field.

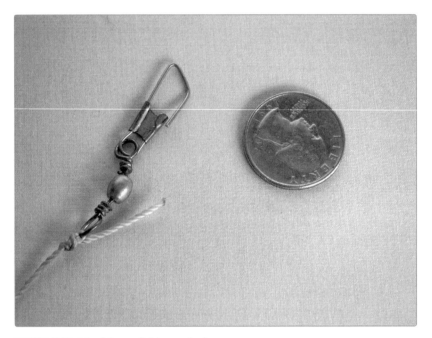

FIGURE 23-24: *A large fishing swivel*

Before you launch either the Box or Diamond Kite, place the bridle ring about 14" from the top of the bridle (the "top" being the point where the bridle connects to the top of the kite). If you dangle the kite by holding the bridle ring, you'll see that the two halves of the bridle form a right triangle (more or less), with the kite as its hypotenuse (Figure 23-25).

FIGURE 23-25: *A good starting place for a bridle ring: the bridle forms a right triangle.*

Depending on wind conditions, you can slide the ring up or down. Sliding it up reduces the amount of sail the kite gives the wind; this is good in steady (if light) breezes, so the kite can climb quickly, skating "on top" of the breeze. Sliding the bridle ring down exposes more sail to the wind; the kite will stay low but will generate more (sometimes much more) lift.

Diamond Kite Pre-flight Tip

It pays to give the Diamond Kite's cross bar a pre-flight bow, as in Figure 23-26. Don't expect the bamboo to hold this bend; the goal is to limber up the center of the horizontal spar so that it will readily bend in the middle. A symmetrically curved surface will encourage air to spill evenly and smoothly off the face of the sail.

Step 1   Hold the kite in front of you with one end of the cross bar in each hand and the frame facing you.

Step 2   Apply pressure, bringing the ends of the cross bar toward you and bowing the center spar away from you.

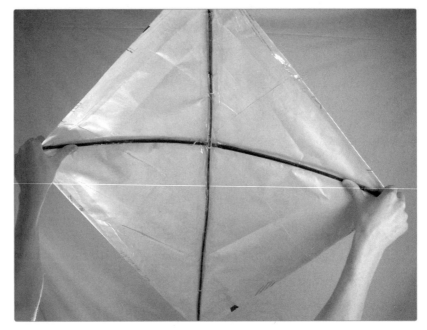

FIGURE 23-26: *Give the Diamond Kite a pre-flight bow.*

Resources

▶   The NASA website hosts an excellent Java-based application that models seven different types of kites and simulates their performance in various conditions. This is helpful information if you need to troubleshoot, modify, or develop a new design: *http://www.grc.nasa.gov/WWW/K-12/airplane/kiteprog.html/*.

▶   "Diamonds in the Sky: The Contributions of William Abner Eddy to Kiting" is a great article about the father of the Eddy bow and includes information about Victorian kite mania (from a 1999 issue of *Kitelife Magazine*): *http://best-breezes.squarespace.com/william-abner-eddy/*.

24 MARSHMALLOW MUZZLELOADER

Guns[1] were the first machines to harness the power of combustion to make stuff go. If you want to do a little armchair international psychoanalysis, consider this: The Chinese discovered gunpowder around 800 AD and used it to make medicine and fireworks. Arabs and Europeans created their version of gunpowder about 500 years later and promptly built guns.

This Marshmallow Muzzleloader isn't all that different from an internal combustion engine: A cylinder is filled with a mix of combustible vapor and air that, when ignited with a spark, drives a piston forward. In this case the cylinder is the chamber of our gun

---

1. A "gun" is any tube-based projectile launching machine with a closed breech, from gigantic ancient cannons to modern artillery, .585-caliber elephant guns to tiny derringers.

(see Figure 24-2), the fuel is breath spray, the spark plug is made from a camera flash, and the piston is a deliciously soft marshmallow.

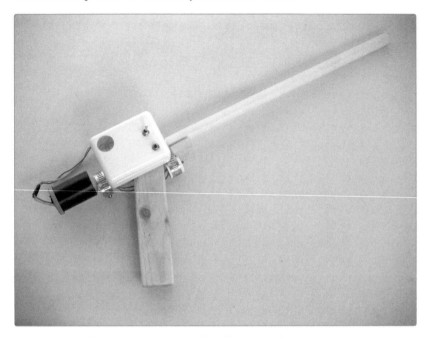

FIGURE 24-1: *The finished Marshmallow Muzzleloader*

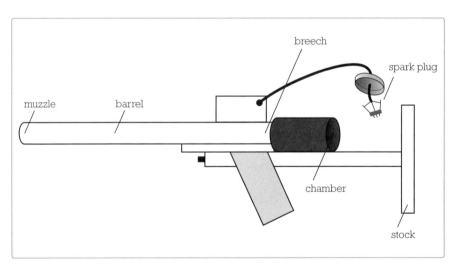

FIGURE 24-2: *The anatomy of our Marshmallow Muzzleloader*

Tools

- a wood saw
- a miter box
- a standard soldering kit (See the appendix.)
- a utility knife
- a tape measure or ruler
- an electric drill with bits
- a pair of insulated test leads, aka clip jumpers
- a pocket knife
- safety goggles or a face shield
- sandpaper (including medium grit, such as 80–120, and fine grit, such as 150)
- (optional) an electric sander
- (optional) a very small Philips head screwdriver, aka a jeweler's screwdriver
- (optional) a multimeter with clip leads

Supplies

- 2' of 1/2" CPVC pipe (Few hardware stores sell this in lengths of less than 5'.)
- one CPVC end cap
- a 6" length of 1" by 2" pine board
- a 5" length of 1" by 1/2" pine trim
- two #12 hose clamps (about 5" long, used on hoses 11/16" to 1 1/4" in diameter)
- two 1" wood screws
- two 1/2" wood screws
- a small, nonconductive enclosure, such as a throat-lozenge or candy box
- a disposable 35 mm camera with a flash
- an empty 35 mm camera film canister
- one 10k ohm resistor (coded with brown-black-orange stripes)
- one SPST (single pole, single throw) momentary push-button switch, such as RadioShack part #275-1571
- one SPST mini-toggle switch, such as RadioShack part #275-612

- ▶ duct tape

- ▶ 22- or 24-gauge insulated, stranded-core hook-up wire

- ▶ three straight pins

- ▶ a pencil with brand new eraser

- ▶ Gorilla Glue

- ▶ electrical tape

- ▶ 2' of 1/4" dowel (or a 2' scrap of bamboo garden stake, leftover from making FedEx Kites in Project 23)

- ▶ a canister of Binaca breath spray

- ▶ a bag of mini marshmallows (for ammunition)

- ▶ (optional) a AA battery holder and a second SPST mini-toggle switch

- ▶ (optional) double-sided, foam-backed tape

- ▶ (optional) a second SPST momentary push-button switch, which makes RadioShack part #275-1571 a good buy, since it includes two identical switches

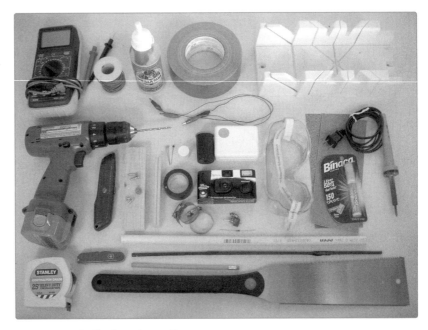

FIGURE 24-3: *Tools and supplies*

Building It

Step 1   Start by making the barrel. Cut an 18" length of CPVC.

          ✳ WARNING: *Wear safety goggles or a face shield when cutting CPVC, because flecks of the material are sharp and can get in your eyes. The friction from your saw can also break down the polyvinyl chloride, releasing toxic fumes—flip to Project 11, the Electro-Didgeridoo, for more info on the dangers of heating PVC and its relatives.*

Step 2   Use your finger to clear away all the burrs and sharp edges from the ends, as these will ultimately tear up the marshmallows and annoy you.

Step 3   Measure 3/4" from one end and mark it, as shown in Figure 24-4. This end of the barrel is the *breech*, where the explosion happens. The other end is the *muzzle*, where the marshmallow flies out.

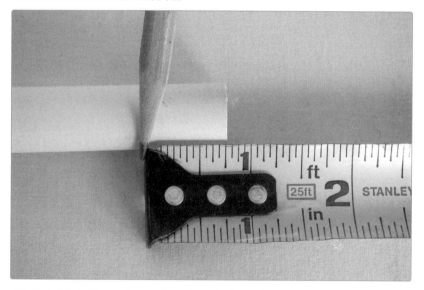

FIGURE 24-4: *Measuring and marking the breech*

Step 4   To make the chamber, use your utility knife to cut a roughly 1/2" hole in the bottom of a film canister, as in Figure 24-5. These are devilishly hard to cut, so don't beat yourself up if you make a mess of it; Gorilla Glue will conceal a multitude of sins.

Step 5   Slide the breech of the barrel into the hole, aligning the bottom of the canister with the line you drew in Step 3, so that the last 3/4" of the breech is inside the film canister.

Step 6   Smear the entire bottom of the canister's exterior with glue. Slide the canister about 1/8" up and down the barrel to spread the glue into the seam. As the Gorilla Glue cures, it will expand quite a bit, sealing the chamber.

FIGURE 24-5: *The prepared canister (left)—notice how ragged the hole is—and the barrel and chamber (right)*

Step 7   Wipe up any excess glue, immobilize the barrel and chamber with a strip of duct tape, and set it aside to dry overnight. (Incidentally, once this is dry, it makes a pretty nifty mini-marshmallow blowgun. Give it a try.)

Step 8   While the barrel and chamber are drying, you can start building the gun's grip and firing mechanism. Start with the grip, which is easy. Use a miter box to guide you in cutting off the top of the grip at a 22.5-degree angle.

Step 9   Whittle down the sharp edges of the grip (just to round it a bit, making it easier on the hand), and then sand these and the cut edges smooth, first with medium-grit sandpaper and finishing up with fine-grit. Sand any rough edges off the 5" piece of trim while you're at it.

Step 10   Center the handle on the piece of trim, drill a pair of guide holes through the trim and into the handle (as in Figure 24-6), and then screw the two together with the 1" screws.

Step 11   Now for the firing mechanism, which is definitely the trickiest part of this project. *Put on your safety goggles*; they might seem like overkill right now, but *keep them on*. Pull the cardboard packaging off the disposable camera. You'll probably find a latch on the end of the camera, which easily opens the body. If not, take a flathead screwdriver to the camera body and pop it open.

Step 12   Remove the battery (a standard AA).

     * **WARNING:** *Do not touch any of the contacts on the circuit board! This is very important!*

Step 13   Pull out the film and set it aside. (It's still perfectly usable and can be loaded into any 35mm camera. Or you can use up all of the film before opening the camera, and then take it in for processing; you might lose the last couple pictures to light exposure, but most of the roll should print up fine.)

FIGURE 24-6: *Drilling a guide hole in the grip*

Step 14   You should be able to access the circuit board (Figure 24-7). A disposable camera includes only one circuit, which is dedicated to running the flash unit. (The picture-taking portion of the camera is entirely mechanical.)

FIGURE 24-7: *On the left is an open disposable camera. On this model, the big capacitor is tucked behind the flash (the flash is in the upper-right corner of the unit shown in the left picture). The right photo shows the back of the flash circuit; the AA battery gives a sense of how large that capacitor is—be careful! The two springy strips of copper on the left of the unit in the right photo (circled) form a rudimentary switch that triggers the flash. Remember this for later.*

✻ WARNING: *A camera flash relies on a large electrolytic capacitor, which can hold its charge for a long time. These capacitors are usually unmarked. Camera flash specs call for a capacitor around 470 µF—which is pretty hefty as is—but many of these look much larger to me, perhaps 1,000–3,000 µF. In any case, the camera uses a step-up transformer to charge this capacitor to upward of 300 volts. This wouldn't necessarily be so bad by itself: a 470 µF capacitor charged to 300 volts holds 0.12 coulomb of electric charge, which isn't life-threatening. A coulomb is equivalent to discharging 1 amp for 1 second,[2] and 1 amp is a hefty current (household wall current is 10–15 amps). Since it is difficult to predict how much resistance a finger will offer, we can't know how quickly a clumsy brush of your thumb will discharge a large capacitor; it will take under a second, perhaps a tenth or hundredth of a second, which means that the 0.12 coulomb in the flash-unit capacitor might end up being 1.2, or even 12 amps. (If this is confusing, just remember this: With capacitors, faster discharge = higher current.)*

Fortunately, the capacitor's legs are so close together that it is unlikely this current will go through an important internal organ if you do get shocked—but it will hurt. A lot. If you scrape the capacitor's leads with a screwdriver, it will let out a big fat spark that can blast little flecks of solder off the board (and into your eye; hence the required goggles).

On top of all of this, disposable camera flash circuits are cheap and a little unpredictable: Sometimes they ship charged, and even with the battery removed the capacitor will hold that charge. Always assume that a large capacitor is fully charged—even if you're working with a device that's factory new and that you've never powered up. Big capacitors are the handguns of electronics: Always assume they are loaded.

Step 15 Start by making sure that capacitor won't hurt you. If you have a multimeter, you can check how much voltage the capacitor is holding; otherwise, skip directly to bleeding the circuit in Step 17.

Step 16 While your soldering iron is warming up, turn on your multimeter and set it to the thousands of DC volts range. *Being sure to hold your probes by their insulated handles and careful not to touch anything but a single leg with each,* touch one probe to either leg (or to the solder pad where each leg is connected to the circuit board—whichever is easiest to reach). A fully charged capacitor will read upward of 300 volts. (A negative sign means you've inadvertently reversed the probes—but it doesn't matter: in this context, −300 volts is just as bad as 300 volts.) Anything larger than a few volts can give you a painful jolt. If the voltage is near zero, you can skip to Step 18—although I urge you to bleed the circuit (as described in the next step), just to be safe.

---

2. As a formula, $Q=C×V$, where Q is the coulombs of charge, C is the capacitor's value in farads, and V is the voltage it's holding. Also note that $Q=A×s$—in other words a coulomb equals 1 amp times 1 second. This means that if the cap takes more than a second to discharge, the current is reduced, but the faster the discharge, the more the current is amplified. This fact is important to Taser and defibrillator manufacturers, as well as tinkerers messing with camera flashes.

Step 17   To bleed the capacitor, clip one end of each jumper to either leg of the 10k resistor. Then, taking pains to touch only the insulated part of the clips, connect each jumper to one leg of the capacitor, being *very careful* not to short the two legs of the capacitor or touch any other exposed metal (Figure 24-8). This will safely drain the capacitor in just a few seconds. (If you have a multimeter, check the capacitor again or even watch it drain.) You can then remove the clip jumpers.

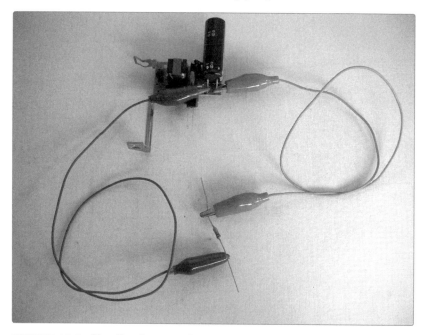

FIGURE 24-8: *Bleeding the capacitor*

Step 18   Now you can add a bleeder circuit to the flash (which will function as the gun's safety—the finished circuit is shown in Figure 24-9). Start by making sure your SPST toggle switch is off (either using the continuity setting on your multimeter or by rigging up a little LED-resistor-battery-switch circuit, such as those featured in Project 2, the Switchbox).

Step 19   After you are sure the switch is off, solder the 10k resistor to one terminal of the SPST toggle switch. Strip the ends of two 4" or 5" lengths of insulated wire (depending on the size of your enclosure), and solder one to the remaining switch terminal and the other to the open leg of the resistor. Then carefully solder the wires to each leg of the capacitor.

Step 20   Test the bleeder circuit. If your multimeter has clip leads (probes that end in tiny alligator or hooked clips), clip one to each capacitor leg now, and you can monitor the capacitor's charge-discharge cycle.

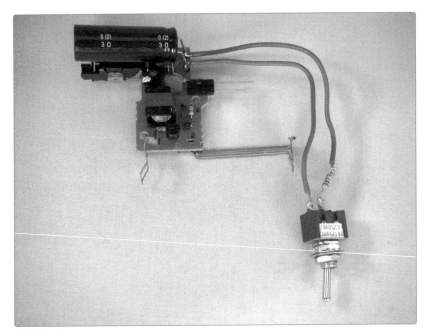

FIGURE 24-9: *The installed bleeder circuit*

Step 21   Replace the battery and charge the flash as normal; you'll hear a high-pitched whine. After about 30 seconds, the indicator light will come on. (The multimeter will read upward of 250 volts when the light comes on; you'll notice that even after the indicator lights up, the whine's pitch continues to rise and the capacitor charges until it exceeds 300 volts.)

Step 22   Trigger the flash and it will fire. Some flash models automatically begin recharging—you'll hear the whine again. Otherwise, recharge the capacitor to its full 300 volts. Being careful not to touch any exposed wires, flick the bleeder switch; you'll hear the whine drop in pitch, and the multimeter will fall to 50 volts or less. The trigger switch will not be able to make the flash fire. (Closing the trigger will likely drop the voltage back to zero, at which time some flash models will again try to recharge it. As long as the bleeder switch is closed, the capacitor won't be able to go over 50 volts.)

Step 23   After you know you can safely bleed the cap, keep the bleeder switch engaged, remove the battery, and then take out whatever screws are holding down the circuit board. (A tiny jeweler's screwdriver is handy here, but an eyeglass screwdriver or the blade of a pocket knife will work, provided you don't care about nicking up the blade.)

Step 24   At this time, you might decide you want to add an AA battery holder and power switch (depending on how your camera is laid out). You'll likely want to replace the charging button with a heartier SPST push button (again, depending on how your board is laid out). If you decide to do the latter, cut two 2" pieces of insulated wire, strip the ends, solder one of each of the ends to each terminal of a push-button switch and the other ends to the copper pads corresponding to the charging switch.

Step 25 You need to add a usable trigger (since the camera's built-in trigger is usually just a pair of flexible copper tongues sticking off the edge of the board; see Figure 24-7) and build a trigger housing. Start by wiring the new trigger switch: cut two 6" pieces of wire, strip the ends, and solder one wire to each of the two terminals of the push-button switch.

Step 26 For the housing, take the 1/2" CPVC cap and drill a small hole through the bottom. (A 3/16" bit will create a tight fit for the RadioShack push-button switch, as shown in Figure 24-10.) Install the switch inside the cap, and then solder the two insulated wires to the two sides of the original trigger switch on the flash-unit circuit board; the camera flash with its new bleeder circuit, charging switch, and trigger is shown in Figure 24-11. (Because most enclosures will require threading the trigger wires through a hole, you might want to hold off on soldering the trigger connections until the end.) Reinstall the battery and test all of your new switches before moving on to the next step.

FIGURE 24-10: *The new trigger with housing*

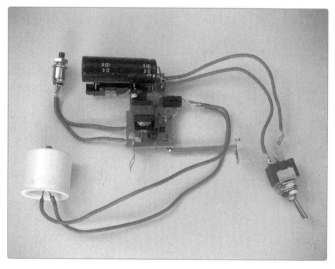

FIGURE 24-11: *The flash circuit board with new safety switch (on the right), charging switch (the button on the upper left), and the trigger (the unit on the lower left)*

Step 27 Now to build the spark plug. You're basically re-creating the internal structure of the flashbulb in the open air so that the spark can ignite the propellant and fling the marshmallow toward heaven or foe. Start by building electrodes from the three pins: Cut three 9" lengths of wire and strip both ends. Solder each wire to one pin, 5/8" from the pin's sharp tip (as shown in Figure 24-12).

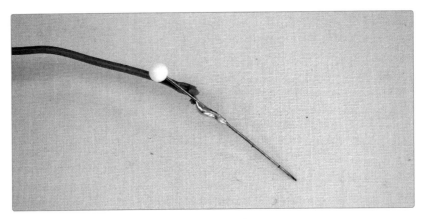

FIGURE 24-12: *A finished electrode spark point*

Step 28   Now pull the eraser off a new pencil, and drive one pin through the middle of the eraser's side.

Step 29   Insert the other pins about 1/4" to either side, and at an angle. Slide the three back and forth until the spark gap between the tips of the middle pin and either side pin is less than 1/16" (see Figure 24-13). This is your three-electrode spark plug, where the ignition spark will actually form.

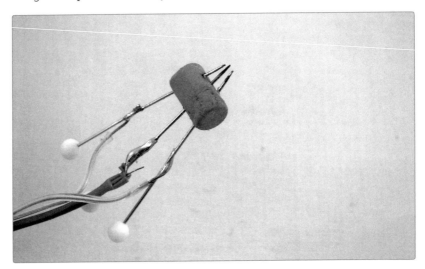

FIGURE 24-13: *The finished three-electrode spark plug*

Step 30   Pop a hole in the middle of the film canister lid, and thread the wires through so that the spark plug is on the inside of the lid.

Step 31   To connect the spark plug to the flash unit, remove the battery, engage the bleeder circuit, and use your multimeter to confirm that no voltage remains in the capacitor.

Step 32   Carefully remove the camera's flash bulb; notice which wire goes to the center of the reflector on the back of the bulb (the other two are interchangeable—see Figure 24-14).

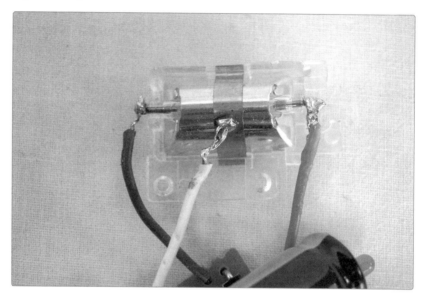

FIGURE 24-14: *The back of the flashbulb*

Step 33   Twist together the middle wire from the flash bulb and the lead to the middle pin in the spark plug, and wrap the connection with a little electrical tape. Do likewise with each of the two outer wires from the flash bulb and each of the two outer wires on the spark plug. (You'll solder all of these later, after installing the firing unit in its enclosure.)

Step 34   Test the sparker: Put on goggles, load the battery back into the camera flash, deactivate the bleeder, and charge the flash circuit. After it is fully charged, hit the trigger. You'll see a very bright spark, accompanied by a loud *crack!* and possibly the smell of brimstone. If the spark doesn't jump (and don't be disappointed if it doesn't; it's normal to need to fine-tune the spark gap), check to make sure that

- the battery is installed properly
- the flash circuit whines as it's charging
- the capacitor is getting its full 300-plus volts
- no bare wires are shorting the circuit.

If these are all okay and you still don't get a spark, you should cut the power, bleed the capacitor, and carefully push the pins further into the eraser, getting the tips as close to each other as possible without touching.

Step 35 Once you've gotten a few good sparks, set aside the firing unit and take out the wooden grip and the barrel (provided the glue is dry). Use the two hose clamps to bind together the grip, trigger, and barrel, as shown in Figure 24-15.

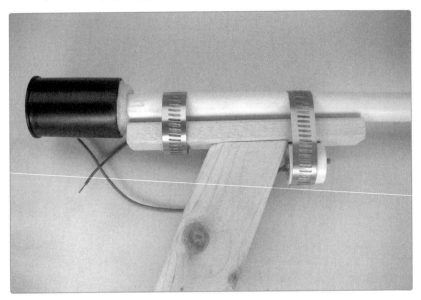

FIGURE 24-15: *The barrel, grip, and trigger bound with hose clamps*

Step 36 Decide how best to orient the firing unit's plastic enclosure (probably just in front of the film-canister chamber is best, so it doesn't obstruct access to the trigger). Drill holes in the enclosure's lid for the charging button and bleeder switch. (I like to orient the switch so that when it's pointed toward the end of the barrel, the firing circuit is live, and when it is pointed back, the safety is engaged.) If you're using the RadioShack switches, then a 3/16" or 1/4" bit is about right for these holes.

Step 37 Drill a hole for the power switch (if you added one) and the wires going to the spark plug (I suggest running the spark plug wires out of the back of the enclosure, as show in Figure 24-16, rather than the lid).

Step 38 Drill a hole so you can see the "ready" LED on your flash unit (unless your enclosure has a handy window, as mine does).

Step 39 Finally, drill guide holes through the bottom of the enclosure and into the piece of 1/2" trim running along the top of the grip. Then attach the enclosure to the grip using two 1/2" wood screws.

Step 40 Detach the spark unit, thread its wires into the enclosure, solder them permanently to the old flash bulb wires, and wrap them in a little electrical tape, insulating them from each other and the rest of the circuit. Now is the time to look for any other potential short circuits as you mount the remaining switches and circuit board in the enclosure. (You can use double-sided tape or glue to secure the board.)

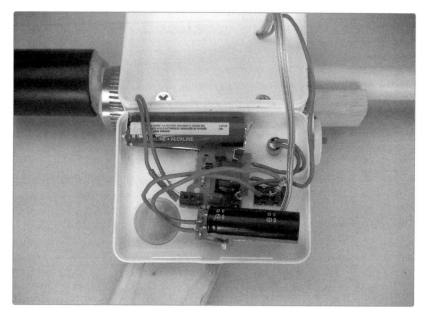

FIGURE 24-16: *The enclosure, with all electronics mounted on the lid; the set of wires threaded out the topmost hole run from the flash bulb's wires to the spark plug*

Step 41   Slide the film canister lid up the wires so that it rests just behind the spark plug, and use a little piece of electrical tape to cover the hole (Figure 24-17).

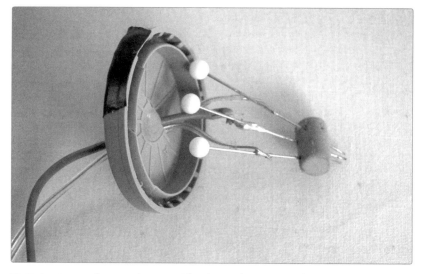

FIGURE 24-17: *Proper placement for the canister cap and spark plug*

Step 42   Retest everything, adjusting the spark gap or other wiring as needed.

Firing Instructions

Turn off the bleeder circuit, charge up the gun, and squeeze the trigger. If the spark gap is tight enough (without electrodes touching!), you'll get a crack and a spark. Otherwise, engage the bleeder circuit, tighten the gap, disengage the bleeder, charge, and try to fire again.

Once you're getting a good spark, the firing mechanism should be fine for the duration of a shooting session, although you will need to adjust the gap periodically and, after a lot of firing, clean and even sharpen the electrodes, since the sparks will char and deform their tips.

After you are sure that the firing mechanism is in working order, engage the bleeder circuit and give the capacitor a few seconds to discharge.

* WARNING: *Always have the bleeder on when loading or adjusting the spark gap! Think of it as the Marshmallow Muzzleloader's "safety."*

Here's how to fire:

Step 1   Make sure the bleeder switch is on.

Step 2   Open the chamber.

Step 3   Put a mini marshmallow in the gun's muzzle and tamp it all the way to the breech using a dowel. Look into the chamber to be sure it is all the way back but hasn't fallen into the chamber.

Step 4   Spray a spritz or two of Binaca into the chamber. Don't overload the chamber, because the propellant needs to mix with air to burn.

Step 5   Put the lid on the chamber.

Step 6   Deactivate the bleeder and press the charging button.

Step 7   After the LED light comes on, you can fire at will.

With this firing unit, misfires are rare; occasionally the unit sparks but doesn't ignite the propellant because there isn't enough air in the chamber. This can almost always be addressed by "burping" the chamber: Lift one edge of the lid just enough to let some air in, then seal it again.

If the inside of the barrel becomes damp (perhaps from a stray shot of propellant or loading error), the moisture will make the marshmallow bullets tear and smear and otherwise foul the barrel. Swab the barrel by placing a small square of paper towel on top of the muzzle and then, using the 1/4" dowel as a tamping rod (Figure 24-18), force the paper towel through the entire barrel and out the breech.

Other propellants—such as hairspray or plain rubbing alcohol spritzed through a mister—will work, but Binaca, which is a mix of denatured alcohol and isobutane, is a great propellant and it has a refreshing minty scent.

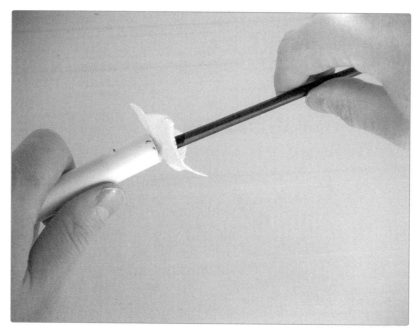

FIGURE 24-18: *Swabbing the barrel*

Despite the bang and muzzle flash, this gun is safe for indoor use (provided you aren't pushing the muzzle right into highly inflammable[3] sheer curtains), but it can be sort of messy. Dogs hate the noise, but they love to chase and eat the ammo.

How It Works

Getting a spark to jump through air is pretty challenging and takes a great deal of energy, even to bridge a gap of just a few millimeters. A disposable camera flash is a pretty impressive little piece of energy ingenuity, squeezing 300 volts out of a 1.5-volt AA battery nearly indefinitely. The flash circuit consists of a fat capacitor, a transistor, a large step-up transformer (which converts the 1.5 volts in the battery to the 300 volts needed to charge the capacitor), and a small step-up transformer (which steps up the 300 volts in the capacitor to almost 1000 volts to trigger the flash—for more information on how transformers work, flip back to Project 7, the Ticklebox).

When you press the charging button, the 1.5-volt battery begins feeding the first transformer, using a transistor to create an oscillating current (since the transformer needs a flowing current to work). The high-pitched whine is the sound of that oscillator speeding up as the capacitor nears 300 volts. Once the capacitor is charged, you press the trigger; this sends a small jolt to the secondary transformer,

3. "*Flammable.* An oddity, chiefly useful in saving lives. The common word meaning 'combustible' is *inflammable*. But some people are thrown off by the *in-* and think *inflammable* means 'not combustible.' For this reason, trucks carrying gasoline or explosives are now marked FLAMMABLE. Unless you are operating such a truck and hence are concerned with the safety of children and illiterates, use *inflammable*."—*Elements of Style*, William Strunk and E.B. White.

which in turn pumps a big jolt to the middle contact in the spark plug. In a camera flash, this is attached to a metal plate that runs along the back of the bulb, between the two leads. This sudden burst of voltage ionizes the Xenon inside the flash tube (or, in our gun, the tiny air gap between the two points), making it conductive enough for the 300-volt spark to jump between the two end leads. *Shazam!*

Going Commando

Since you'll probably have plenty of spare CPVC sitting around after this project, you might want to trick out your muzzle loader with a nifty shoulder stock. The stock shown in Figure 24-19 is made from a few extra lengths of CPVC pipe (left over from the barrel), a pair of CPVC end caps (just like the one used for the trigger housing), and a CPVC T-connector.

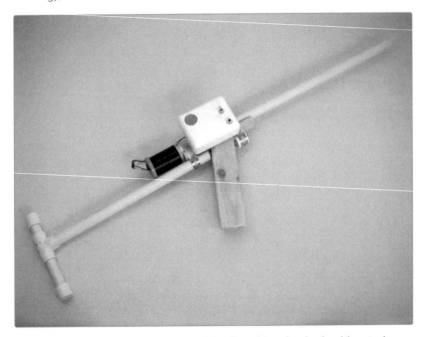

FIGURE 24-19: *A Marshmallow Muzzleloader with a simple shoulder stock*

After you've built the stock, you may be tempted to shoulder your firearm, lay your cheek against the chamber, and sight down the barrel like Ralphie with his official Red Ryder carbine-action 200-shot range-model air rifle on Christmas morning—but beware: It's really not well advised to press your face against a thin-walled plastic canister filled with inflammable vapor that you are about to blast with a 300-volt spark.

Although it's almost always cheaper to buy electrical components and tools online, if you happen to live near a shop catering to electrical tinkerers or ham radio enthusiasts, always go there first. These shops generally offer excellent deals and are invariably staffed by wise old folks with a bottomless reservoir of tips, tricks, and quick fixes—in addition to occasional stories about being stationed at South Pacific remote listening posts during World War II.

Almost anything you purchase at RadioShack will work about as well (with a higher sticker price), with one exception: jacks. Normal operation puts a great deal of strain on jacks, especially the springy metal tongue that presses against the plug's tip. In a cheap jack this tongue deforms over time, leading to a loose, noisy connection. Do yourself a favor and buy a high-quality jack to begin with. Jacks made by Switchcraft are the gold standard, and Mouser part #502-L-11 is suitable for all of the projects in this book.

Components

Many components (especially capacitors and some resistors) have wattage and voltage ratings printed on them; all you need to know is that any 1/4- or 1/2-watt component is fine for these projects, as is anything rated more than 9 volts. (Most will be 16 or 35 volts; you should use components rated higher than the amount of voltage you plan on applying to them.)

✳ **WARNING:** *Because the batteries used in the projects in this book are small and supply relatively low currents, every project featured here is safe. You should not rework anything to run on more than a 9-volt battery, and please don't use the information in this book as permission to start messing with wall current!*

Resistors: Fixed and Variable

Resistors are electrical components that conduct current but impede its forward flow. Resistance is measured in *ohms* (abbreviated with the symbol Ω), with values usually in the hundreds or thousands. *Fixed resistors* (Figure A-1) are labeled with four colored bands, grouped as a set of three, then a space, and then the fourth (which is always silver or gold).

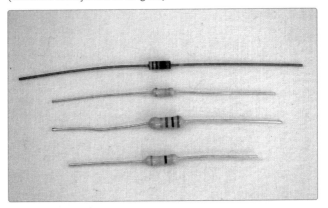

Fixed resistor

FIGURE A-1: *Several fixed resistors and the resistor symbol (right) used on circuit diagrams*

If you hold the resistor so that the three-band group is to the left, the first three bands give the resistor's *value* (its resistance in ohms) and the last band tells you its *tolerance* (how close to that value it really is). Resistors are cheap, so you should always purchase those with a gold fourth band, which corresponds to a tolerance of ±5 percent. When you're reading a value, the first two bands provide the numerical value, and the third tells you how many 0's to tack onto the end, as shown in Table A-1. For example, a resistor with brown-black-orange bands has a value of 1 (brown) and 0 (black), followed by three 0's (orange), and is thus 10,000 ohms, or 10k ohms. If you need to find a 470 ohm resistor in your bin, look for the one that is marked with a yellow band (4), a purple band (7), and a brown band (add one 0).

✱ **NOTE:** *If this is confusing (and it usually is at first), Google "resistor value decoder"; the Internet abounds with Java-based resistor decoder applications.*

TABLE A-1: Resistor value decoder

Color	Value
Black	0
Brown	1
Red	2
Orange	3
Yellow	4
Green	5
Blue	6
Purple (aka Violet)	7
Gray	8
White	9

There is a popular mnemonic device for remembering this table, but it is callous, misogynistic, racist, pointless, and wantonly defames girls named Violet. Note that the order of the colors in the chart is the same as the order of the colors in the rainbow (ROY G BV); in other words, the system has a built-in, inoffensive mnemonic: just remember "black-brown-ROY G BV-gray-white," and you'll remember the values from 0 through 9.

Variable resistors (Figure A-2) can be adjusted to offer different amounts of resistance—generally between 0 ohms and their marked value.

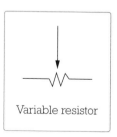

Variable resistor

FIGURE A-2: *Variable resistors: two potentiometers on the left, three trim potentiometers on the right, and the variable resistor symbol*

The larger variable resistors, which are usually accessible from the outside of the finished project's enclosure, are meant to be adjusted often and are called *potentiometers*, or *pots*. Very small variable resistors, which are meant to be adjusted only during the initial building stage (sometimes referred to as "set-and-forget"), are usually called *trim pots*, or *trimmers*. Any variable resistor can have either an *audio* (also called *logarithmic*) *taper*, or a *linear taper*. (For more details on this, see "Audio Tapers vs. Linear Tapers" on page 190.)

The pot's value is usually printed on its face, with an *A* prefix for audio tapers, and either a *B* or no prefix for linear tapers; unless specified otherwise, you should always use linear tapers. In this book, a pot's lugs are numbered from left to right when the pot is viewed from the front with the lugs on top, like a crown. (This means they are numbered from right to left when viewed from the back, which is the view you'll normally have when you're soldering; see Figure A-3.)

FIGURE A-3: *Variable resistors, viewed from the front and back, with lugs labeled*

The shafts on pots are often much longer than you want for your final project. A good way to deal with this is to measure the depth of the knob cover you want to use (usually around 1/4"), mark this on the pot's shaft, clamp the shaft in a vice, and cut it down with a hacksaw. If you're worried about getting grit in the pot (not usually a problem, since most modern pots are fully enclosed), you can wrap the body of the pot in masking tape before sawing.

Pots often have small anchors protruding from their bodies; you can either drill an extra hole in your enclosure to accommodate the anchor or snap it off with a pair of pliers (Figure A-4).

FIGURE A-4: *Snapping off an anchor*

* **NOTE:** *Resistors—fixed, variable, and otherwise—are basically indestructible; you don't need to treat them with TLC as you start soldering.*

Capacitors

Capacitors (Figure A-5) are composed of two wires separated by a thin insulating layer (called a *dielectric*). When voltage is applied to a capacitor, it stores energy. (It's a bit like a water tower: pump the water in, and it stays there until you open the valve, at which time it forcefully pours back out.) *Capacitance* (a component's ability to hold this charge) is measured in farads (abbreviated F). Because a farad is a huge amount of capacitance, most components are labeled in terms of picofarads (pF), which are larger than nanofarads (nF), which are larger than microfarads (µF). The smallest fixed capacitors—those commonly used in intro-level projects like these—are often marked in a frustratingly opaque code (which is why I've included Table A-2 of common values). For clarity's sake, this book always deals in terms of microfarads.

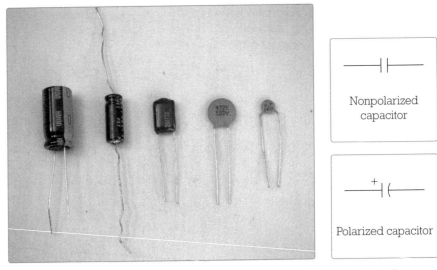

Nonpolarized capacitor

Polarized capacitor

FIGURE A-5: *Here are some capacitors and their symbols. The two on the left are electrolytic—that is,* polarized. *The middle one is a Mylar-film capacitor, and the two on the right are ceramic discs.*

TABLE A-2: Commonly used ceramic/Mylar capacitor markings and their values

Marking	Value
102	0.001 µF
202	0.002 µF
472	0.0047 µF
103	0.01 µF
104	0.1 µF
105	1 µF
205	2 µF

For the most part, small capacitors are little beige ceramic disks, or occasionally Chiclet-shaped plastic lozenges (these latter are called *Mylar capacitors* because they use a thin Mylar film as their dielectric). The larger capacitors are barrel-shaped electrolytic capacitors. The only difference we care about is that although ceramic discs and Mylar-film capacitors are *nonpolarized* (that is, it doesn't matter which way which leg goes), electrolytic capacitors are *polarized* and must be oriented properly. The negative leg of an electrolytic capacitor is always marked with a thick stripe. Also, happily, electrolytic capacitors are large enough to be labeled with their value, rather than relying on the terrible code. In general, any cap under 1 µF is ceramic/Mylar, and anything over 2 µF is electrolytic.

Like resistors, capacitors are hardy components. Although it is theoretically possible to heat an electrolytic capacitor to such a degree (or apply so much current) that it pops, I've never known anyone who did so accidentally.

Diodes, LEDs, and Transistors

Thus far, we've discussed only *passive components* (those that obstruct the flow of electricity, decreasing or slowing a signal). Diodes and transistors are *active components*—they can be used to construct circuits that produce a *power gain* and increase the level of a signal. They can do this because they are *semiconductors*. While *conductors* (such as a piece of wire or a resistor) allow current to pass through them, and *insulators* (such as the plastic coating on a 24-gauge wire) stop all flow of current, semiconductors pass current in special ways.

Diodes and *LEDs* (light-emitting diodes), shown in Figure A-6, allow voltage of only a certain level or greater to pass (that is, the voltage must exceed the diode's *forward voltage*) and will let current travel in only one direction (in other words, they have *polarity*). Like all polarized components, they must be mounted in the proper direction to work. The stripe on a physical diode is closest to the diode's negative leg (its *cathode*) and corresponds to the crossbar at the tip of the triangle on the diode symbol. On an LED, the negative leg is the shorter leg (which is on the side closest to the flat spot on the LED lens's edge).

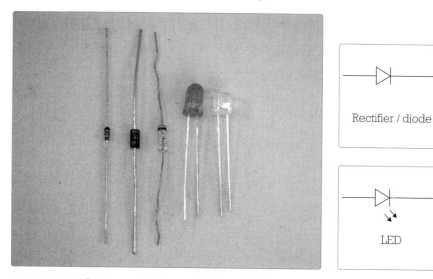

Rectifier / diode

LED

FIGURE A-6: *Diodes and LEDs, and their symbols*

Transistors are the diodes' fancy big brothers. Like diodes, they let current flow in one direction and only if it exceeds the transistor's forward voltage. But the three-legged transistor works like a valve: A low-current signal at the *base* controls a higher current that flows from the *collector* to the *emitter*. (There are many kinds of transistors, but because all the projects in this book use common *NPN*, negative-positive-negative, transistors, that's what is depicted in Figure A-7 and described here.)

All semiconductors are sensitive to heat and static electricity. If you're concerned about damaging them, use a *heat sink* when soldering them (details in "Tools" on page 322).

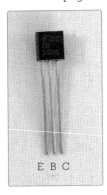
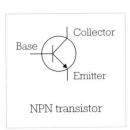

FIGURE A-7: *An NPN transistor and its symbol*

Integrated Circuits

Integrated circuits (ICs)—shown in Figure A-8—are compact packages of microscopic diodes, transistors, and resistors, prewired to perform a given task. (Anything an IC can do, a fistful of transistors, diodes, and other basic components, plus a few yards of bus wire and some circuit boards, can also accomplish.) As such, ICs are semiconductors and are thus heat- and static-sensitive, so you must handle them carefully.

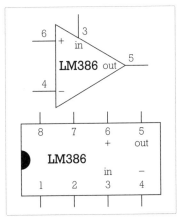

FIGURE A-8: *On the left are two DIP-style ICs, and on the right are symbols for the lower chip, which is the LM386 op-amp used in the Dirt-Cheap Amp, Project 12. An IC in a circuit diagram is usually depicted as a triangle (or a series of triangles for each of its logic sections). For clarity, I've used little drawings of the ICs in circuit diagrams throughout this book.*

When ordering ICs from a catalog or website, you should always be sure to get the *DIP (dual in-line package)* version (like those in Figure A-8), as opposed to the *surface-mount* version. DIPs look like little rectangular insects standing on 8, 14, 16, or more straight little legs and are relatively easy to work with. Surface-mount chips are flat with short legs; they are usually mounted on circuit boards by machines (you'll find them on your computer's motherboard); you will go insane trying to learn to solder on surface-mount chips.

Wire

In electrical work, wire is described in terms of *gauge*, *insulation*, and *core*.

The gauge of a wire is its thickness, with thinner wire having a higher gauge than thicker wire. For example, the 42-gauge winding wire used in guitar pickups is as thin as a human hair, while 18-gauge copper wire is nearly the thickness of a plastic cocktail straw. Conducting wire is measured using the American Wire Gauge (AWG) Standard (e.g., the guitar pickup winding wire will be labeled *42 AWG*).

All About AWG

Historically, the AWG number referred to the number of dies through which the wire needed to be drawn to be reduced to the desired diameter. A drawing die is a steel plate with a hole in it. A copper rod is forced through a die with a diameter slightly smaller than that of the rod, squeezing the rod down to the smaller diameter. This continues with increasingly smaller dies until the wire reaches the desired gauge. For example, 18-gauge wire would undergo 18 reduction steps from fresh rod to ready wire, while the pickup winding wire would go through 42 different steps. Roughly speaking, when the wire's diameter is doubled, the AWG decreases by 6, so 12 AWG wire is actually twice as thick as 18 AWG wire. (This is why you can't wind a pickup from common 20 AWG magnet wire; it's actually four times thicker than real pickup wire and thus significantly more difficult to induce a current through.) Incidentally, the body modification community often uses AWG to measure the gauge of needles and jewelry, especially smaller gauge accoutrements.

Any wire can be either *insulated* or *bare* (uninsulated). Thicker insulated wire usually has flexible plastic insulation, but thinner wire (20 to 30-something AWG) may be enameled—coated in a shiny polyurethane varnish—instead. Finer insulated wires (high 30s and above) are usually enameled.

Finally, a wire is either *solid-core* or *stranded*. Solid-core wire is composed of (surprise!) a single solid strand, and stranded wire comprises several strands whose total combined cross-sectional area corresponds to the wire's AWG. Solid-core insulated wire is often called *bell wire*, and stranded insulated wire is called *hook-up wire*.

Solid-core wire is a little easier to solder into printed circuit boards (PCBs), because it fits nicely through the holes, but it can break easily with repeated bending (such as flexing when you open and close a case to check a circuit, change batteries, or make other adjustments). Stranded wire can occasionally be a headache to thread through the holes on a circuit board. As a rule, use solid-core wire for connections that won't move much (such as point-to-point connections on a board, or when running between pieces of hardware mounted on the same surface), and use stranded wire if the wires need to flex a lot (such as for connections to a battery or to hardware running from a circuit mounted on the side of the box to hardware mounted to its top).

Bare 22- or 24-AWG solid-core wire is often called *bus wire* and is great for running grounds, repairing broken traces on prefabricated printed circuit boards, making jumpers, replacing lost eyeglass screws, and so on; it's the all-purpose bailing twine of hobby electronics.

Quarter-Inch Phone Plugs and Jacks

These 1/4" jacks and plugs (commonly thought of as a "guitar jack") were first developed for manual telephone switchboards and are often called *phone jacks*, which is confusing, since RCA plugs and jacks are called *phono* jacks, because they were the old standard on hi-fi stereo phonograph systems.

Mono 1/4" phone jacks are also called *TS connectors*, because they have two lugs—one that carries the audio signal and makes a circuit with the *tip* of a plug when connected and another that connects the *sleeve* of the plug to ground (see Figure A-9).

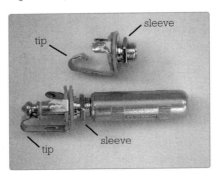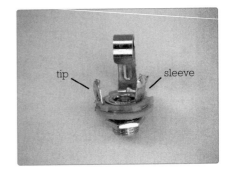

FIGURE A-9: *On the left are two 1/4" mono jacks—one with a plug inserted. Notice how the jack's bent metal tongue fits into the notch at the plug's tip. On the right, a jack with labeled lugs; as you can see, the right lug is connected to the sleeve (which connects to the circuit's ground), and the other lug connects to the tip.*

Stereo phone jacks and plugs are sometimes called *TRS connectors*. In this configuration, the sleeve still connects to ground, but the tip and ring each connect to an independent audio channel, allowing for stereo sound through a single cable.

Batteries, Clips, and Holders

A variety of battery clips and holders are shown in Figure A-10. It's easy to forget to buy these, and then you either end up running back to RadioShack when you'd rather be testing your latest project or trying to tape leads to a battery (which makes troubleshooting frustrating, as it's hard to be sure if the problem is the circuit or your cruddy battery connection). Make a practice of buying a bunch of these when you find them cheap, so that you have plenty on hand when you need them.

✳ **WARNING:** *Never solder directly to a battery! Heating a battery can cause it to burst, releasing a mélange of chemicals that will burn exposed skin or, depending on the type of battery, catch fire when they contact air or moisture!*

Invest in some rechargeable batteries. Newer nickel-metal hydride (NiMH) cells might seem pricey, but they are ultimately worth the cost: They are less toxic than the old nickel-cadmium rechargeable batteries, they can be recharged hundreds of times, and they actually out-perform regular alkaline batteries in high-drain applications (such as ultra-bright flashlights and digital cameras).

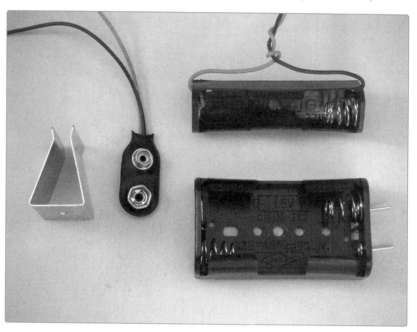

FIGURE A-10: *Assorted battery holders and clips: the piece of metal at the far left is a 9-volt battery clip holder that keeps the battery from rattling around the enclosure.*

Tools

The only mandatory tools you'll need to build the electronics projects in this book are those included in the standard soldering kit (and even some of those can be faked).

The Standard Soldering Kit

You'll need a 25-watt soldering iron with a chisel or pencil tip (shown in Figure A-11). You can work on electrical projects with irons of 15 to 40 watts, but a 25-watt iron is probably the handiest: Cooler irons are great for soldering little components but will be a royal pain for soldering hardware, and hotter irons (great for quickly soldering plugs and jacks) can ruin ICs, LEDs, and diodes in a flash.

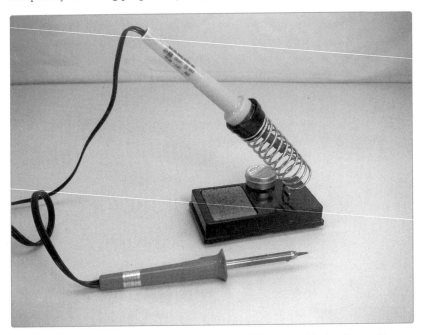

FIGURE A-11: *Here are a 15-watt (bottom) and 25-watt soldering iron with stand (top). The damp sponge in the stand is used for cleaning the tip, although many tinkerers prefer to use a copper scrubbing pad or old bolt instead.*

In terms of value, your best bet is a Weller soldering iron. This brand is often sold at hardware stores, and a $25 Weller (their entry-level model) will vastly outperform any $10 generic counterpart: It will last longer, heat more regularly, and its replacement tips are cheap and easy to find (usually at the same hardware store that sold you the iron). You should also acquire a soldering iron stand; otherwise you *will* burn yourself. You could just lay the hot iron across a china plate or tile, but you will eventually absent-mindedly pick up the hot barrel instead of the insulated handle. (I vividly recall the hot July night that I seared my index finger and thumb prints into the chrome of my first soldering iron. Fortunately, I was working in an un-air-conditioned third-floor room, and my hands were so sweaty that I dropped the iron before all the moisture seared off my fingers. I bought a stand the next day, but my prints were etched into that iron a decade later when I finally invested in a decent Weller.)

Use thin *rosin-core solder.*[1] Anything you buy at RadioShack will fit the bill. It's actually difficult to get the wrong kind of solder nowadays, but you should avoid the acid-core solder sold at hardware stores. That stuff is used for working with copper plumbing, and it will ultimately corrode your electronic projects. Lead-free solder is a good idea, but even old solder doesn't pose much of a threat, as long as you aren't chewing on it. Always wash your hands after soldering and before eating. (Incidentally, you should always wash your hands before eating. What would your mother think?)

Several hand tools are vital when soldering: diagonal cutters, wire strippers, needle-nose pliers, and clamps (all shown in Figure A-12).

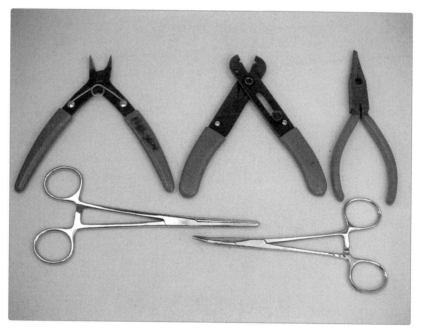

FIGURE A-12: *Clockwise from top left: diagonal cutters, wire strippers, needle-nose pliers, and two types of clamps*

Diagonal cutters are fine snips used to cut the legs off of components after you've soldered them. Don't confuse diagonal cutters with heavy-duty wire

---

1. The smell of melting solder might remind Catholic hobbyists of Midnight Mass; the rosin used in solder is a pine product and is similar to the resins used in making the incense still used during Catholic and Greek Orthodox services. In solder, the rosin serves to clean the contacts while you work, thus helping to ensure a good joint.

snippers sold in hardware stores—these are a different sort of diagonal cutters, often called *dikes*. Dikes are too beefy to get in close to a circuit board. On the other hand, fine diagonal cutters are too delicate to be used on thicker gauge wires (such as guitar strings), which will notch and ruin them. In a pinch, you can often use a pair of nail clippers if you don't have actual diagonal cutters.

Wire strippers are notched snips used for cutting through the plastic insulation of electrical wires while leaving the core intact. You can substitute a small pair of scissors, provided you're very careful not to nick the wire's core (which will weaken them). Like diagonal cutters, wire strippers are a very good investment.

Needle-nose pliers are great for bending wires and component legs, seating components into hard-to-reach places, and loosening stubborn nuts and plugs. Any set of small pliers will work well, and any cheap pair of needle-nose pliers will probably fit the bill.

The items at the bottom of Figure A-12 are locking clamps, the same sort used by doctors (who call them *forceps*, *hemos*, or *hemostatic clamps*). They come curved or straight, in a variety of sizes, and are really handy for holding components while soldering.

Although a *desoldering tool* is not mandatory, if you suspect you'll be working on more than a project or two, you should invest in one. Desoldering tools come in a variety of forms, including *desoldering braids*—also called *solder wicks*—and comical squeezy bulbs, but the spring-loaded *desoldering vacuum* (shown in Figure A-13) is by far my favorite. You'll use your desoldering tool very infrequently,

FIGURE A-13: *A desoldering vacuum, or "solder sucker"*

but the moment you realize you've soldered a transistor backward, you'll be very glad you bought one. (You'll learn more about desoldering in "Skills" on page 328.)

Finally, buy a roll of *electrical tape*; this black, rubberized tape can be used to secure wires, cover their soldered joints, and insulate bare solder points from each other. Insulation becomes especially important as you cram your projects into inconveniently sized enclosures. (As a rule, any enclosure that looks like the perfect size when you are planning a project will turn out to be a hair too small.)

Helpful Additions to the Standard Kit

A *heat sink* (on the left of Figure A-14) is clipped into the leads of a heat-sensitive component between the solder point and component to prevent the component from getting overheated. (You can get by using an alligator clip or a spare set of clamps as stand-ins, as shown in Figure 16-4 on page 191.) You probably won't need a heat sink very often in the course of normal soldering, but it comes in handy during desoldering (which tends to go slower and take more heat than soldering) or if you are working with an expensive component and you don't want to fry it.

FIGURE A-14: *A heat sink (left) and "helping hands" (right)*

Although you can hold all your soldering with clamps, clothespins, your elbows, and stacks of books, most hobbyists eventually buy a *helping hands* jig (shown on the right of Figure A-14). These are also used by model builders and fly fisherman, so they might pop up for cheap at garage sales. They come with and without the integrated magnifying glass; I've never had call to use the magnifier, so

I don't consider it mandatory—but I'm getting terribly near-sighted, more so with every year, so maybe I should have been using that lens all along.

Several common hand tools shown in Figure A-15 make frequent appearances on the electronic tinkerer's workbench, especially *jeweler's screwdrivers*[2] (for tiny screws or for prying ICs out of their sockets), a *tapered half-round file* (the round side is great for clearing burrs from holes drilled in metal cases, and the flat side takes the rough edges off of trimmed pot shafts), and a small *hacksaw* (for cutting down those pot shafts).

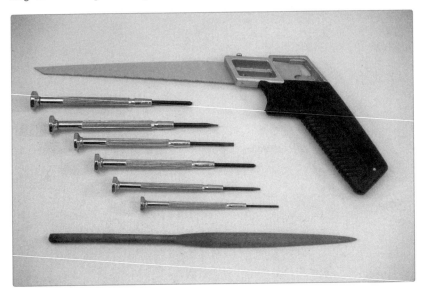

FIGURE A-15: *Jeweler's screwdrivers (center), a tapered half-round file (bottom), and a hacksaw (top)*

After you've decided you like creating electronics gadgets, go out and buy a *digital multimeter* (like the one in Figure A-16). Do not get an analog meter (the kind with the old-timey dial gauge on it, rather than an LCD display). These are no longer cheaper than digital meters (which start at around $20), and they are far more confusing to use.

Even the cheapest multimeters will measure DC voltage, resistance, and current and will do the job well. Slightly nicer meters have special settings for testing continuity (handy) and testing the forward voltage on diodes (only occasionally called for but a big time-saver), and they can be used on AC circuits, which might come in handy down the road if you need to fix something around the house or install a light fixture.

2. If electronic tinkering is really turning you on, now is probably the time to invest in a multi-bit Torx driver like the Husky 8-in-1 Precision Screwdriver; Torx-headed screws are sometimes called "star-driver screws," "star keys," or "those goddamned things!" and are increasingly popular on small consumer electronics that the manufacturer would prefer you just throw away and replace, rather than attempt to fix or monkey with yourself.

Most multimeters come with a normal set of *probes* (these look like thin knitting needles with bulky insulated handles; see Figure A-17) and will serve most purposes as you poke around testing batteries and trouble-shooting circuits. Occasionally you'll need a pair of *clip leads*, which will free up your hands as you run tests—again, you won't need them often, but you'll be glad to have them when you do.

Also handy for troubleshooting or mocking up circuits are several sets of *insulated test leads.* (These are also called *jumpers, clip jumpers, alligator jumpers,* and *clip leads,* and they look a lot like miniature automotive jumper cables.) You can buy these at RadioShack (part #278-1156 is a set of ten color-coded, insulated test leads for less than $8) or buy two sacks of insulated alligator clips (part #270-378) and get some practice soldering (although you save only a buck going that route).

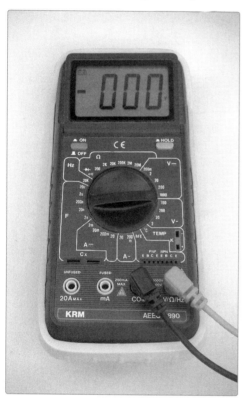

FIGURE A-16: *A digital multimeter*

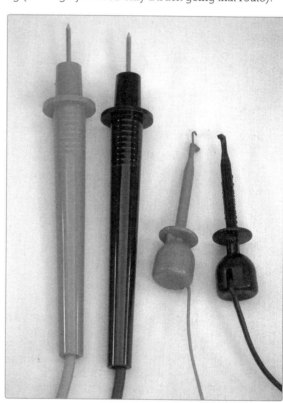

FIGURE A-17: *A set of probes (left) and mini-clip leads (right); the latter are retractable hook leads, also called mini-clip jumpers, and are easy to clip to the leg of a single PCB-mounted component without creating a short circuit*

Skills

The keystone skill for an electronics tinkerer is soldering (and, of course, its dark twin, desoldering). This section will also discuss using a multimeter, building circuits, and troubleshooting projects.

Soldering

Figure A-18 shows good and bad soldered joints. In general, good soldering requires four steps, illustrated in Figures A-19 and A-20: make a mechanical connection, apply heat, apply solder, then cool and trim.

✳ **NOTE:** *If your soldering iron has a brand new tip, you should* tin *the tip before using it. Plug in the iron, and when the tip is nice and hot, melt some fresh solder onto it to coat the tip and prevent corrosion (which will otherwise eat away the tip pretty quickly).*

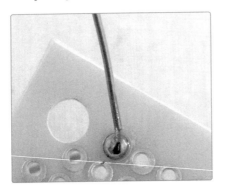 

FIGURE A-18: *Good (left) and absurdly bad (right) solder joints*

Before you can start, you need to preheat your iron. Then:

Step 1   Make a solid mechanical connection between the components to be soldered.

Step 2   Wipe the iron's tip clean of excess solder using a damp sponge or some scrap metal, and then apply heat to the joint for a few seconds.

Step 3   Touch solder to the heated joint. (Do not touch the solder directly to the hot tip of the soldering iron! Forcing hot solder onto cold joints will always make a bad solder joint.) Solder will flow over and into the joint like quicksilver. It's very pretty. Don't apply too much solder.

Step 4   Let the joint cool, and then snip off the excess wire. Don't move the joint until it has cooled: don't wiggle it to see if it's ready, and don't blow on it to speed up the process.

If you are doing point-to-point (aka *dead-bug*) construction (Figure A-19), Step 1 mean twisting the legs of the components together.

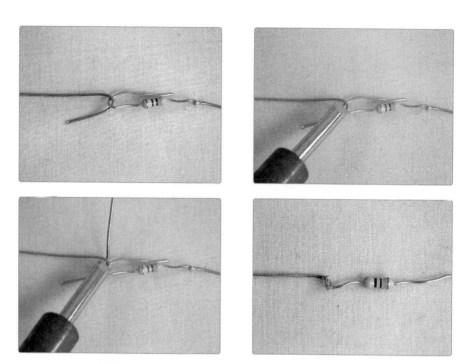

FIGURE A-19: *Point-to-point soldering in four steps*

If you are using a circuit board (Figure A-20), making a "solid mechanical connection" means sliding the component's lead through the appropriate hole in the circuit board and bending the leg to one side so that it is making contact with the board's copper pad (but not touching other components or pads, since the solder will tend to slide up the hot wire and stick to whatever other metal it finds).

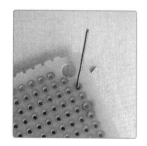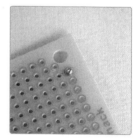

FIGURE A-20: *Circuit-board soldering in four steps*

Any time you use standard wire, you should start by *tinning* the wires—stripping off the insulation, twisting together the strands, heating the wire, and melting solder into it, as shown in Figure A-21. This will make the wire easy to solder to other components or a PCB.

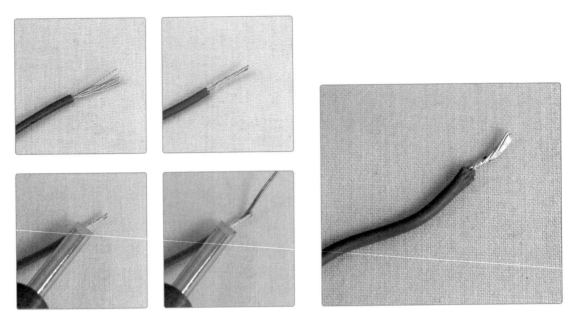

FIGURE A-21: *Tinning in four steps: strip, twist, heat, apply solder.* Voila!

Small components whose thin legs have very little volume will heat and solder very quickly, but the lugs on hardware, especially switches and 1/4" jacks, will take a good long while to heat up and melt the solder. If you've invested in a chisel-tip soldering iron, you'll find that the sharp edge of the tip is best for working with small or heat-sensitive components, while the broad, flat face, which has more surface area to conduct heat, can make soldering hardware much faster.

Desoldering

Desoldering is even easier than soldering (and you'll do it much less frequently):

Step 1   Heat up your soldering iron, clean off the tip, and then apply heat to the soldered joint.

Step 2   When the solder flows, use your desoldering vacuum to suck up as much as you can. (The tips of these vacuums are usually made of heat-resistant plastic.)

Step 3   Repeat once or twice.

Step 4   Let the joint and component cool, and then wiggle the component free with a pair of needle-nose pliers.

The soldering vacuum can also be used to remove a *solder bridge*, which is any place that hot solder has inadvertently flowed between two components, causing a short circuit. Just heat the offending solder and suck it up. Although you can desolder heartier components without the aid of a solder vacuum (just put on goggles, heat the solder joint, and tug at the component with your pliers, being careful not to flick hot beads of molten metal anywhere sensitive), killing a solder bridge without the aid of a desoldering tool can be very tricky.

If you are desoldering a heat-sensitive component (such as a transistor), play it safe and use a heat sink (as shown in Figure 16-4 on page 191).

Using a Multimeter

For the most part, you'll use a multimeter for three tasks: testing batteries; identifying resistors, potentiometers, and speakers; and testing continuity.

Testing a Battery

Set your meter for the proper DC voltage range. On most meters, you'll need to use the 20-volt range for 9-volt batteries, because the batteries will overwhelm the lower 2-volt range and blow your fuse. Connect the black lead to the negative terminal and the red to the positive (Figure A-22), and see if the voltage is in the neighborhood of what it ought to be. (Advanced skill: If a circuit is misbehaving, connect the black lead to the circuit's ground, and then start poking around with the red lead and see if the voltage levels throughout the circuit make sense. If you find an area that's being starved of voltage, a short circuit is likely the culprit.)

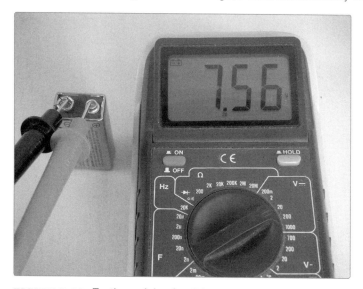

FIGURE A-22: *Testing a dying 9-volt battery*

Identifying Resistance

If you have an unlabeled variable resistor, you can find its maximum resistance by setting the meter to one of the ohm ranges (corresponding to your best guess of what the resistor may be), and then connecting the leads to the edge lugs, as in Figure A-23. (It doesn't matter which goes to which; just ignore the center lug.) The multimeter will read the maximum voltage for the resistor.

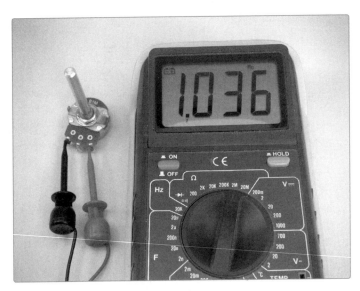

FIGURE A-23: *Identifying a potentiometer*

You can use this same method to identify unlabeled speakers (the projects in this book all call for 8-ohm speakers, so you should be looking for speakers that give 8 ohms of resistance between their lugs) or to figure out the *turns ratio* of a mystery transformer you find at a garage sale or scrounge from an old piece of gear. The ratio of turns between the primary and secondary coils—which is also the ratio of the input to output voltages—is roughly equivalent to the ratio of the square roots of the resistances of each coil (you'll want to round to two significant digits or so). To generalize this (where *P* stands for *primary* and *S* for *secondary*):

$$\frac{Turns_P}{Turns_S} = \frac{Volts_{in}}{Volts_{out}} = \sqrt{\frac{\Omega_P}{\Omega_S}}$$

So, if you need to figure out the turns ratio on a transformer, measure the resistance on each side, take the square root of each, and then reduce the fraction so that the smaller term is a 1 (in other words, divide the big number by the small one). For the audio transformer used throughout this book:

$$\sqrt{\frac{8\Omega_P}{1000\Omega_S}} = \frac{2.83}{31.62} = \frac{1}{11.17}$$

Is it exactly right? Clearly not, but it's a very useful approximation and spot on after you round to the nearest turn.

Testing Continuity

To test continuity (as shown in Figure A-24), choose an ohm range and connect one lead to each end of something that should conduct electricity (such as the tip or ground connectors at the ends of a guitar cable). If the meter reads anything other than 0, there's a problem. This is also a good way to figure out which lugs are which on a complicated switch (such as the many-pole, many-throw selector knobs that can be salvaged from old medical and computer equipment).

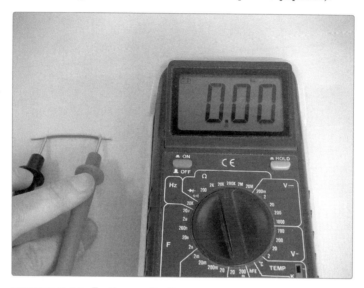

FIGURE A-24: *Testing continuity*

Building a Circuit

A *circuit diagram* is a map of the functional relationship among electrical components, drawn using symbols (such as those shown in Figure A-25). A circuit diagram doesn't tell you the actual physical layout of the circuit. In most simple projects, if the components are connected correctly, it doesn't really matter what is where. In some designs—especially for audio circuits—the physical layout of some parts of the circuit are sensitive; if that's the case, it will be noted in the build notes, or the designer will provide a separate *layout diagram* showing exactly which physical component should be placed where on the circuit board. Most circuit diagrams flow either from top to bottom or left to right, with positive voltage or signal sources at the top or left and ground connections and signal outputs at the bottom or right.

It's a good idea to mock up a new circuit on a *solderless breadboard* (see Figure A-26—you won't find this in the kitchen) before getting out your soldering iron. Breadboards are cheap and come in many sizes. Most include a selection of pre-cut jumpers to connect everything together as you prototype your project. A nice feature of the breadboard is the central divider, which is spaced just right to hold an IC, giving easy access to each pin. This makes it a lot easier for you to hook things up correctly when you start tinkering with ICs.

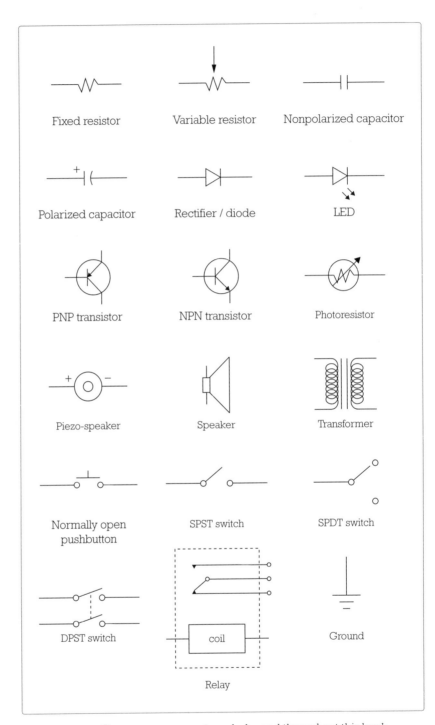

FIGURE A-25: *Common component symbols used throughout this book*

To build a circuit, begin by gathering all the components you need for the project and sort them out. You don't want to grab the wrong resistor or IC inadvertently in the heat of the moment. A cardboard egg carton is great for sorting components for a small project; avoid Styrofoam cartons if you are using ICs in your project—Styrofoam can hold a static charge on a dry day, and ICs are sensitive to static electricity. After you've sorted your components (and labeled them, if you want to be a suspenders-and-a-belt kind of tinkerer), build up the circuit. It's usually easiest to start by placing the ICs or transistors and then building out from there.

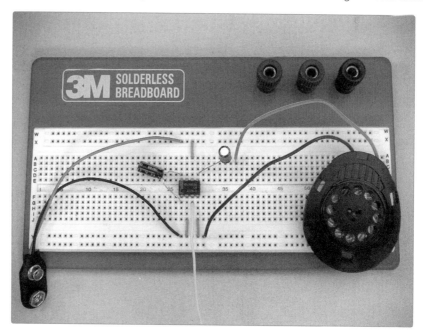

FIGURE A-26: *A breadboard with a sample circuit. Specifically, this is the Dirt-Cheap Amp from Project 12, with the optional gain-maximizing capacitor running from pin 1 to 8. The white wire running from pin 3 out of frame at the bottom carries the input signal. Notice that the bottom and top rails of the breadboard are being used as a common ground and power source, respectively.*

After you have the circuit working on the breadboard (and you understand why it works), you can build it, either dead-bug style—soldering the components directly to each other (this is very compact but often ugly and difficult to repair or troubleshoot)—or on a printed circuit board (PCB), a sturdy, nonconductive board with copper pads and traces etched onto one side (Figure A-27).

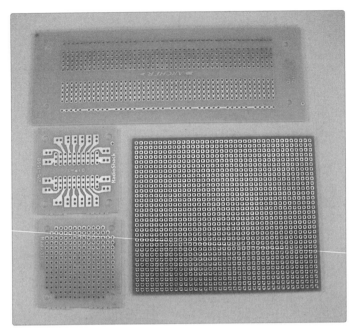

FIGURE A-27: *A selection of PCBs*

Troubleshooting

If a circuit worked fine on the breadboard but malfunctions when it's built, check for the following:

▶ properly-seated ICs

▶ shorts and solder bridges

▶ bad solder points (a good solder point is smooth and shiny; bad ones are rough, brittle, or chunky; see Figure A-18)

▶ reversed polarized components (e.g., electrolytic caps, diodes, LEDs, transistors, and ICs)

▶ missed ground connections

▶ reversed pots

▶ shorts to ground (especially in tight enclosures—when you close the box, something could get pressed against a bare bus ground; you can prevent this by running lengths of shrink tube over the bare bus in problem areas or by using a judicious application of nail polish, which will act as an insulator when it dries)

If an audio project is noisy or is picking up AM radio, check to ensure that the audio signal lines are either shielded or less than 8" long. (I like to err on the side of caution and keep all wires carrying audio signals under 6", with the exception of lines running from the amp to the speaker, since the amplifier signal is strong enough to drown out any interference that might creep in at that point.)

Resources

▸ If any single man is responsible for launching a thousand electronic tinkerers, it's Forrest M. Mims III. RadioShack has sold his clear, readable, and cheap Engineer's Mini Notebook series for decades. *Getting Started in Electronics*, as the title implies, is a great place to start. In addition to providing a solid framework for both the practical skills and theoretical foundations of electronics, the book also offers 100 neat, easy-to-build circuits. Mims's website can be found at *http://www.forrestmims.org/*.

▸ When buying components online, most folks go with either Digi-Key (*http://www.digikey.com/*) or Mouser Electronics (*http://www.mouser.com/*). Mouser is often slightly cheaper, but Digi-Key offers the cheapest shipping options as of this writing. I've never ordered from Jameco Electronics (*http://www.jameco.com/*), but they come fondly recommended by friends and colleagues, and have an easily navigable website. Alternatively, you can use a tool like Octopart (*http://octopart.com/*) to track down the absolute cheapest component prices. On the other hand, if you live close to a RadioShack, you might want to stop in: Although these parts are usually more expensive, you can often get common components (such as those used throughout this book) right away.

▸ Once you've built a couple of the electronics projects in this book, you're perfectly qualified to build any of the supercool kits sold by Adafruit Industries (*http://www.adafruit.com/*), *MAKE* magazine's Maker SHED (*http://www.makershed.com/*), SparkFun Electronics (*http://www.sparkfun.com/*), and Evil Mad Science (*http://evilmadscience.com/*).

▸ Keep an eye out for neat components that you might use for future projects of your own. Check the American Science & Surplus website (*http://www.sciplus.com/*), garage sales, resale shops, and freecycle groups.

Snip, Burn, Solder, Shred is set in Rockwell. The book was printed and bound at Malloy Incorporated in Ann Arbor, Michigan. The paper is Glatfelter Spring Forge 60# Smooth, which is certified by the Sustainable Forestry Initiative (SFI). The book uses a RepKover binding, which allows it to lie flat when open.

The LEGO® MINDSTORMS® NXT 2.0 Discovery Book
A Beginner's Guide to Building and Programming Robots

by LAURENS VALK

The crystal-clear instructions in *The LEGO MINDSTORMS NXT 2.0 Discovery Book* show you how to harness the capabilities of the NXT 2.0 set to build and program your own robots. Author and robotics instructor Laurens Valk walks you through the set, showing you how to use its various pieces and how to use the NXT software to program robots. Interactive tutorials make it easy for you to reach an advanced level of programming as you learn to build robots that move, monitor sensors, and use advanced programming techniques like data wires and variables. You'll build eight increasingly sophisticated robots like the Strider (a six-legged walking creature), the CCC (a climbing vehicle), and the Hybrid Brick Sorter (a robot that sorts by color and size). Numerous building and programming challenges throughout encourage you to think creatively and to apply what you've learned as you develop the skills essential to creating your own robots.

MAY 2010, 336 PP., $29.95
ISBN 978-1-59327-211-1

The LEGO® Technic Idea Book: Simple Machines

by YOSHIHITO ISOGAWA

The LEGO Technic Idea Book: Simple Machines offers hundreds of color photos of the author's original, Technic-based creations, with text only at the beginning of the book. Rather than tell you what to think, you're encouraged to use your imagination as you pick apart each model just as you would any work of art. Each photograph demonstrates various ways to combine Technic gears as starting points for your own creations. *Simple Machines*, the first in the three-volume *LEGO Technic Idea Book* series, begins with basic combinations of gears, shafts, and connectors and then displays more complex models, like winches, chains, and cranes. You'll learn how to change rotational motion into linear motion, launch projectiles with rubber bands, change speed and direction, and even create musical instruments. The *LEGO Technic Idea Book* series is for anyone who wants to create a moving masterpiece with LEGO Technic, whether that's a simple machine, a kinetic sculpture, or a LEGO MINDSTORMS robot.

OCTOBER 2010, 168 PP., *full color*, $19.95
ISBN 978-1-59327-277-7

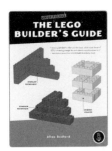

The Unofficial LEGO® Builder's Guide

by ALLAN BEDFORD

The Unofficial LEGO Builder's Guide combines techniques, principles, and reference information for building with LEGO bricks that go far beyond LEGO's official product instructions. You discover how to build everything from sturdy walls to a basic sphere, as well as projects including a mini space shuttle and a train station. The book also delves into advanced concepts such as scale and design and includes essential terminology and the Brickopedia, a comprehensive guide to the different types of LEGO pieces.

SEPTEMBER 2005, 344 PP., $24.95
ISBN 978-1-59327-054-4

Forbidden LEGO®
Build the Models Your Parents Warned You Against!

by ULRIK PILEGAARD **and** MIKE DOOLEY

Written by a former master LEGO designer and a former LEGO project manager, this full-color book showcases projects that break the LEGO Group's rules for building with LEGO bricks—rules against building projects that fire projectiles, require cutting or gluing bricks, or use nonstandard parts. Many of these are backroom projects that LEGO's master designers build under the LEGO radar, just to have fun. Learn how to build a catapult that shoots M&Ms, a gun that fires LEGO beams, a continuous-fire ping-pong ball launcher, and more! Tips and tricks will give you ideas for inventing your own creative model designs.

AUGUST 2007, 192 PP., *full color*, $24.95
ISBN 978-1-59327-137-4

The Manga Guide™ to Physics

by HIDEO NITTA, KEITA TAKATSU, **and** TREND-PRO CO., LTD.

The Manga Guide to Physics teaches readers the fundamentals of physics through authentic Japanese manga. Megumi, an all-star tennis player, is struggling to pass her physics class. Luckily for her, she befriends Ryota, a patient physics geek who uses real-world examples to help her understand classical mechanics. Readers follow along with Megumi as she learns about the physics of everyday objects like roller skates, slingshots, braking cars, and tennis rackets. As the book progresses, Megumi begins to master even the toughest concepts of physics, like momentum and impulse, parabolic motion, and the relationship between force, mass, and acceleration. Using a lively and quirky approach, *The Manga Guide to Physics* combines a whimsical story with real educational content so that readers will quickly master the core concepts of physics with a minimum of frustration.

MAY 2009, 248 PP., $19.95
ISBN 978-1-59327-196-1

PHONE:
800.420.7240 OR
415.863.9900
MONDAY THROUGH FRIDAY,
9 AM TO 5 PM (PST)
FAX:
415.863.9950
24 HOURS A DAY,
7 DAYS A WEEK

EMAIL:
SALES@NOSTARCH.COM
WEB:
WWW.NOSTARCH.COM
MAIL:
NO STARCH PRESS
38 RINGOLD STREET
SAN FRANCISCO, CA 94103
USA

Updates

Visit *http://www.nostarch.com/snipburn.htm*
for updates, errata, and other information.